WITHDRAWN
NEBRASKA CHRISTIAN
COLLEGE LIBRARY

10-18-89 M. Johnson

D1804514

ENDANGERED HERITAGE

ENDANGERED HERITAGE

An Evaluation
of
Church of Christ
Doctrine

Walt Yancey

College Press Publishing Company, Joplin, Missouri

Copyright © 1987
College Press Publishing Company

BX
7323
-Y36
1987

Printed and bound in
United States of America
All Rights Reserved

Library of Congress Catalog Card Number: 0-89900-283-8
International Standard Book Number: 87-070450

CONTENTS

PROLOGUE 9

PART I. ASSESSING THE SITUATION

Chapter

1   Motivations for Producing This Document 15
      The Author's Perspective 15
      Objective Bible Study 21
      The Author's Investigation 25
      The Author's Objectives 28

2   20th Century Church of Christ Doctrine 31

3   19th Century Church of Christ Doctrine 35
      Brief Historical Background 35
         Introduction 35
         Early Beginnings 36
         Barton W. Stone 38
         Thomas Campbell 45
         Alexander Campbell 48
         Walter Scott 54
         Union of the Stone and Campbell
         Movements 59
         Divisions Within the Restoration
         Movement 59
      List of 19th Century Doctrinal Items 65
      Two Separate and Distinct Church of Christ
      Traditions 67

PART II. MAJOR ELEMENTS OF BOTH 19TH
         AND 20TH CENTURY TRADITIONS

4   Baptism 73

5   The Lord's Supper 93

6   Summary of Our Best Attributes 117

PART III. MAJOR ELEMENTS UNIQUE TO THE 20TH CENTURY TRADITION

7 The Problem Concepts 123

8 Instrumental Music Used in Worship Is a Sin .. 125
    A Fresh Approach 126
    Pattern, Blueprint, Liturgy 129
    Authority in Silence 134
    Necessary Inference 138
    The Author's Study Regarding Music 146
    Summary of the Arguments Against
    Instrumental Music 147
    Is Congregational Singing Authorized? 151
    Solo Singing in a Congregational Setting 154
    Judging 155
    Summary 158

9 The Church of Christ Is not a Denomination .. 163

10 Only Church of Christ Members Can
    Go to Heaven 173
    Introduction 177
    The Definition of a Christian 177
    Opinion 179
    Are There Any Christians in the
    Other Denominations? 183
      A Collection of Short Quotes 184
      The Lunenburg Letters;
      Alexander Campbell 194
      The Limits of Religious Fellowship;
      Isaac Errett 204
      What Has Been the Custom Among Us?
      W. K. Pendleton 209
      Do the Unimmersed Commune?
      Moses E. Lard 211
      Opinion; Barton W. Stone 213

Union; Barton W. Stone 216
Comments by Walter Scott 221
Additional Thoughts on Limits of
Fellowship; Alexander Campbell 222
Summary 227

PART IV.   EPILOGUE

11   The Validity of the Restoration Principle......235

12   Conclusion................................241
      Summary of Our Problems 241
      Christian Forbearance 247
      Where Do We Go from Here? 252

Bibliography 259

Index..265

PROLOGUE

This document is dedicated to all members of the Church of Christ. It is dedicated to all those who, like the author, sincerely believe with all of their heart and soul that in our Christian walk we should take the Bible (the Holy Scriptures) as our only rule of faith and duty, that we should speak where the Bible speaks and be silent where the Bible is silent, that we should not add to or take away from the Word of God, that the Bible is the inspired Word of God, that the Bible is all sufficient and thus provides all that we need to know regarding our soul's eternal salvation, that we should never replace Christ's simple gospel message with the traditions of men, that the opinions of men should never be elevated in importance above or even equal to the inspired Word of God and that it should be our constant goal to restore, in matters of faith and worship, the old ways, the old paths, the ancient order of things in New Testament Christianity.

ENDANGERED HERITAGE

Those of us who are members of the Church of Christ are heirs to a religious reformation which took place in the United States, in a broad region centered roughly around Ohio and Kentucky, during the early years of the last century. The goals of this reformation have been most often stated as "the restoration of New Testament Christianity." It has been variously styled as the restoration movement, the Stone-Campbell movement or the American restoration movement. Since it is the only such movement with which we are concerned in this document, I will usually refer to it for the sake of simplicity as the restoration movement. The restoration movement began with strong sentiments for Christian unity. The founders of the movement believed that returning to the New Testament as the only source of Christian authority would quickly bring about the unity of all of Christendom. As we look back on the movement from our vantage point 150 to 180 years after its inception we unfortunately observe that the "unity movement" has divided into three major churches: the Christian Church (Disciples of Christ), the Independent Christian Church, and the Church of Christ. In this study I will specifically address only one of these splinter groups, the Church of Christ. We in the Church of Christ claim that we are the only group which has remained true to the goals, the ideals and the heritage of the movement. The investigation of the validity of this claim is one significant aspect of this study.

In the process of investigating this claim, that the Church of Christ has remained absolutely true to the goals and ideals of the restoration movement, I have studied many of the writings of the early pioneer preachers who were the founders of the movement. In the process of presenting the results of this investigation, I will quote quite extensively from these writings. I am confident that this is entirely appropriate, especially since we generally claim to have remained true to their ideals. I feel it necessary to make one thing very clear, however, from the very beginning. I place no authority in anything that any of these pioneer preachers have written. This is a very fundamental part of my Christian philosophy. I place no ultimate religious authority in anything

PROLOGUE

written or said by any human being since the last book of the New Testament was penned. However, I wish to make a second point which I think is just as important: that it is acceptable and appropriate to read what these men have written. It is just as appropriate to read what Alexander Campbell or Barton W. Stone wrote 150 years ago as it is to listen to our local preacher expound for one hour each and every Sunday morning on his personal opinion as to what the Bible really means. The average conscientious Church of Christ member probably listens to at least two hours of sermons or lectures per week, fifty-two weeks per year. This is roughly 100 hours of human opinion that we listen to per year. This means that by the time a person reaches the age of forty he has listened to approximately 4000 hours of personal human opinion regarding the Bible. I am making no criticism of this whatsoever. My point is that it will be no deviation from our accepted practices to spend a few short moments reading material written by some of our Church of Christ preachers of another era. We should only remember to measure everything that they say against the Scriptures, in the same way that we should measure everything that our contemporary preachers say against the Bible, our ultimate authority.

 A great deal of care was taken in the selection of the historical material which is quoted in this document. The objective was to quote the minimum amount, from each selected passage, necessary to convey the intended message. Even though this goal was constantly kept in mind, some eight or ten of the selections are still quite lengthy. I ask the reader's patience in dealing with these long passages, but also strongly encourage that each of these historical documents be read carefully. They have been selected from a large field of material and each article has a message of importance to convey. I believe that a familiarity with this historical material is crucial to those of our particular religious heritage and that most of it is not otherwise readily available to the average reader. I would like to add that every attempt has been made to copy this historical material exactly as it appeared in the source documents; including outdated styles of punctuation, old and inconsistent rules for capitalization, archaic spelling and even typographical errors.

PART I

ASSESSING THE SITUATION

1

MOTIVATIONS FOR PRODUCING THIS DOCUMENT

THE AUTHOR'S PERSPECTIVE

I am a member of the Church of Christ. For all practical purposes I have always been a member of the Church of Christ. My mother probably took me to the worship services the very first Sunday after she brought me home from the hospital. To be more technically correct, I should say that I have been a member since I was baptized in my early teens. I still have vague memories from those early years of how proud I was of my church, how proud I was to be a member of the Church of Christ, how proud and lucky I felt to be a member of the one and only true church. That was in another time and another place. Today, while I am still a member of the Church of Christ, I have developed an awareness of how the Church is perceived from the outside. I gradually came to realize that we in the Church of Christ have a bad reputation, a very bad reputation, among most of the members of Christendom who are not a part of our particular group. It is not among the heathen that I believe we are particularly disliked. The nonbelievers probably show us no special attention relative to the other professors of Christianity. What I am saying is that among our friends and neighbors in the community, our colleagues at work, and those around us who are members of other churches that profess to be followers of Jesus Christ, that among these we are not well respected. I am not saying only that they don't agree with our doctrine. They could reject all of our doctrine and still respect us for what we are trying to do or be. I am saying that we are strongly disliked by many at a more emotional level.

This attitude manifests itself in many ways. When I meet someone new and the conversation gets around to religion, and I say that I am a member of the Church of Christ, I often see the countenance change, the discussion falter and an awkward situation result. If I walk into a group of people having a religious discussion at work or in a social situation, and if I sooner or later make it known that I belong to the Church of Christ, the discussion seems to no longer be quite as open and free. At least two or three times in the last two years I have heard people sitting at a table next to me in a restaurant say derogatory things about the Church of Christ. Four years ago a man with whom I was sharing an office at work, a man who had in-laws who were Church of Christ members, told me that the Church of Christ was definitely not a thinking man's religion. These things bother me. Now I realize that if we are persecuted for righteousness' sake we will receive our reward in heaven (Matt. 5:10), and I suppose that verbal persecution probably counts here; however, we must be very careful that we are being maligned for our support of righteousness and not for our support of some artificial doctrinal point which we may have contrived or some self-righteous attitude which we might have acquired. To suffer for either of the two latter reasons would certainly not add any stars to our crown in heaven.

MOTIVATIONS FOR PRODUCING THIS DOCUMENT

Another thing that I gradually came to realize over a period of time was that as a youth I had not received a very good Christian education. I grew up in a church where we were taught that we went strictly by the book, the Bible, rather than relying on the traditions of men as other churches did. That sounded good and it made us feel good. We even verbalized this concept in a hymn that we often sang in the rural Church of Christ that was my first church home. Unfortunately this song is missing in the newer hymnal that we use in the congregation which I now attend. Even the title described the theme, "Back to the Bible for it All." The first verse and the chorus we sang read:

> Vainly we seek after men for guiding light,
> Or in dreams for a heavenly call;
> Man, of himself, cannot set his soul aright;
> So it's back to the Bible for it all.
> Back to the Bible! The God given Bible!
> For grace and duty, great or small;
> Each one may know what to do and where we go,
> But it's back to the Bible for it all.[1]

I believe that the concept expressed here is a valid one, and these sentiments ring just as true today as they did when I was a child. In fact this is the very essence of what the Church of Christ has always stood for. It is because of this that, if we look back to the early years of the Church of Christ, we have a rich heritage. It is a heritage of which we can be proud, and worth our best efforts to maintain. The problem was that although we talked a lot about getting back to the Bible, we never really studied it in a comprehensive, coordinated manner. In our high school Bible class we used little gospel quarterlies in which we first read the Scriptures which had been extracted for us and then we filled in the blanks. This made it very easy to

---

1. "Back to the Bible for it All," by Vana R. Raye and L. O. Sanderson, from *Christian Hymns Number Two,* Nashville: Gospel Advocate Co., 1948, p. 346.

prepare our Sunday morning lesson, but it also made it easy to not learn very much. We learned a doctrine, of course, from hearing hundreds of sermons, but we didn't have enough knowledge about the Bible to know whether what the preacher told us the Bible said and what the Bible actually said were one and the same thing. In fact it probably never occurred to most of us to even ask that question.

Let me be quick to assure the reader, lest any become offended by the fear that I might generalize too much, that I am sure that there are now and that there were then better educational programs than the one which I experienced. Other congregations, larger assemblies and other circumstances could result in improved conditions. However, even after living in several parts of the country during my lifetime, I have seen nothing to cause any significant change in my assessment of the overall quality of the Church of Christ Bible educational programs. The pioneer preachers who founded the movement from which the Church of Christ emerged were Bible scholars par excellence. One of their basic guidelines was that each person should read, study and interpret the Bible for himself. Somehow, between then and now, we seem to have become a people who depend upon a few elders, paid preachers, or magazine editors to tell us what the Bible really means. This is a very dangerous tendency. The result of such a tendency, if unimpeded, is the emergence of a system of church government such as that seen in the Roman Catholic church where the church leadership actually constitutes the ultimate source of authority on spiritual matters, rather than the Bible being the source.

Our growth rate is another item which has attracted my attention. The Churches of Christ seem to not be growing very fast. Most of our meeting houses are half empty, even on Sunday morning. In fact, in the last few years I have heard several reports which claim that our overall numbers are actually decreasing at an alarming rate. If we are declining in numbers, or even merely stagnant, that in and of itself is cause for concern.

MOTIVATIONS FOR PRODUCING THIS DOCUMENT

But that it should be happening at this particular time in history I find even more alarming. I believe that during the last 20 years there has been a renewed interest in this country in individual Bible study. This may have been fueled in part by some of the anti-materialism sentiments of the 1960s or by some of the associated Jesus movements. It may seem ironic, based upon a cursory evaluation, that we should be in decline during a period of increased Bible study. If we are really simply a people of the "Book," as we claim to be, then an increasing interest in the Bible should give rise to an improvement in our reputation and an increase in our membership. That this isn't happening should immediately raise a red flag in our minds and cause us to ask why.

At this time I would like to address a question which might appear in the minds of some readers. Most books written in Church of Christ circles are written by well known preachers, elders, editors or men who are combinations of two or more of the above. Why then should anyone read a book which purports to deal with serious theological issues, which is written by a competely unknown author? If we were Roman Catholics such a book would certainly have to come from an established theologian, perhaps a Bishop or Cardinal. Even in most Protestant denominations, where there is a declared and distinct separation between the clergy and the laity (and where members of the clergy must be ordained by the proper authorities before assuming their duties) such a book should probably most appropriately come from a member of the clergy. However, we in the Church of Christ are in a very unique position. We claim to have no separation between the clergy and the laity. One of our foundational tenets is that we have, in fact, no clergy at all. We claim that any Christian who has the knowledge and the ability can preach the gospel of our Lord and Savior Jesus Christ to anyone at any available opportunity. Thus the Church of Christ is perhaps one of the few religious groups wherein a person who is not a member of the currently acknowledged circle of leadership could write a book relating to church doctrine and expect it to receive serious consideration.

The Jewish historian Josephus, in the opening pages of the "Life of Flavius Josephus,"[2] written in approximately A.D. 100, felt it necessary to establish his credentials. This was probably done to establish his credibility as an historian. In a similar vein, but hopefully with a much more modest flair than that exhibited by Josephus, I would like to present my genealogy as relates to the Church of Christ. I am fourth generation Church of Christ. My maternal great-grandparents were members of the Church of Christ. Their lifespan reaches back to around 1855. Prior to that I have no information. My grandparents and my mother were and are, respectively, also members of the Church of Christ and I, myself, was baptized when I was a teenager. My mother was in a family of six sisters and two brothers. Both of her brothers are now Church of Christ preachers. One of my uncles (the husband of my mother's sister) is a preacher and his family boasts several Church of Christ preachers. Thus my background is deeply rooted in the Church of Christ. Tradition is a powerful influence, and I have all of the reasons that tradition affords to want to support, cherish, and defend the Church of Christ.

Some men from among us who have believed that they have found some errors in our teaching have reacted by seemingly rejecting everything in their heritage. They have either left the Church of Christ and struck back at us very harshly, or have remained but seemingly abandoned all of our conservative principles. I am cast from a different mold. I see nothing wrong with our basic theology. I believe it to be theologically accurate, academically sound, and the only safe approach toward the understanding and practice of Christianity. My main criticism

---

2. Josephus, "Life of Flavius Josephus" (approx. A.D. 100), *Josephus' Complete Works* (translated by William Whiston, A.M.), Grand Rapids: Kregel Publications, p. 1.

is that we have allowed some of the opinions of men to be elevated until they are almost on a par with the inspired word, and this is not consistent with our conservative heritage. We must begin to admit this to ourselves and to the world.

OBJECTIVE BIBLE STUDY

Approximately seven years ago I began a program of very serious personal Bible study. I finally initiated an effort to correct my deficiency in Bible education. I was trying to make up for lost time, to make up for the Bible study that I didn't do during the years when I was getting my secular education. I wanted to find out what the Bible really said about everything. I wanted to find out whether or not all of the things that I had been taught in the Church of Christ were true, or if not, which were true and which were false. The thing utmost in my mind was objectivity in my study. This, it seems, is a goal very difficult for most people to achieve. Many people study to find words in support of what they already believe. In fact it seems that this is the way the majority of people study, otherwise there would be less division in the religious world. I used to say that one should study the Bible as if he had lived all of his life on a desert island, with no religion, and one day a Bible washed ashore in a bottle—or that one should study as if he lived in a world with no religion and one day in a dusty old trunk in his grandmother's attic he found an old Bible packed away beneath a pile of old clothes. In either of these cases he should then open this strange book and read it from cover to cover having no preconceived ideas to clutter up his mind. He would in this way probably end up with an objective view of what the Bible really said. As I proceeded in my study I found that this concept was not new with me, only that perhaps I had picked new situations for the setting. Robert Richardson, in his book *Memoirs of Alexander Campbell,* written in the late 1800s, says of Mr. Campbell:

> Acting himself upon the principles he taught to others, he was accustomed to contemplate the Bible as if it had just fallen into his hands from heaven, and utterly disregarding all systems and theories, and even his own previous conclusions, he was wont to study it constantly with a free and unbiased mind.[3]

A few pages later in the same book Richardson, speaking of the recommended method of Bible study, quotes Alexander Campbell:

> Beware of having any commentator or system before your eyes or your mind. Open the New Testament as if mortal man had never seen it before.[4]

Putting these principles into practice is not easy. There are really two major tasks inherent in the accomplishment of this objective. The first task, and a very important one, is to consciously decide that one must disregard his previous conclusions each time he studies. To get this far is very commendable, but this is the easy part. The more difficult task, I am convinced, is to actually put this into practice. When I first began my study, with all of my determination to be objective, I wrote down a small list of topics which I thought I would pay very close attention to because of their importance. In reflecting back on this a couple of years later I realized that even the items on this list which I used while I was "being objective" were influenced heavily by my prior Church of Christ training and thus, to an extent, prevented me from being completely objective. If my background were Roman Catholic I would certainly have compiled a different list. I think that complete objectivity in any human study is impossible, but also not essential to the success of that study. What is necessary is that we realize the need to

---

3. Robert Richardson, *Memoirs of Alexander Campbell,* Vol. 2, p. 42.
4. Ibid., p. 97. Richardson quotes Alexander Campbell from an undisclosed location in the *Christian Baptist.*

MOTIVATIONS FOR PRODUCING THIS DOCUMENT

be objective and that we are constantly, throughout the course of our lives, trying to work toward this goal. Along with this we must realize that even today, after our most recent and best efforts at being objective, we might still (not just other people in other religious groups but even we, ourselves) be less than objective on some particular idea or point of doctrine and that because of this possibility we might have misinterpreted or misapplied or even been absolutely wrong on something.

Assume then that we embark upon a course of study with such goals of objectivity. What if our study leads us to a tentative conclusion that something which we have been previously taught is wrong? How are we to react to this situation? Should we conclude that our recent discovery must be somehow in error because of the fact that many very godly and well educated men have believed the majority doctrine for many years and therefore it must be correct? If the pioneer preachers of our own restoration movement had taken this attitude there never would have been a Church of Christ as we know it today. They questioned many things which had been taught by many very godly and well educated men for centuries as sound doctrine (such as baptism of infants by sprinkling). We must always allow all points of doctrine to be placed under the microscope in a serious and objective Bible study. What is good and true will never suffer from a careful examination, but rather stand stronger for it in the end. Only those things which are not true need fear the eye of the careful sleuth. In 1823 in his first monthly periodical, the *Christian Baptist,* Alexander Campbell phrased this idea as follows:

> But shall we be deterred from examining any principle because good and great men have espoused it? Nay, verily! Should we adopt this course, all examination of principles is at an end.[5]

---

5. Alexander Campbell, *Christian Baptist,* Oct. 6, 1823, p. 19.

ENDANGERED HERITAGE

A few years later, in 1842, from the pages of his second monthly periodical the *Millennial Harbinger,* Mr. Campbell said further:

> It is always more or less detrimental to the ascertainment of truth to allow our previous conclusions to assume the position of fixed and fundamental truths, to which nothing is to be at any time added, either in the way of correction or enlargement. On the contrary, we ought rather to act under the conviction that we may be wiser today than yesterday, and that whatever is true can suffer no hazard from a candid and careful reconsideration. In this view of the subject, I am accustomed to examine all questions—literary, moral or religious; because I am, from much reflection and long observation, constrained to regard it as the only safe and prudential course.[6]

Suppose now that we have accepted some new idea as a result of our objective Bible study. It still may not be an easy task to present this idea to others. We may be quite afraid to speak up in a classroom situation where a group of our peers are listening and we don't know whether or not anyone else will agree with us. The Church of Christ of my day has not encouraged the questioning of any points of doctrine in the classroom. The study of doctrine has been conducted more like indoctrination than like objective, academic investigation. But we must not wait for everyone else to agree with us before we speak the truth. If we followed that course of action the truth would never be heard. The Christian martyrs of centuries past did not wait for all present to agree with them before they stood up for their Lord. Can we do less when we risk so much less? Thomas Campbell, the father of Alexander, penned a document in 1809 called the "Declaration and Address." This document has been called the Magna Carta of our restoration movement. He calls on people of all religious groups to study their Bibles objectively and to return to the Bible as their only source of authority. In this document Thomas Campbell addresses our immediate topic as follows:

---

6. Alexander Campbell, "Nature of the Christian Organization," *Millennial Harbinger,* 1842, p. 327.

It is not the voice of the multitude, but the voice of truth, that has power with the conscience; that can produce rational conviction and acceptable obedience. A conscience that awaits the decision of the multitude, that hangs in suspense for the casting vote of the majority, is a fit subject for the man of sin. This, we are persuaded, is the uniform sentiment of real Christians of every denomination.[7]

And so we must not, we can not, remain silent if we know that our leaders are teaching anything which is not true; because, in a situation like this, silence constitutes agreement[8] and makes us just as guilty as they.

THE AUTHOR'S INVESTIGATION

Approximately the first two and one-half years of my study were spent studying the Bible alone, without any aids or commentaries. I wanted the foundation of my Bible knowledge to be based on the Bible only, and not on what some man told me that it said. I tried to use the same study techniques which I had used while earning a Masters Degree in Physics during my university days. These techniques included extensive reading, voluminous note taking, making my own outlines and summaries and doing a comprehensive investigation of each subject in some appropriate order. By the time I had finished this phase of my study I had drawn some tentative conclusions. Some of the things that I had always been taught and which I had always believed to be true were confirmed by my study and my confidence in these basic points of doctrine was thus increased. Some of the things that I had always been taught, but on which I had suspected that we might be in error or at least too dogmatic, turned out to be true and valid, after all, and thus my doctrinal base was strengthened and broadened. However, unfortunately,

---

7. Thomas Campbell, "Declaration and Address," St. Louis: Mission Messenger, p. 50.
8. Ibid., p. 40.

there were some things which I had been taught which I could not find any support for in the Bible. This can be very disheartening to one who has been taught from childhood that his church is always correct. However I did not falter for a moment at this point because something had happened about a year earlier which pointed me immediately to the next phase of my study.

While on a business trip several hundred miles from my home, I had occasion to attend the Wednesday evening assembly of the local congregation of the Church of Christ. The preacher of that congregation was presenting a series to the class assembled in the auditorium entitled "Restoration History." My schedule only permitted me to hear one or two sessions of this series but I was fascinated by what I heard. He was talking about the history of the Church of Christ. He talked about Thomas Campbell, Alexander Campbell, Barton W. Stone and Walter Scott, among many others. These were names that I had never even heard of except for one vague memory of a friend calling us Campbellites when I was a child. The most amazing thing was his description of what these men believed and how they did not all believe exactly the same thing about every subject. I determined right then that I needed to study this subject. After one of the sessions, thinking that I might want to ask him some questions someday, I introduced myself to the preacher in order to get his name.

Approximately one and one-half years later I decided to study Church of Christ history in order to compare the Church of Christ doctrine of the early 1800s to the Church of Christ doctrine of the mid and late 20th century. Since I had no books on our church history, and did not know what was available on the subject, I called this preacher to see if he would send me his notes from the class he had taught. When I introduced myself on the phone this man did not remember who I was, and had no reason to, but he was very gracious and said that he would try to collect his notes and send them to me. In

MOTIVATIONS FOR PRODUCING THIS DOCUMENT

the meantime he gave me the name of two books which were currently in print which addressed the subject. I then looked through local Church of Christ bookstores until I found these books. What I read kindled my interest even more. I read the first book and then began looking for books that were referenced in the footnotes. This began a two year search for available literature describing the religious reformation which took place in the early 1800s in the eastern-central United States, best known as the restoration movement, which became the movement from which the Church of Christ eventually emerged. This movement has now splintered into three churches; the Disciples of Christ Christian Church, the Independent Christian Church, and the Church of Christ. I soon limited my study primarily to the period prior to the Civil War, roughly 1792-1862. This was the period during which the movement began, matured, and realized its most rapid growth. I wanted to see what was believed and taught during this successful period prior to any of the splits which later ruptured this unity movement. What I found thrilled my heart beyond measure. I found thousands of people, an entire movement, who appear to have actually lived up to what the Church of Christ of today claims to be, but unfortunately rarely measures up to. It is a history and a heritage of which we can all be very proud. It should be studied by all of our people to help ensure that we do not drift away from our very noble goal of getting back to the Bible.

My preacher friend never did send me his class notes. But it did not matter because in a very short time I had no need of them. But he did become, by long distance telephone over a period of years, one of my very dearest friends in Christ. He offered me help and encouragement in my Christian study during a time when I needed it very much, when there was no once else to fill that need, and he gave this free time, these hours on the phone, to a man whose face he could not even recall. I owe him a debt that I might never be able to repay, but then, I guess debts to true friends don't require repayment.

THE AUTHOR'S OBJECTIVES

I have engaged in a very determined effort to do a completely objective study of 20th Century Church of Christ doctrine. For reasons which we discussed earlier I have probably, to some degree, fallen short of this goal. There was a time during my study of the Bible when I had convinced myself that if my study led me away from the Church of Christ and into some other church affiliation that I would go. However this didn't happen. I found so much that is good and true in what we claim to be, and so much evidence from our heritage that these goals are really achievable, that it reaffirmed my commitment to the Church of Christ. I want to make whatever contribution I can to the Lord's cause, whether it be large or small, from within this framework. I think that on all points that relate to what I would consider basic New Testament gospel our Church of Christ doctrine is sound, solid and true.

The problem is that over the years we have allowed some opinions, opinions of men, to become elevated in stature to the point where they are almost considered to be of equal importance with Scripture. In some cases it almost seems that we had rather part with the Bible than part with our opinions. Our opinions have become tradition and tradition becomes quickly cast in concrete. In stressing our opinions so strongly we have actually endangered our heritage. The very essence of what the pioneer preachers of our restoration movement taught was that we must always distinguish very clearly between explicit Bible teaching and man's opinion of what the Bible means. For the first 60 or 70 years of the movement they seemed to keep this distinction clearly in focus. Around the time of the Civil War some of the newer second generation teachers in the movement allowed this distinction to become blurred in their minds and in their teaching and writing. This caused the beginning of a long series of divisive problems for the movement. The results have been disastrous for the Church of Christ. The reputation

MOTIVATIONS FOR PRODUCING THIS DOCUMENT

that we have established over the last 100 years is seriously hampering our efforts today to spread the gospel of our Lord and Savior Jesus Christ to the rest of the world. No one takes our pleas for Christian unity seriously when our own movement is itself divided into somewhere between 25 and 50 separate groups. The arrogant, self-righteous attitudes of many of our Church of Christ members have turned thousands of people against us, people who might otherwise have benefited from our knowledge of the Scriptures.

I am tired of having to apologize for what my brethren have taught. I am tired of having to explain to people that I really do not believe all of the things that they have probably heard that the Church of Christ teaches. By contrast, when I study what the Church of Christ believed, taught and stood for 150 years ago, I feel nothing but extreme pride. I find nothing of any significance that was taught by the leaders of our early restoration movement with which I disagree. I would have been very proud to have been a part of that group.

It is the objective of this document to point out the difference between some of the teachings of the Church of Christ today and those of the Church of Christ 150 years ago. With these differences clear in our minds, we can begin to correct some of the damage that has been caused by the deviations which have been taken from the earlier course. The corrective action needed is really quite simple. We must, once again, recognize the vast difference between what the Bible expressly declares and man's opinion as to what the Bible means.

2

20TH CENTURY CHURCH OF CHRIST DOCTRINE

The method of study which is used in this document is to first identify the major items of doctrine of the contemporary 20th century Church of Christ, and then to carefully examine each item. Each item is measured against both Biblical teaching and against the teachings of the Church of Christ of the early restoration movement some 150 years ago. Since the Church of Christ claims to have no creed there is no official list of doctrinal items to which reference can be made. Of course, most members will admit privately to themselves that the Church of Christ does have a creed, a very strong creed (in fact probably stronger than that of most other religious groups), to which both individuals and congregations must subscribe in order to be accepted as a member of the community. The creed appears in countless books, sermons, periodicals, Sunday school literature and other places where Church of Christ people write about their doctrine. But there is, indeed, no official list.

The list of doctrinal items to be used in this study will be a list such as that which might be assembled by a person who is not a member of the Church of Christ. This would be a person in the community who knows of or about the Church of Christ through association with friends, neighbors, relatives or business associates but who is not himself a member. This is an appropriate perspective because the present study is concerned, in part, with the reputation of the Church of Christ within the community. However, this same list probably reflects the effective order of priority placed on doctrinal items by a composite profile of at least the vocal elements of contemporary Church of Christ leadership. The five most important items on this list, listed in descending order of importance (i.e., most important first) are suggested to the reader as follows:

1. You must be a member of the Church of Christ in order to go to heaven.
2. You must sing a cappella in the Lord's worship in order to go to heaven.
3. The Church of Christ is not a denomination.
4. You must partake of the Lord's supper each Sunday in order to go to heaven.
5. You must be baptized in the proper way by the proper people in order to go to heaven.

This list, of course, does not stop with the fifth item and could be increased until it was quite lengthy. The five items listed, however, are the ones which will be given specific attention in the present study. This is my list, of course, and although I believe it to be very representative of existing conditions some readers might prefer to make some slight adjustments to the contents or the order of arrangement of the items in the list. That is perfectly acceptable and appropriate. The reader is welcome to make any alterations he chooses to such a list based on his personal background and experience. Neither the study presently undertaken nor any of the conclusions drawn from it would suffer in any significant way from some slight rearrangement of the list.

An explanation is in order at this time of why the items in the list are arranged in the particular order given. Each item will be addressed separately and in the order given.

ITEM 1. "You must be a member of the Church of Christ in order to go to heaven." Anyone who knows anything at all about us knows that we think we are the only ones going to heaven. It might be argued that not everyone in the Church of Christ believes this, and not everyone does, but at least for the last 30 to 60 years most have appeared to believe it. At least most teaching from the pulpit during this period has been to this effect. It is the one thing which is most widely known about us. I think that there is no question but that this item belongs at the top of the list.

ITEM 2. "You must sing a cappella in the Lord's worship in order to go to heaven." This item ranks high on the list for two reasons. First, because it is so conspicuous in our assemblies. Anyone visiting one of our congregations for the first time can plainly see that we do not use mechanical instruments of music. A person might visit us several times without hearing our views on baptism. And even though he would, on a first visit, see us partaking of the Lord's supper he might not know that we do that on every Sunday. But he can certainly see, even in a single visit, that we sing a cappella. The second reason that this item ranks so high on the list is because we have emphasized it so much in our teaching and practice. Sometimes it seems that we have almost made it the most important sign of a Christian people or assembly. No matter how close some other group of people might come to mirroring our teaching and practice in every other regard, we would never even consider the possibility of fellowshipping them as Christians if they used an instrument to accompany their singing.

ITEM 3. "The Church of Christ is not a denomination." This item ranks so high on the list because this concept is so ever present in our writing and in our rhetoric. There is scarcely a sermon, a paper, or a chapter in one of our books that does not reference this idea in some way.

ITEM 4. "You must partake of the Lord's supper each Sunday in order to go to heaven." Any visitor who attends our assemblies two or more weeks in a row will realize that we partake of this memorial feast on a weekly basis. This is contrary to the practices of many of the other major religious organizations. Thus this practice sets us apart.

ITEM 5. "You must be baptized in the proper way by the proper people in order to go to heaven." This item might seem to be the most important of the five to us. It is ranked fifth here because it is probably not as apparent to the casual outside observer as the other four items. He might have to know us a little longer or study with us a little more in order to understand this concept. It is ranked below the Lord's supper only because a visitor might not see a baptism or hear a lesson on baptism every Sunday, but he will see that the Lord's supper is observed weekly.

The basic framework for the study which is done throughout the remainder of this document is the careful analysis of the validity of each of these five items.

period Alexander Campbell often spoke to Baptist congregations located within a sixty mile radius. The Baptists encouraged them to join their Redstone Association. This they did in the fall of 1813, with the qualification that they be allowed to teach and preach whatever they learned from the Holy Scriptures, regardless of any creed or formula in Christendom. This began a long and somewhat uneasy alliance with the Baptists, lasting for approximately eighteen years (1813-1831).

Eventually there were efforts underway to expel Alexander Campbell from the Redstone Association. In order to avoid this expulsion he and thirty-one other members of the Brush Run church (on August 31, 1823) withdrew (in good standing) to form the second church of the Campbell reformation in the town of Wellsburg. This second congregation was not a part of the Redstone Association and thus it had no jurisdiction over the members. In September of 1824 the Church of Christ at Wellsburg, now consisting of forty members, solicited and was granted membership in the "Mahoning Baptist Association." In relation to the Baptists, Alexander Campbell once said, "I do intend to continue in connection with this people so long as they will permit me to say what I believe; to teach what I am assured of, and to censure what is amiss in their views or practices."[19] In the years 1830-1831 the association of the Campbell reformers with the Baptists essentially came to an end. The hostility of many of the Baptists toward the reformers had reached a critical level and in many cases the Baptists themselves effected the schism. During this same time period many among the reformers began to question whether or not there was any Biblical authority for the Baptist associations. The Mahoning Association, in 1830, dissolved itself into nothing more than an annual meeting of worship.

During the course of his ministry Alexander Campbell engaged in five major public debates. The first was with Mr. John Walker in

---

19. Ibid., Vol. 2, p. 134.

June of 1820, on the subject of baptism. In this debate Campbell made a connection between baptism and the remission of sins, but he had not yet made a firm commitment to this concept. In his second debate, with Mr. McCalla, a Presbyterian, in October of 1823, the subject of baptism was again examined. By this time the concept of baptism for the forgiveness of sins had become a matter of firm conviction with Alexander Campbell, although he apparently still did not fully understand the ramifications of his new position. Robert Richardson comments on this:

> Thus, in 1823, the design of baptism was fully understood and publicly asserted. It was, however, reserved for Walter Scott, a few years later, to make a direct and practical application of the doctrine, and to secure for it the conspicuous place it has since occupied among the chief points of the Reformation.[20]

In April of 1829 Campbell debated Robert Owen, a world renowned atheist. This debate elevated Mr. Campbell to a very high position in the estimation of the entire religious community. In January of 1837 he debated Bishop Purcell, a Catholic, and in November of 1843 the Rev. N. L. Rice, a Presbyterian, on the subject of baptism. These debates did much to help make both Alexander Campbell himself, and the reformation of which he was a part, well known throughout the land.

In August of 1823 Alexander Campbell began the publication of a monthly periodical called the *Christian Baptist*. There was some degree of debate associated with the adoption of this title. The publication would probably have been simply called the *Christian,* had the reformers not been associated with the Baptists at this time. It was thought expedient to make this concession to the Baptists. In the prospectus the nature and objectives of the publication were stated as follows:

> The "Christian Baptist" shall espouse the cause of no religious sect, excepting that ancient sect "called Christians first at

---

20. Ibid., Vol. 2, p. 84.

Antioch." Its sole object shall be the eviction of truth and the exposing of error in doctrine and practice. The editor, acknowledging no standard of religious faith or works other than the Old and New Testament, and the latter as the only standard of the religion of Jesus Christ, will, intentionally at least, oppose nothing which it contains and recommend nothing which it does not enjoin. Having no worldly interest at stake from the adoption or reprobation of any articles of faith or religious practice, having no gift nor religious emolument to blind his eyes or to pervert his judgment, he hopes to manifest that he is an impartial advocate of truth."[21]

The *Christian Baptist* is a priceless storehouse of ideas and information for anyone interested in the restoration of New Testament Christianity. It was published through July, 1830. At that time Campbell became concerned that the label "Christian Baptist" might become attached to the members of the restoration movement. In 1830 he began the publication of a new periodical under a new title. It was called the *Millennial Harbinger*. This paper was edited by Alexander Campbell and others from 1830 through 1870. The various co-editors were W. K. Pendleton, Robert Richardson, A. W. Campbell, R. Milligan, Isaac Errett and C. L. Loos.

Alexander Campbell was without a doubt the single most influential person in the restoration movement. His monthly papers, first the *Christian Baptist* and then the *Millennial Harbinger,* were major influences in the spread of the reformation. He was a prolific writer. On the last page of the *Memoirs of Alexander Campbell,* Robert Richardson gives a list of Mr. Campbell's published works. He says that in all it totaled about sixty volumes. Alexander Campbell had an outstanding ability (one which unfortunately seems to be rare among religious leaders) to vigorously teach and promote what he believed to be Biblical truth, but simultaneously to be tolerant, understanding and forbearing towards those who did not totally share his point of view. It was

---

21. Ibid., Vol. 2, p. 50.

this ability, without a doubt, which enabled his mellowing influence to prevent any major divisions within the restoration movement during his lifetime. He died on March 4, 1866.

Walter Scott

Walter Scott was a Scotch Presbyterian who was educated at Scotland's Edinburgh University. He immigrated to America in 1818. He soon moved to Pittsburg, Pennsylvania and became an assistant in a school run by George Forrester. Forrester soon convinced Walter Scott to be immersed. Scott first met Alexander Campbell in 1821 and the two subsequently became close friends and co-workers in the restoration movement. Walter Scott wrote for the *Christian Baptist* under the pen name of Philip. Scott's church in Pittsburg was not Baptist and he was not a member of the Mahoning Association. His church was simply called a Church of Christ, as were some of the reformed churches in his native Scotland. They were immersionists but not Baptists.

In the year of 1827 the Baptist churches of the Mahoning Association were not doing well, they were not growing. The Association decided to assign an itinerate preacher to travel among the churches in order to stimulate growth. In 1827, upon the recommendation of Alexander Campbell, Walter Scott was thus selected as "Evangelist upon the Western Reserve." It was in this capacity that he made his unique contribution to the restoration movement and earned the designation as one of the "big four" of the restoration movement, along with Thomas and Alexander Campbell and Barton W. Stone.

In 1827, in Braceville, Jacob Osborne asked Walter Scott if he had ever thought that baptism in the name of the Lord is for the remission of sins.[22] A few days later in Howland, Adamson

---

22. Dwight E. Stevenson, *Voice of the Golden Oracle* (A biography of Walter Scott), Written in 1946; College Press Publishing Company, Box 1132, Joplin, MO 64802, p. 60.

Bentley preached, based on Acts 2:38, that no one had the promise of the Holy Spirit until baptism. "From this moment," says Richardson, "Mr. Scott's mind seemed to be engrossed with the consideration of the consecutive order appropriate to the various items in the gospel, and being greatly given to analysis and arrangement, he proceeded to place them thus: 1. faith 2. repentance 3. baptism 4. remission of sins 5. Holy Spirit. This view relieved at once his previous perplexities, and the gospel, with its items thus regularly disposed, seemed to him almost like a new revelation. He felt that he had now obtained a clue which would extricate men's minds from the labyrinth in which they were involved in relation to conversion, and enable him to present the gospel in all its original simplicity."[23]

In the October, 1828, *Christian Baptist,* in the ninth installment of the "Ancient Gospel," on page 486, Alexander Campbell (who by this time had picked up on Walter Scott's emphasis) gives a smiliar list, but with an interesting augmentation. He in effect presents the "Six steps of the gospel."

> In the natural order of the evangelical economy, the items stand thus;— 1. Faith; 2. Reformation; 3. Immersion; 4. Remission of sins; 5. Holy Spirit; and 6. Eternal life. We do not teach that one of these precedes the other, as cause and effect; but that they are all naturally connected, and all, in this order, embraced in the glad things of salvation. In the apostolic age these items were presented in this order.

A. S. Hayden, in recounting the story of Walter Scott in the book *A History of the Disciples of the Western Reserve,*[24] written apparently around 1871, gives exactly the same list of six steps as those recorded by Campbell in the previous reference. One historian suggested that Walter Scott shortened his original six

---

23. Robert Richardson, *Memoirs of Alexander Campbell,* Vol. 2, pp. 208, 209.

24. A. S. Hayden, *A History of the Disciples on the Western Reserve,* written approx. 1871; Reprinted by Religious Book Service, 722 North Payton Road, Indianapolis, Indiana 46219, p. 71.

steps to five steps so that when he came into a new town for a meeting he could teach them to children on the fingers of one hand. In any case, it is interesting to compare Walter Scott's original "Five (or six) steps of the gospel" to the "Five steps" that we have heard so often preached in the 20th century Church of Christ. Notice that the first three of Scott's steps; 1. Faith, 2. Reformation, 3. Immersion, are things done or action taken by man. The last three of Scott's steps; 4. Remission of sins, 5. The gift of the Holy Spirit, 6. Eternal life, are things granted or done by God. Thus there is a sort of balance in emphasis between man's response by faith to the Scriptural teaching of the Word of God and God's granting, through his grace, salvation, the indwelling of his Holy Spirit and eternal life. By contrast, now, examine the 20th century five steps; 1. Hear, 2. Believe, 3. Repent, 4. Confess, 5. Be baptized. Notice that there has been a drastic change from Scott's original five steps. The modern list is a different set of five and they are all things done by man. No mention is made of God's part in this process of salvation. It might be profitable for 20th century Church of Christ members to contemplate any significance which might be attributable to the differences between these lists. If Walter Scott's original five or six steps had survived the passage of time, perhaps there might have been more of an emphasis on the indwelling of the Holy Spirit in the life of a Christian in the 20th century Church of Christ theology.

Alexander Campbell continues in an interesting vein in the ninth installment of the "Ancient Gospel" mentioned above, on page 487 of the *Christian Baptist*.

> To derange this order in the reign of Favor, is an error of no ordinary magnitude. Yet it is a common error. The Presbyterian arrangement of the items is as follows, viz—1st. Baptism; 2d. The Holy Spirit in effectual calling; 3d. Faith; 4th. Forgiveness of sins; 5th. Reformation. Some Regular Baptists arrange the items thus;—1st. The Holy Spirit; 2d. Faith; 3d. Repentance; 4th. Forgiveness of sins; 5th. Baptism. The Quaker has it the Holy Spirit throughout, and no immersion. Other Baptists have

it—1st. Regeneration, or the Holy Spirit; 2d. Repentance; 3d. Faith; 4th. Forgiveness of sins; and 5th. Baptism. A very different tune is played upon the same notes when the arrangement of them is changed, and so different gospels are preached upon the different ordering of these items. Those who proclaim faith in the Lord Jesus Christ and reformation in order to immersion; and immersion in order to forgiveness and the Holy Spirit, proclaim the same gospel which the Apostles proclaimed.

Walter Scott had at last broken the spell which had long been cast over much of Christendom by Calvinism. Believers no longer had to agonize for weeks, months or years while waiting for some mystical, external, direct operation of the Holy Spirit to indicate to them that finally God had decided to allow them to "get religion" or to be saved. Scott now taught that if a man believed the gospel message, and if he obeyed the teachings of Scripture, he could immediately have confidence in his salvation. It was at New Lisbon, on November 18, 1827, that Walter Scott made his first successful application of his newly acquired understanding. After the manner of Acts 2:38, he called on those in the audience to "Repent, and be baptized every one of you in the name of Jesus Christ for the forgiveness of your sins; and you shall receive the gift of the Holy Spirit." One lone man came forward on this occasion. Scott took his public confession and baptized him that same day in a local stream. At the time of baptism Scott uttered the words, now so familiar to Church of Christ members but then unheard of, "For the forgiveness of sins." This occurrence caused a great commotion in the town. Before the close of the meeting seventeen persons accepted the primitive faith and baptism. This was the beginning of a vigorous and successful evangelistic thrust for the reformers. Thus the restoration movement is indebted to Walter Scott for its single most distinguishing feature, the concept of baptism for the forgiveness of sins. Walter Scott died on April 23, 1861.

One of the most valuable lessons to be learned from a study of restoration history (perhaps the most valuable lesson) is a realization of the fact that it took the pioneer preachers of the restoration movement at least eighteen years to come to their final understanding of the full significance of baptism. In the "Declaration and Address" Thomas Campbell declared in 1809 his intention to reject all human inventions and get back to the Bible. It was June of 1812 before he and his son Alexander decided that their infant sprinkling was not sufficient and that they needed to be immersed. It was 1820 or 1823 before Alexander Campbell was publicly on record as believing that baptism was for the forgiveness of sins, although he still did not comprehend the significance of this relationship. It remained for Walter Scott in 1827 to make the final connection.

Thus if we take 1809 as the starting point it took these highly educated Bible scholars eighteen years to develop this new concept, even after they had made a conscious commitment to get back to the Bible in all things. We in the Church of Christ who have been taught this doctrine since our days in the cradle seem to think that everyone should accept it completely as soon as it is presented to them. We seem not to realize (in our attempts to recruit persons of other religious persuasions) that long held and highly cherished religious beliefs die hard, even if they are false. It often takes many years to change a particular belief. We sometimes expect a prospective convert to completely accept our ideas after hearing one sermon, or at least after a short series of Bible studies. We might be more effective if we could come to realize that seed once planted often sleeps many seasons ere it germinates and brings forth life. It is also interesting to note that all of these pioneer preachers considered themselves to be Christians (saved persons with the expectation of eternal life) throughout this entire period while their understanding of the Scriptures was growing toward maturity. Even after they had arrived at what they considered a full understanding of the significance of baptism (after 1827) they did not consider themselves to have been in a lost condition in the previous years when their understanding was less clear.

Union of the Stone and Campbell Movements

The two religious reformations, one led by Barton W. Stone and the other by Thomas and Alexander Campbell, were entirely separate in their origins. They both, however, occurred in the same general geographical area and they both shared a common theme. They both rejected all human authority in religion and called for a return to the Bible as the only standard. In time the two groups came to realize that they had so many things in common that they should be worshiping God together and working together to promote the cause of Christ. This union became a reality in 1832. First, congregations of the two movements united in Georgetown, Lexington and Paris, Kentucky. Soon this union was effected throughout the state and eventually almost all of the congregations throughout the country became united. These united churches, constituting what we now refer to as the restoration movement, began several decades of highly successful growth in their efforts to promote the restoration of New Testament Christianity.

Divisions Within the Restoration Movement

From 1832 until the mid 1880s the movement continued without any overt divisions. There were disagreements, sometimes heated debate, but the movement did not divide. The movement, in general, seemed to relegate a large number of issues to the realm of personal opinion and to allow differences of opinion on such matters without demanding a cessation of fellowship between the parties involved. These were the values espoused by all of the first generation leaders. However, in the second generation of the movement there arose a group of men who began to expand the list of what they considered to be fundamental Christian doctrine. There was a very small group of influential editors of some of the brotherhood papers who agitated regarding these issues through their periodicals and thus kept the controversies alive. The efforts of this small group of men were instrumental in undermining the spirit of forbearance that had prevailed in the first generation leaders, sowing the seeds of the division which was to come in the third generation. Without the efforts of this small group, perhaps none of the issues would ever have caused the movement to divide. The list of problem issues of the period included: instrumental music, missionary societies, open communion, pew renting, dancing, theatre going, located preachers (such as congregations use today), multiple cups for communion, Sunday schools, salaries for preachers and baptisteries inside the church buildings. The two most persistent problem issues turned out to be instrumental music and missionary societies. History shows that instrumental music caused the most devastating controversies, probably because of its conspicuous presence in the worship assembly.

During the second generation of the movement there were three editors who championed the opposition to the use of instrumental music used to accompany the singing during congregational worship. Moses E. Lard (1818-1880) was the most militant of the three. He taught that the use of instrumental music was a grievous sin and as early as 1864 he called for a complete separation from all who used the instrument.[25] Benjamin Franklin (1812-1878) was perhaps slightly less militant but he also taught that instrumental music was sinful and thus supported the call for separation.[26] J. W. McGarvey (1829-1911) was opposed to the use of instruments;[27,28] however, he maintained fellowship with those who did use them.[29]

---

25. Moses E. Lard, "Instrumental Music in Churches and Dancing," *Lard's Quarterly,* March 1864, Vol. 1, p. 330.

26. Earl West, *The Search for the Ancient Order,* Vol. 2, pp. 88, 89.

27. J. W. McGarvey, "Instrumental Music in Churches," *Millennial Harbinger,* 1864, p. 510.

28. J. W. McGarvey, "Bro. Hayden on Expediency and Progress," *Millennial Harbinger,* 1868, p. 213.

29. Earl West, *The Search for the Ancient Order,* Vol. 3, p. 51.

Historians tell us that the first confirmed introduction of a musical instrument into a restoration movement church was in the year 1859.[30,31] L. L. Pinkerton introduced it into his congregation in Midway, Kentucky. In the years that followed, some congregations adopted the use of the instrument while some did not. There was controversy, but no division. The Stone-Campbell restoration movement even survived the ravages of the Civil War, which divided many Protestant denominations, without experiencing division. This situation might have continued indefinitely, and division might never have come, without the efforts of a protege of Benjamin Franklin, Daniel Sommer, who will be examined later.

The controversies over missionary societies and instrumental music were carried on more or less in parallel. D. S. Burnet (1808-1867) was largely responsible for the emergence of societies within the movement. He organized the American Christian Bible Society in Cincinnati in 1845.[32] It existed for eleven years but was never very successful.

In October, 1849, in Cincinnati, the American Christian Missionary Society was formed.[33] It was Alexander Campbell who finally called for a general convention but the previous work of D. S. Burnet laid the groundwork. Campbell was absent from the convention because of illness but he sent W. K. Pendleton, his son-in-law, in his place. Campbell was elected president in his absence, and D. S. Burnet was elected vice-president. Campbell served as president of the society for the next sixteen years, until his death in 1866. In the beginning the missionary society did not appear to be very controversial. It was formed by messengers from many congregations and it had the support of almost all of the leaders of the time. Even the staunch

---

30. Homer Hailey, *Attitudes and Consequences,* p. 199.
31. Earl West, *The Search for the Ancient Order,* Vol. 1., p. 311.
32. Ibid., p. 164.
33. Bill Humble, *The Story of the Restoration,* p. 39.

conservative Benjamin Franklin was an enthusiastic supporter, though he later changed his mind and opposed it. Jacob Creath Jr. was the leading voice of opposition at this time.[34,35] Two factors caused serious problems for the American Christian Missionary Society. One was the fact that the society had issued two resolutions against slavery during the Civil War, which made the society appear to be as politically minded as missionary minded, even to some northerners. The second was the defection of Benjamin Franklin, then a popular editor in the movement. A different scheme for organization, called the Louisville Plan, was an attempt to save it but was not successful.

The Foreign Christian Missionary Society was formed in 1875 as a result of the efforts of W. T. Moore and Isaac Errett.[36] This was the missionary society for the instrumental music branch of the movement, the Christian Church or the Disciples of Christ, as they moved into the 20th century.

Daniel Sommer (1850-1940) was probably more influential in causing the emergence of the Church of Christ as a separate organization than any other single individual. His Sand Creek Address, August 18, 1889, at Sand Creek, Illinois, was a pivotal event in the history of the restoration movement.[37] The previous paragraphs have shown that prior to this time the movement had handled serious controversies without division. At Sand Creek Sommer preached at length to a large crowd of conservative brethren, condemning what he considered to be innovations. After his sermon a document was read called "An Address and Declaration." This document spoke very strongly against many "innovations." It was amended by the conservatives in 1892 with a clause, recommended for use in the property deeds of churches, that would forbid the use of instrumental music or other innovations on the premises.[38] In the conclusion of this

---

34. Earl West, *The Search for the Ancient Order,* Vol. 1, pp. 193, 201.
35. Bill Humble, *The Story of the Restoration,* p. 41.
36. Ibid., p. 61.
37. Matthew C. Morrison, *Like a Lion,* p. 85.
38. Ibid., p. 97.

address was a call to no longer consider as brethren (thus to disfellowship) all who would not, in effect, pledge allegiance to this document.[39] Thus, for the first time in the restoration movement, a major effort was underway to make a test of fellowship over things which had previously been considered by the majority to be matters of personal opinion. Matthew C. Morrison, in his biography of Sommer, says the following:

> Daniel Sommer's Sand Creek Address not only marked the high point of his strength and popularity as a preacher, but it precipitated inevitable division and thereby publicly defined two incompatible brotherhoods—the Churches of Christ and the Disciples of Christ.[40]

David Lipscomb (1883-1917) was both an editor and an educator. He founded Nashville Bible College (now David Lipscomb College)[41] and served for 46 years as editor of the Gospel Advocate.[42] Lipscomb was opposed to both instrumental music and missionary societies. He at first resisted efforts to separate from the Christian Church but later changed his mind and called for division. In the third generation of the restoration movement these two men, Daniel Sommer in the North and David Lipscomb in the South, were major catalysts in bringing about the emergence of the Church of Christ as a separate body. They built upon the foundation laid by Lard, Franklin and McGarvey in the second generation. In 1906 David Lipscomb and J. W. Shepherd provided information to the U. S. Census Bureau listing the Churches of Christ as an organization entirely separate from the Christian Church. This is usually considered by historians as the official date for the beginning of the Church of Christ as a separate body, although the events at Sand Creek in 1889 might be a better date.

It is clear from the history that a relatively small percentage of the Stone-Campbell restoration movement separated themselves

---

39. Ibid., p. 96.
40. Ibid., p. 99.
41. Earl West, *The Search for the Ancient Order,* Vol. 2, p. 368.
42. Bill Humble, *The Story of the Restoration,* p. 64.

from the main body of the movement to form the Church of Christ. The 1906 census report listed 892,701 members of the Christian Church and 159,658 members of the Church of Christ.[43] These numbers say that at the time of the official separation the Church of Christ only consisted of approximately fourteen percent of the size of the previously combined group, a quite small minority. However, in the decades that followed the separation, the Church of Christ became very evangelistic and experienced a rapid growth. This next generation was the era of G. C. Brewer, N. B. Hardeman and Foy E. Wallace Jr., among many other significant leaders, when the Church of Christ grew and flourished. Unfortunately, this was also an era of divisions. Some have claimed that there are over 25 divisions within the Church of Christ today, although all except the mainstream group are relatively small. These divisions have been over such issues as Sunday schools, one cup vs. multiple cups for the Lord's supper, wine vs. grape juice for the Lord's supper, and non-cooperation between congregations.

After the Church of Christ became a separate organization, the main body of the restoration movement was generally called the Christian Church or the Disciples of Christ. During the first half of the 20th century a very liberal element emerged within this body. The new liberal theology and modern Biblical criticism, which had arisen in Germany late in the 1800s, and which touched most of the American Protestant denominations, had an impact on the Disciples. Some even began to question such fundamentals as the inspiration of the Bible and the virgin birth of Christ. Open membership (accepting members into their congregations without requiring immersion) began to be practiced by some. Cooperating with or uniting with other denominations became more important than their restoration heritage. In 1968 the liberal wing of this body restructured itself into an "official" denomination with its own hierarchial intercongregational organization. This Church is now known as the Disciples of Christ (or the Christian Church-Disciples of Christ).

---

43. Ibid., p. 66.

There was a conservative segment of the Disciples which resisted these liberal trends and remained more true to their restoration heritage. They have now separated from the Disciples of Christ and are now known generally as the Independent Christian church (also sometimes as Christian Churches-Churches of Christ). The emergence of the Independent Christian Church as a separate fellowship during the first half of the 20th century resulted in the establishment of three separate churches from within the original restoration movement. The "Independent" or "Conservative" Christian Churches are doctrinally very conservative and just as committed to the restoration principle as are the Churches of Christ. They practice baptism for the forgiveness of sins and weekly communion. They have autonomous congregations ministered to by elders and often wear the name "Church of Christ." The most important difference between the Independent Christian Church and the Church of Christ is the use of instrumental music by the Independent Christian Church. They have an annual "North American Christian Convention," similar to the Christian college lectureships of the Churches of Christ.

LIST OF 19TH CENTURY DOCTRINAL ITEMS

In the process of studying the history of the Stone-Campbell restoration movement of the early 1800s I realized that their teachings did not correspond exactly to the Church of Christ teachings of the 20th century as stated in the five items of chapter two above. Two of the items of chapter two were not taught at all in the early 19th century restoration movement and were advocated by only a relatively small minority toward the end of the 19th century. At least three of the oft stated beliefs of the founders of the restoration movement I had never heard taught in a 20th century Church of Christ. I have prepared a composite list which I feel is a fair description of the teaching of the early restoration leaders. I do not claim this list to be comprehensive, although it is accurate. I have identified ten major items which are listed below.

1. The belief that Jesus Christ is the Son of God and that man without Christ is eternally lost; however, because of the death of Christ on the cross as an expiation for our sins, man can have eternal life in heaven, by the grace of God, through faith in Jesus Christ and obedience to his teachings.
2. The belief that the primary evidence that a man is a Christian is the demonstration of a Christlike character in his life, what they sometimes called a vital piety, without which they felt no man could inherit eternal life.
3. The belief that in addition to the Christlike life the Christian institution on this earth consisted of three primary elements:
   a. The weekly observance of the Lord's day (the first day of the week).
   b. The weekly observance of the Lord's supper.
   c. The concept of baptism by immersion for the forgiveness of sins.
4. Back to the Bible as the only rule of faith and duty.
5. The right and duty of each individual to study and interpret the Bible for himself; and that each person must obey the teachings of Scripture to the limit of his own understanding (not to the limit of someone else's understanding).
6. Opposition to ecclesiastical organizations, including their use of the official clergy and their abuse of the use of human creeds.
7. The firm and oft stated belief that there were some Christians to be found among the membership of all of the denominations, including even the Roman Catholic.
8. The belief that the Holy Spirit does not cause an individual to be converted to Christ by some mystical, external, direct operation on his body or on his mind. Rather they taught that for the unconverted sinner the Holy Spirit, in the process of conversion, acts only through the word of God, the Bible.

They taught that man is a free moral agent and that he must make a free will decision to accept Christ. Then, after making this commitment to Christ, and after baptism by immersion for the forgiveness of sin, through the grace of God by faith in Jesus Christ, they believed that the new Christian received the gift of the Holy Spirit, the Comforter, with all of its attendant benefits.

9. They were non-pentecostal and non-charismatic. They were opposed to the idea of a second, separate baptism of the Holy Spirit subsequent to water baptism. They believed that Jesus Christ is all-sufficient and that baptism into Christ left the Christian lacking in nothing. They were opposed to such mystical manifestations of the Holy Spirit as tongue speaking, faith healing and direct revelations from God to man, in the present age.

10. They believed and taught that our God is a prayer-hearing and a prayer-answering God. They believed that the presence of the Holy Spirit in the life of a Christian was a very real and active thing. They taught that the Christian should pray to God for assistance and have a very real hope that it would be granted, provided that the request was consistent with God's will.

TWO SEPARATE AND DISTINCT CHURCH OF CHRIST TRADITIONS

If we compare the doctrine of the 19th century Church of Christ (as listed in chapter three) with the doctrine of the 20th century Church of Christ (the five items of chapter two) we will see that there are some distinct differences. A careful study will show that the differences are of such a nature and of such significance as to indicate that there are in reality two separate and distinct Church of Christ traditions. The contemporary Church of Christ tradition could be appropriately termed the 20th century tradition and the tradition established during roughly the first half of our movement could be called the 19th century Church of Christ tradition. There is some overlap between the two just before and around the turn of the century, but in their character and their impact on the world they are separate and distinct.

It is thus interesting to realize that some of what we today may have considered to be traditional Church of Christ doctrine is really of fairly recent origin, perhaps less than one hundred years old. In fact, some of the smaller, more conservative congregations have doctrinal traditions which are only about thirty years old.

One item must be mentioned for the benefit of all heirs of the restoration movement who are not members of the Church of Christ. We realize full well that in the 19th century the label "Church of Christ" was not the exclusive name for those within the restoration movement. They were also often called the "Christian Church" or sometimes "Disciples" or in the early days "Reformers." The exclusive use in this document of the name Church of Christ when referring to the 19th century movement is nothing more than a matter of convenience.

PART II

MAJOR ELEMENTS OF BOTH 19TH AND 20TH CENTURY TRADITIONS

In this section we will examine some of the major elements of the restoration movement of the 19th century which have remained as major elements of our 20th century Church of Christ doctrine. These are items or concepts which we believe to be fundamental characteristics of a church which is fashioned after the church of New Testament times. If any person or persons should feel disposed to reject these few basic points of doctrine there would then be no reason for them to claim any allegiance whatsoever to the Stone-Campbell restoration movement. They would be rejecting the very characteristics which made this religious reformation unique.

I believe that the vast majority of Church of Christ members in all of the various sub-groups still believe in these basic points of doctrine. However, I believe that in some circles we have produced a generation which is not very well educated in these fundamentals nor very adequately able to defend our position or teach it to others. In some congregations we seem to teach more psychology and positive thinking concepts than Christian doctrine. I don't think this is by design, I think that it is rather a result of something else. Some of our people have become embarrassed by the fact that some of the standard 20th century Church of Christ doctrine has a negative tone and is not conducive to positive church growth. They have tried to solve the problems, not with the proper approach of correcting any errors in our doctrine, but by not teaching much doctrine at all. In the long run this will be a self-destructive approach.

The ordinances of baptism and the Lord's supper were given special emphasis by the early restoration leaders, and they are still considered fundamental by the Church of Christ of today. Both of these are given somewhat detailed examinations in this section, based on the Scriptures. In each case, after our present doctrine is authenticated based on the Bible, sufficient quotations are provided from the early restoration leaders to establish that they were unquestionably "sound" and "conservative" regarding these issues.

4

BAPTISM

It has always been maintained by those within the Stone-Campbell restoration movement that Christian baptism is to be administered to believers, by immersion, for the forgiveness of sins. The early restoration leaders were as committed to this principle as our most conservative brethren of today. Where they differed from some of our contemporary brethren was on the subject of how to relate to or deal with other people who claim to be Christians but who do not completely agree with us regarding baptism. In later chapters we will quote many of our pioneer leaders on the subject of Christian fellowship. In order to lay a foundation for these later discussions we will present in this chapter sufficient quotes from the same sources to show that the early leaders were sound, conservative and uncompromising regarding the doctrine of baptism, by immersion, for the forgiveness of sins.

ENDANGERED HERITAGE

We in the Church of Christ have been accused by many of preaching a spiritless, graceless, faithless, water salvation. This has never been a fair nor an accurate description of our doctrine. What we have taught is that baptism by immersion in water, in connection with repentance of our sins and a true faith in Christ, brings about the forgiveness of our sins. This is by the grace of God, made available by the death of his Son and our Saviour Jesus Christ, on the cross, as an expiation for our sins. We have never taught that baptism was more important than faith or grace or repentance or confessing his Holy name or the living of a Christlike life. What we have strongly resisted, and rightly so, is the teaching of some other religious groups that salvation is somehow related to faith, grace, repentance, and the blood of Christ but not at all related to baptism.

Throughout the centuries since the time of Christ those who have claimed allegiance to his name have often been inclined to extremes on the subject of baptism, some in one direction and some in the other. It seems to be a common tendency of man to try with such zeal to avoid one extreme that he winds up positioned completely at the other end of the spectrum, in a position exactly opposite to, but no less extreme than, the other. The Roman Catholics in former times considered the mere act of immersion or sprinkling, irrespective of the sentiments, faith, or feelings of the subject, as being capable of washing away sins. They supposed that the mere pronunciation of the names constituting the "Holy Trinity," together with two or three drops of water from the baptized finger of a Priest, forgave all sins, whether "original or actual," and therefore contended, "no baptism, no salvation." Because they carried their theology to this immense extreme, many Protestants following the Reformation ran to an equal extreme on the other side of the equator of truth; and therefore gave baptism, however administered, no connection with the remission of sins. They hated the errors of Catholicism so much that they would scarcely mention "the forgiveness of sins" on the same day on which they "administered baptism." This is not the only instance in which the Protestants were driven to an extreme, because of a Catholic practice. Thus, as the Catholics laid so much stress upon fasting, as to make it almost more than "a sacrament," many Protestants would not fast at all, in order not to appear like the Catholics.

The founders of the Stone-Campbell restoration movement had the history of both the Roman Catholics and the Protestants before them for evaluation during the period when they were searching the Scriptures in their efforts to determine the true nature of Christianity. It seems that the Lord smiled on their efforts and allowed them to gravitate to a well balanced position more or less equidistant from the two extremes. They did not allow themselves to lose sight of the forgiveness of sins in baptism (by immersion) simply because the Roman Catholics had made a savior of a mere ceremony. Similarly, they did not lose sight of the importance of faith in salvation just because some Protestant groups claimed that salvation is based on faith alone and is completely unrelated to baptism. They taught that faith is absolutely essential to salvation and that baptism is meaningless without it. We in the Church of Christ, as heirs of the restoration movement, have inherited this well-balanced view of baptism and its sigificance in the Christian economy. This is one of the reasons why we have a heritage worthy of our study and a message of tremendous value which we must effectively communicate to the world.

In order to lay a foundation for our study of baptism it will be useful to show the relationship between the old and the new covenants (the law of Moses and the kingdom of Christ) and to recognize the part played by the death of Jesus Christ in God's overall plan for mankind. These things are recognized and understood by most within Christendom today and are addressed at this time only to lay a proper groundwork for our study of baptism.

Under the law of Moses the Levitical priests offered sacrifices yearly (the blood of goats and bulls) for the sins of their people.

This covenant, the law of Moses, was only a shadow of the things to come. Jesus Christ offered himself as a sacrifice for mankind, once and for all, by shedding his blood in death on the cross. He thus established a new covenant, more perfect than the old. The ninth chapter of Hebrews tells this story: [quotations from the Revised Standard Version]

Heb. 9:1 Now even the first covenant had regulations for worship and an earthly sanctuary. (2) For a tent was prepared, the outer one, in which were the lampstand and the table and the bread of the Presence; it is called the Holy Place. (3) Behind the second curtain stood a tent called the Holy of Holies, (4) having the golden altar of incense and the ark of the covenant covered on all sides with gold, which contained a golden urn holding the manna, and Aaron's rod that budded, and the tables of the covenant: (5) above it were the cherubim of glory overshadowing the mercy seat. Of these things we cannot now speak in detail.

(6) These preparations having thus been made, the priests go continually into the outer tent, performing their ritual duties; (7) but into the second only the high priest goes, and he but once a year, and not without taking blood which he offers for himself and for the errors of the people. (8) By this the Holy Spirit indicates that the way into the sanctuary is not yet opened as long as the outer tent is still standing (9) (which is symbolic for the present age). According to this arrangement, gifts and sacrifices are offered which cannot perfect the conscience of the worshiper, (10) but deal only with food and drink and various ablutions, regulations for the body imposed until the time of reformation.

(11) But when Christ appeared as a high priest of the good things that have come, then through the greater and more perfect tent (not made with hands, that is, not of this creation) (12) he entered once for all into the Holy Place, taking not the blood of goats and calves but his own blood, thus securing an eternal redemption. (13) For if the sprinkling of defiled persons with the blood of goats and bulls and with the ashes of a heifer sanctifies for the purification of the flesh, (14) how much more shall the blood of Christ, who through the eternal Spirit offered himself without blemish to God, purify your conscience from dead works to serve the living God. (15) Therefore he is the

BAPTISM

mediator of a new covenant, so that those who are called may receive the promised eternal inheritance, since a death has occurred which redeems them from the transgressions under the first covenant. . . .

(22) Indeed, under the law [the law of Moses] almost everything is purified with blood, and without the shedding of blood there is no forgiveness of sins. (23) Thus it was necessary for the copies of the heavenly things to be purified with these rites, [blood sacrifices] but the heavenly things themselves with better sacrifices than these. (24) For Christ has entered, not into a sanctuary made with hands, a copy of the true one, but into heaven itself, now to appear in the presence of God on our behalf. (25) Nor was it to offer himself repeatedly, as the high priest enters the Holy Place yearly with blood not his own; (26) for then he would have had to suffer repeatedly since the foundation of the world. But as it is, he has appeared once for all at the end of the age to put away sin by the sacrifice of himself. (27) And just as it is appointed for men to die once, and after that comes judgment, (28) so Christ, having been offered once to bear the sins of many, will appear a second time, not to deal with sin but to save those who are eagerly waiting for him.

And now a few related verses from the tenth chapter of Hebrews:

Heb. 10:9 . . . He [Christ] abolishes the first in order to establish the second. (10) And by that will we have been sanctified through the offering of the body of Jesus Christ once for all. . . .
(14) For by a single offering he has perfected for all time those who are sanctified.
(16) "This is the covenant that I will make with them. . . . (17) . . . I will remember their sins and their misdeeds no more."
(19) Therefore, brethren, since we have a confidence to enter the sanctuary by the blood of Jesus, (20) by the new and living way which he opened for us through the curtain, that is, through his flesh, (20) and since we have a great priest over the house of God, (22) let us draw near with a true heart in full assurance of faith, with our hearts sprinkled clean from an evil conscience and our bodies washed with pure water.

From this basic presentation it is already evident that we have redemption (i.e., forgiveness of sins; salvation; eternal life) in

Christ or in his body, through his death and by his blood. But to pursue this fundamental point even farther, the following verses establish that redemption, in fact every spiritual blessing, is *in Christ*: [all italics are, of course, inserted by the author for emphasis].

Romans 8:1	There is therefore now no condemnation for those who are *in Christ* Jesus.
2 Cor. 1:20	For all the promises of God find their Yes *in him*. That is why we utter the Amen through him, to the glory of God.
2 Cor. 5:17	Therefore, if any one is *in Christ*, he is a new creation; the old has passed away, behold, the new has come.
Eph. 1:3	Blessed be the God and Father of our Lord Jesus Christ, who has blessed us *in Christ* with every spiritual blessing. . . .
Col. 1:13	He [the Father] has delivered us from the dominion of darkness and transferred us to the kingdom of his beloved Son, (14) *in whom* we have redemption, the forgiveness of sins.

Now to continue in a similar vein, the Scriptures repeatedly emphasize that all of these spiritual blessings can be spoken of not only as being "in Christ" but also as being in, or through, or by *his blood*:

Romans 5:8	But God shows his love for us in that while we were yet sinners Christ died for us. (9) Since, therefore, we are now *justified by his blood,* much more shall we be saved by him from the wrath of God.
Eph. 1:7	In him we have *redemption through his blood,* the *forgiveness of our trespasses,* according to the riches of his grace. . . .

BAPTISM

Eph. 2:13	But now *in Christ Jesus* you who once were far off have been *brought near in the blood of Christ.*
1 Pet. 1:18	You know that you were ransomed from the futile ways inherited from your fathers, not with perishable things such as silver or gold, (19) but *with the precious blood of Christ,* like that of a lamb without blemish or spot.
1 John 1:7	. . . if we walk in the light, as he is in the light, we have fellowship with one another, and *the blood of Jesus his Son cleanses us from all sin.*
Rev. 7:14	. . . These are they who have come out of the great tribulation; they have washed their robes and made them *white in the blood of the Lamb.*
Rev. 12:11	And they have conquered him [Satan] *by the blood of the Lamb* and by the word of their testimony, . . .

If, indeed, all of the spiritual blessings are "in Christ" then that is certainly where we need to be. The next question is, then, how do we get into Christ, into his body, into his kingdom or come in contact with (gain the benefits of) his shed blood? The following verses from the inspired writers give us the answer:

John 3:3	Truly, truly, I say unto you, *unless one is born anew,* he cannot see the kingdom of God.
John 3:5	Truly, truly, I say to you, *unless one is born of water and the Spirit,* he cannot enter the kingdom of God.
Romans 6:3	Do you not know that all of us who have been *baptized into Christ Jesus* were *baptized into his death*?
1 Cor. 12:13	For by one Spirit we were all *baptized into one body.*
Gal. 3:27	*For as many of you as were baptized into Christ have put on Christ.*

Thus it is through the waters of baptism that we get into Christ, where every spiritual blessing lies. But this is only a part of the data to be presented. There is a direct parallel between the death of Christ on the cross, his burial in the tomb, and his resurrection to reign victorious over death; and our burial in the waters of baptism, our death thereby to the old man of sin, and our rising to walk victorious over sin through Christ. We now present two verses which show this parallel:

Romans 6:4 — *We were buried therefore with him by baptism into death, so that as Christ was raised from the dead by the glory of the Father, we too might walk in newness of life.*

Col. 2:11 — In him also you were circumcised with a circumcision made without hand, by putting off the body of flesh in the circumcision of Christ; (12) *and you were buried with him in baptism, in which you were also raised with him through faith in the working of God, who raised him from the dead.* (13) And you, who were dead in trespasses and the uncircumcision of your flesh, God made alive together with him, having forgiven us all our trespasses, (14) having cancelled the bond which stood against us with its legal demands; this he set aside, nailing it to the cross. (15) He disarmed the principalities and powers and made a public example of them, triumphing over them in him.

Reference in these verses to burial seems to answer the question regarding the mode of baptism: sprinkling, pouring or immersion? Although there may be no statement in the common English translations of the New Testament which explicitly says immersion, the conditions surrounding the examples of baptism which are recorded for us establish beyond any doubt that immersion was the mode by which baptism was administered in New Testament times, as recorded by the inspired Apostles. If, indeed, this was how the first century Christians administered baptism then we would be foolish to do it in any other way.

First of all John tells us that baptism required *much* water.

BAPTISM

John 3:23 — John also was baptizing at Aē'nŏn near Sālĭm, *because there was much water there;* and people came and were baptized.

It would not have required much water for pouring, certainly not for sprinkling. Next we observe that persons were sometimes baptized "in," not "near" a river and that on other occasions they *went down into the water* and *came up out of the water.* Sprinkling would not require any of these circumstances.

Matt. 3:6 — ... and they were baptized by him *in the river* Jordan, confessing their sins.

Matt. 3:16 — And when Jesus was baptized, *he went up immediately from the water.*

Mark 1:9 — In those days Jesus came from Nazareth of Galilee and was baptized by John in the Jordan. (10) *And when he came up out of the water,* immediately he saw the heavens opened and the Spirit descending upon him like a dove; (11) and a voice came from heaven, "thou art my beloved Son; with thee I am well pleased."

Acts 8:38 — And he commanded the chariot to stop, and *they both went down into the water,* Philip and the eunuch, and he baptized him.

Acts 8:39 — And when they came *up out of the water,* the Spirit of the Lord caught up Philip; and the eunuch saw him no more, and went on his way rejoicing.

Having thus concluded that the earliest mode of baptism was immersion, we could ask next about its design. What is the purpose of baptism? Several passages answer this question clearly and directly. We are told in language so simple and direct that it is difficult to see how men could misunderstand that baptism is: for the forgiveness of sins, in order to be saved, in order to receive the gift of the Holy Spirit, to wash away sins and as a washing of regeneration. Notice carefully the following:

Mark 1:4 — John the baptizer appeared in the wilderness, preaching a baptism of repentance *for the forgiveness of sins.*

Mark 16:15	And he said to them, "Go into all the world and preach the gospel to the whole creation. (16) *He who believes and is baptized will be saved*:
Luke 3:3	... and he went into all the region about the Jordan, *preaching a baptism of repentance for the forgiveness of sins.*
Acts 2:38	Repent, and be baptized every one of you in the name of Jesus Christ *for the forgiveness of your sins; and you shall receive the gift of the Holy Spirit.*
Acts 22:16	And now why do you wait? Rise and *be baptized and wash away your sins,* calling on his name.
Eph. 5:25	Husbands, love your wives, as Christ loved the church and gave himself up for her, (26) that he might sanctify her, *having cleansed her by the washing of water with the word,* (27) that he might present the church to himself in splendor, without spot or wrinkle or any such thing, that she might be holy and without blemish.
Titus 3:3	For we ourselves were once foolish, disobedient, led astray, slaves to various passions and pleasures, passing our days in malice and envy, hated by men and hating one another; (4) but when the goodness and loving kindness of God our Savior appeared, (5) *he saved us, not because of deeds done by us in righteousness, but in virtue of his own mercy, by the washing of regeneration and renewal in the Holy Spirit,* (6) which he poured out upon us richly through Jesus Christ our Savior, (7) so that we might be justified by his grace and become heirs in hope of eternal life.
1 Pet. 3:20	... when God's patience waited in the days of Noah, during the building of the ark, in which a few, that is, eight persons, were saved through water. (21) *Baptism, which corresponds to this, now saves you,* not as a removal of dirt from the body but as an appeal to God for a clear conscience, through the resurrection of Jesus Christ.

These verses clearly indicate what has been long maintained by those within the restoration movement, that the New Testament clearly teaches that a very well defined and intimate relationship exists between baptism and the forgiveness of sins.

But someone with a different church background may say I didn't quote the verses that deal with faith. They may say they can show me more verses that say faith saves than I have assembled regarding baptism. But, I can counter their argument by simply acquiescing to them on this point and saying, "yea verily, perhaps you can; and I believe every such verse you can find." Some people, in effect, embrace what I call an "OR" theology. They concentrate on or accept the verses stressing faith "OR" the verses stressing baptism. I prefer an "AND" theology, in which our doctrine should be consistent with all of the verses found in Scripture. The restoration movement has historically accepted both the verses which teach of faith "AND" those which teach of baptism; because, they all blend together harmoniously into the gospel of our Lord and Saviour Jesus Christ, as revealed in the Holy Scriptures.

It is a childlike faith that leads one to search the Scriptures from cover to cover, throughout a lifetime, for a more complete understanding of God's will. It is this diligent search that leads one to a more thorough understanding of baptism, as well as faith and grace. The faith that saves, often referred to as "saving faith," is not simply a faith that says, "I believe that God exists and that Jesus Christ is his Son." The Bible tells us that even the demons believe this, and tremble at the thought. A "saving faith" is a faith that leads a person to make a commitment to recreate the image of Jesus Christ in his own life. A part of this commitment is a continuous search of the Scriptures to better understand God's will for our lives. A faith that saves is a faith that will lead one to obey each directive or command when it comes to be comprehended and understood. One of the truths which is clearly propounded in God's word is that baptism, by immersion, is the initiation process into the Lord's Kingdom.

It brings us into Christ, into contact with the blood of Christ, and avails us of the forgiveness of our sins, the comforting aid of the Holy Spirit and the hope of eternal life.

The development presented above, regarding the nature of baptism, is completely consistent with the doctrine taught within the early restoration movement. One of the most well known leaders of the movement, and the major spokesman for the first fifty or sixty years, was Alexander Campbell. The periodicals which he published were widely circulated and contributed to the successful growth of the movement. Many historians credit his influence as the major factor in preventing any open divisions in the movement during his lifetime. He wrote extensively on the subject of baptism. In his second monthly periodical, the *Millennial Harbinger,* he published a comprehensive treatise on the subject of baptism in the Extra No. I, which appears in the back of the 1830 volume. It is entitled "Remission of Sins." This is probably the most comprehensive treatise on baptism to come out of the restoration movement. We will examine some carefully selected segments from this article. The purpose here is to show how strongly Alexander Campbell believed and taught the orthodox, Church of Christ, doctrine on this subject. The reader must understand how very "sound" Campbell is regarding baptism in order to be able to view his later writings on the subject of Christian fellowship from a proper perspective. The writings of Campbell on this subject are representative of the thinking and the teaching of most of the major leaders of his period.

We will now examine a series of excerpts from the *Millennial Harbinger* Extra No. I, "Remission of Sins," by Alexander Campbell, dated Monday, July 5, 1830. On page 30 of this article Campbell is commenting on John 3:5.

> Some curious criticisms have been offered, to escape the force of the plain declaration of Jesus and his Apostles, upon this subject. Some say, that the words, "Except a man be born of water and Spirit," are not to be understood literally. Surely, then, if to be born of water does not mean to be born of water,

to be born of the Spirit, must mean something else than to be born of the Spirit. This is so fanatical and extravagant as to need no other exposure. He who cannot see the propriety of calling immersion a being born again, can see no propriety in any metaphor in common use. A resurrection is a new birth. Jesus is said to be the first born from the dead; because the first who rose from the dead to die no more. And, surely there is no abuse in speech; but the greatest propriety in saying, that he who has died to sin, and been buried in water, when raised up again out of that element, is born again, or regenerated. If Jesus was born again, when he came out of a sepulchre, surely he is born again who is raised up out of the grave of waters.

(p. 34) . . . remission of sins, or coming into a state of acceptance, being one of the present immunities of the kingdom of heaven, cannot be enjoyed by any person before immersion. . . . remission of sins cannot, in this life, be received or enjoyed previous to immersion.

(pp. 34-35) "Conversion" is, on all sides, understood to be a turning to God. Not a thinking favorably of God, nor a repenting for former misdeeds; but an actual turning to God, in word and in deed. It is true, that no person can be said to turn to God, whose mind is not enlightened, and whose heart is not well disposed towards God. All human actions, not resulting from previous thought or determination, are rather the actions of a machine, than the actions of a rational being. "He that comes to God," or turns to him, "must believe that God exists, and that he is a rewarder of every one who diligently seeks him." Then he will seek and find the Lord. An "external conversion" is no conversion at all. A turning to God with the lips, while the heart is far from him, is mere pretense and mockery. But though I never thought any thing else, since I thought upon religion; I understand the "turning to God, taught in the New Institution, to be a coming to the Lord Jesus—not a thinking about doing it, nor a repenting that we have not done it;—but an actual coming to him. The question then is, Where shall we find him? Where shall we meet him? No where on earth, but in his institutions. "Where he records his name," there only can he be found; for there only has he promised to be found. I affirm, then, that the first institution in which we can meet with God, is, the institution for remission. And here it is worthy of notice, that the Apostles, in all their speeches, and replies to interrogatories, never commanded an inquirer to pray, read, or sing, as preliminary to coming; but always commanded and proclaimed immersion as the first duty, or the first thing to be done, after a belief of the testimony. Hence, neither praying, singing, reading, repenting, sorrowing, resolving, nor waiting to be better, was the converting act. Immersion alone was that act of turning to God. Hence, in the commission to convert the nations, the only institution mentioned after proclaiming the gospel, was the immersion of the believers, as the divinely authorized way of carrying out and completing the work. And from the day of Pentecost, to the final Amen in the revelation of Jesus Christ, no person was said to be converted, or to turn to God, until he was buried in, and raised up out of the water. I call upon them who dissent, to specify an instance to the contrary.

If it were not to treat this subject as one of doubtful disputation, I would say; that, had there not been some act, such as immersion, agreed on all hands, to be the medium of remission and the act of conversion and regeneration; the Apostles could not, with any regard to truth or consistency, have addressed the disciples as pardoned, justified, sanctified, reconciled, adopted, and saved persons. If all this had depended upon some mental change, as faith; they could never have addressed their congregations in any other way than as the moderns do: and that is always in the language of doubt and uncertainty—hoping a little, and fearing much. This mode of address and the modern compared, is proof positive that they viewed the immersed through one medium, and we through another. They taught all the disciples to consider not only themselves as saved persons; but all whom they saw, or knew to be immersed into the Lord Jesus. They saluted every one, on his coming out of the water, as saved, and recorded him as such. Luke writes, (Acts ii) "The Lord added the saved daily to the congregation."

(p. 36) No man can, scripturally, be said to be converted to God until he is immersed. How ecclesiastics interpret their own language is no concern of ours. We contend for the pure speech, and for the apostolic ideas attached to it.

(pp. 36-37) Many, seeing so much stress laid upon faith or belief, suppose that all blessings flow from it immediately. This is a great mistake. Faith, indeed, is the principle, and the distinguishing principle, of this economy. But it is only the principle

BAPTISM

of action. Hence, we find the name, or person of Christ always interposed between faith and the cure, mental or corporeal. The woman, who touched the tuft of the mantle of Jesus, had as much faith before as after; but though her faith was the cause of her putting forth her hand, and accompanied it; she was not cured until the touch. That great type of Christ, the brazen serpent, cured no Israelite simply by faith. The Israelites, as soon as they were bitten, believed it would cure them. But yet they were not cured as soon as bitten; nor until they looked to the serpent. It was one thing to believe, that looking at the serpent would cure them; and another to look at it. It was the faith, remotely; but, immediately, the look, which cured them. It was not faith in the waters of Jordan that healed the leprosy of Naaman the Syrian. It was immersing himself in it, according to the commandment. It was not faith in the pool of Siloam, that cured the blind man, whose eyes Jesus anointed with clay; it was his washing his eyes in Siloam's water. Hence, the imposition of hands, or a word, or a touch, or the shadow, or something from the persons of those anointed with the Holy Spirit, was the immediate cause of all the cures recorded in the New Testament. 'Tis true, also, that without it is impossible to be healed; for in some places Jesus could not work many miracles, because of their unbelief. It is so in all the moral remedies and cures. It is impossible to receive the remission of sins without faith. In this world of means, (however it may be in a world where there are no means) it is as impossible to receive any blessing through faith without the appointed means. Both are indispensable. Hence, the name of the Lord Jesus is interposed between faith and forgiveness, justification and sanctification, even where immersion into that name is not detailed. It would have been unprecedented in the annals of the world, for the historian always to have recorded all the circumstances of the same institution, on every allusion to it; and it would have been equally so for the Apostles to have mentioned it always in the same words.

Some captious spirits need to be reminded, that as they sometimes find forgiveness, justification, sanctification, &c. ascribed to grace, to the blood of Christ, to the name of the Lord, without an allusion to faith; so we sometimes find faith, and grace, and the blood of Christ without an allusion to water. Now, if they have any reason, or right to say, that faith is understood in the one case; we have the same reason and right to say, that water or immersion is understood in the other. For their argument is, that in sundry places this matter is made plain enough. This is, also, our argument—in sundry places this matter is made plain enough. This single remark cuts off all their objections drawn from the fact, that immersion is not always found in every place where the name of the Lord, or faith is found connected with forgiveness. Neither is grace, the blood of Christ, nor faith, always mentioned with forgiveness. When they find a passage where remission of sins is mentioned without immersion, it is weak, or unfair, in the extreme, to argue from that, that forgiveness can be enjoyed without immersion. IF THEIR LOGIC BE WORTH ANYTHING, IT WILL PROVE, THAT A MAN MAY BE FORGIVEN WITHOUT GRACE, THE BLOOD OF JESUS, AND WITHOUT FAITH: FOR WE CAN FIND PASSAGES, MANY PASSAGES, WHERE REMISSION, OR JUSTIFICATION, SANCTIFICATION, OR SOME SIMILAR TERM OCCURS, AND NO MENTION OF EITHER GRACE, FAITH, OR THE BLOOD OF JESUS.

As this is the pith, the marrow, and fatness of all the logic of our most ingenious opponents on this subject, I wish I could make it more emphatic, than by printing it in capitals. I know some editors, some of our Doctors of Divinity, some of our most learned declaimers, who make this argument, which we unhesitatingly call a genuine sophism, the alpha and the omega of their speeches against the meaning, and indispensable importance of immersion, or regeneration.

(p. 38) The New Testament would have been a curious book, if, every time remission of sins was mentioned, or alluded to, it had been preceded by grace, faith, the blood of Jesus, immersion, &c. &c. But now the question comes, which, to the rational, it is the emphatic question—WHETHER DO THEY THINK, BELIEVE, TEACH, AND PRACTICE MORE WISELY AND MORE SAFELY; WHO THINK, BELIEVE, AND TEACH, THAT GRACE, FAITH, THE BLOOD OF JESUS, THE NAME OF THE LORD, AND IMMERSION, ARE ALL ESSENTIAL TO IMMEDIATE PARDON AND ACCEPTANCE;—OR THEY WHO SAY, THAT FAITH ONLY, THE BLOOD OF CHRIST ONLY, THE NAME OF THE LORD ONLY—AND IMMERSION, NOT AT ALL? To all men, women, and children, of common sense, this question is submitted.

(pp. 39-40) How comes it to pass, that though once, and only once, it is commanded, that the nations who believe should be immersed into the name of the Father, and of the Son, and of the Holy Spirit; and though we read of no person being immersed into this name in this way; I say, how comes it to pass, that all sects use these words without a scruple, and baptize or sprinkle in this name; when more than once persons are commanded to be immersed for the remission of sins, and but a few of the proclaimers can be induced to immerse for the remission of sins, though so repeatedly taught and proclaimed by the Apostles? Is one command, unsupported by a single precedent, sufficient to justify this practice of christians; and sundry commands and precedents from the same authority insufficient to authorize, or justify us in immersing for the remission of sins? Answer this who can; I cannot, upon any other principle than, that the tyrant Custom, who gives no account of his doings, has so decreed.

I come now to another of the direct and positive testimonies of the Apostles, showing that immersion for the remission of sins, is an institution of Jesus Christ. It is the address of Ananias to Saul. "Arise and be immersed, and wash away your sins, calling upon the name of the Lord." On this testimony we have not as yet descanted in this essay. It has been mentioned; but not examined.

Paul, like the Pentecostian hearers, when convinced of the truth of the pretensions of the Messiah, asked what he should do. He was commanded to go into Damascus, and it should be told him there what to do. It was told him in the words now before us. But say some this cannot be understood literally.

For experiment, then, take it figuratively. Of what was it firgurative? of something already received,—of pardon formerly bestowed! a figure of the past! This is anomalous. I read one writer, and but one, who converted this into a commemorative baptism, like Israel's commemorating the escape from Egypt, or christians commemorating the Lord's death. And, if I do not mistake, some preacher said it was a figurative expression, similar to "This is my body!!" One, whom I pressed out of all these refuges, was candid enough to say he really did not know what it meant; but it could not mean, that Paul was to "be baptized for the remission of his sins."

"To wash away sins" is a figurative expression. Like other metaphoric expressions, it puts the resemblance in place of the proper word. It necessarily means something analogous to what is said. But we are said to be washed from our sins in, or by, the blood of Christ. But even "washed in blood" is a figurative expression, and means something analogous to washing in water. Perhaps we may find in another expression a means of reconciling these strong metaphors. Rev. vii. 14. "They have washed their robes, and made them white in the blood of the Lamb." Here are two things equally incomprehensible—to wash garments white in blood, and to wash away sins in water! An efficacy is ascribed to water which it does not possess; and, as certainly, an efficacy is ascribed to blood which it does not possess. If blood can whiten or cleanse garments, certainly water can wash away sins. There is, then, a transferring of the efficacy of blood to water; and a transferring of the efficacy of water to blood. This is a plain solution of the whole matter. God has transferred, in some way, the whitening efficacy, or cleansing power, of water to blood; and the absolving or pardoning power of blood to water. This is done upon the same principle as that of accounting faith for righteousness. What a gracious institution! God has opened a fountain for sin, for moral pollution. He has given it an extension far and wide as sin has spread—far and wide as water flows. Wherever water, faith, and the name of the Father, Son, and Holy Spirit, are, there will be found the efficacy of the blood of Jesus. Yes; as God first gave the efficacy of water to blood, he has now given the efficacy of blood to water. This, as was said, is figurative; but it is not a figure which misleads, for the meaning is given without a figure; viz. immersion for the remission of sins. And to him that made the washing of clay from the eyes, the washing away of blindness, it is competent to make the immersion of the body in water efficacious to the washing away of sin from the conscience.

(p. 51) . . . there is some connexion between immersion, and the forgiveness of sins. What that connexion is, may be disputed by some; but that such a connexion exists, none can dispute, who acknowledges the New Testament to contain a divine communication to man. With John Wesley we say, it is "to the believing the means and seal of pardon for all previous offences;" and we not only say we think so, but we preach it as such, and practise it as such. Those who think of any other connexion, would do well to attempt to form clear ideas of what they mean: for we are assured there is no meaning in any other connexion. To make it a commemorative sign of past remission is an outrage upon all rules of interpretation, and a perfect anomaly in all the revelation of God. To make it, prospectively, the sign of a future remission, is liable to the same exceptions. Nothing remains, but that it be considered, what it is in truth, the accompanying sign of an accompanying remission; the sign and the seal, or the means and the seal of remission then granted through the water, connected with the blood of Jesus by the divine appointment, and through our faith in it.

We have heard some objections, and we can conceive of new objections which may be presented to immersion for the remission of sins. Some of them are anticipated and attended to in the preceding remarks. We could wish that we had them all drawn up numerically, that we might examine and refute them. There can be objections made to any person, doctrine, sentiment, or practice, natural, moral, political, or religious, which ever existed. But notwithstanding all the objections made to every thing, there are thousands of matters and things we hold to be facts and truths indubitable. Amongst those certain and sure things, not to be shaken, is this christian institution.

Campbell proceeds to address several of the objections to which he has just made reference. Two of these are presented below:

(p. 52) Objection 2. - "It makes void the value, excellency, and importance of both faith and grace." By no means. If a man say, with Paul, we are justified by faith; does it follow that grace is made void? Or, if one say we are justified by grace; does it make the blood of Christ of none effect? Or, if, with Paul, a man say we are justified by his blood; does it make faith, repentance, and grace of no effect? Nay, indeed, this gives to faith its proper place, and its due value. It makes it the principle of action. It brings us to the water, to Christ, and to heaven. But it is as a principle of action only. It was not Abel's faith in his head, or heart; but Abel's faith at the altar which obtained such reputation. It was not Enoch's faith in principle, but Enoch's faith in his walk with God, which translated him to heaven. It was not Noah's faith in God's promise and threatening, but his faith exhibited in building an ark, which saved himself and family from the Deluge, and made him an heir of a new world, an heir of righteousness. It was not Abraham's faith in God's call, but his going out in obedience to that call, that first distinguished him as a pilgrim, and began his reputation. It was not faith in God's promise that Jericho should fall, but that faith carried out in the blowing of rams' horns, which laid its walls in ruins, &c. It is not our faith in God's promise of remission, but our going down into the water that obtains the remission of sins. But any one may see why faith has so much praise, and is of so much value. Because, without it, Abel would not have offered more sacrifices than Cain; Enoch would not have walked with God; Noah would not have built an ark; Abraham would not have left Ur of the Chaldees, nor offered up his son upon the altar. Without it, Israel would not have passed through the wilderness, nor crossed the Jordan; and without it, none receive the remission of their sins in immersion. And, again, we would remind the reader, that when he talks of being saved by faith, he should bear in mind, that grace is not lost sight of; nor blood, nor water, nor reformation, discarded.

(p. 53) Objection 3. - "It is so uncharitable to the Paidobaptists!" And how uncharitable are the Paidobaptists to Jews, Turks, and Pagans!! Will they promise present salvation from the guilt, pollution, and the dominion of sin, with the well grounded hope of heaven, to Jews, Turks, Pagans, or even Roman Catholics? Or will the Roman Catholics to them! How uncharitable are they who cry "uncharitable" to us! Infants, idiots, deaf, and dumb persons, innocent Pagans wherever they can be found, with all the pious Paidobaptists, we commend to the mercy of God. But such of them as wilfully neglect this salvation, and who, having the opportunity to be immersed for the remission of their sins, wilfully neglect or refuse, we have as little hope for them as they have for all who refuse salvation on their own terms of the gospel. While they inveigh against us for laying a scriptural and rational stress upon immersion, do we not see that they lay as great, though an unscriptural and irrational, stress upon their baptism or sprinkling; so much so, as to give it without faith, even to infants, so soon as they are born of the flesh?

The passages quoted above clearly establish the strength of the early restoration movement leaders (as voiced by Alexander Campbell) regarding this concept of believers' baptism by immersion for the forgiveness of sins.

5

THE LORD'S SUPPER

I stated in an earlier chapter that the truth has nothing to fear from a detailed and scrutinizing examination, from a truly objective study. I think that my personal study relating to the Lord's supper provides an excellent example of the validity of this statement. When I began my personal Bible study I fully expected to find that we in the Church of Christ had been too dogmatic in our insistence that the Lord's supper should be observed on each and every Lord's day, the first day of every week. I knew that there was no single statement in the Scriptures which, standing alone on its own merits, specified precisely both the day and the frequency. I had also heard the argument by some of our religious neighbors that when 1 Corinthians 11:25 says, "Do this, as often as you drink it, in remembrance of me" that it means that we can do it as often (as frequently or as infrequently) as we desire, with no specific frequency either expressed or implied. I assumed that they were probably right, that we were probably wrong, and I expected my study to substantiate this assumption.

I was surprised to find that exactly the opposite turned out to be true. My contemporary 20th century Church of Christ religious education had not given me the kind of solid foundation necessary to deal with this subject. However, I found a different situation when I studied the Bible with the help of some of the pioneer reformers of our 19th century restoration movement. Their more open and objective methods of Bible study convinced me that we have a solid basis for our insistence that we should observe the Lord's supper each and every time that we meet on the first day of the week for our corporate worship.

This study, however, held some surprises. I had always been taught that the Bible clearly and distinctly commands us (or at least by an unambiguous approved example directs us) to observe the Lord's supper each and every first day of the week. I am paraphrasing here but this seems to have been the essence of our teaching in recent years. Logically and grammatically this is not really true. It is strongly implied, very strongly implied, but I do not believe that we can conclusively prove our hypothesis based on Biblical evidence. However, even a more alarming observation can be made. It is also not possible, from a study of the Bible, to absolutely prove, by the proper application of good rules of interpretation, that we must assemble on the first day of each and every week for worship, or in fact for any purpose at all. It is strongly implied, very strongly implied, but it is never explicitly commanded that the observance of the Jewish Sabbath should be replaced by the observance of the first day of the week, and neither is it ever clearly and unambiguously exemplified. Throughout the centuries men who have been followers of Christ, with only a few exceptions, have believed that the observance of the first day of every week as the Lord's day was an authentic element of the Christian institution. We in the Church of Christ today, along with the leaders

THE LORD'S SUPPER

of the restoration movement, stand with the multitudes who down through the centuries have believed this to be true. We wish in no way to cast any doubt on the authenticity of this doctrinal position. We stand firmly in its support. However since the purpose of the present study is an attempt to ensure that the Church of Christ methods of Bible study and Bible interpretation are based on sound logic and good academic principles it is appropriate (and in fact obligatory) that any and all principles be reexamined.

When we reexamine the principle of the weekly observance of the Lord's supper we find that there are only four passages in the New Testament which may be used to address the question of how often. It is necessary to take all four of these passages together, in concert, in order to construct our "proof." Even after having constructed this combined "proof" a candid, unbiased, objective observer might still with some propriety say that our proof is not conclusive. It might not immediately appear clear and conclusive to all persons. But before we become despondent over this possibility we must make one other very interesting observation. These same four verses contain the essence of the arguments from the New Testament which are used to justify the observance of the first day of the week, and the first day of every week, for the Lord's day worship. Yes, indeed, this is true. The validity of the weekly participation in the memorial feast known as the Lord's supper and the validity of the weekly observance of the first day of the week as the Lord's day stand or fall together. The arguments for the one are as strong and valid, or as weak and invalid, as the arguments for the other. This now sheds a whole new light on the whole issue. It now becomes apparent that those of us in the Church of Christ, and those in other groups that also contend for the weekly observance of the Lord's supper, are more consistent in our methods of interpretation in these areas than all of the rest of Christendom. To insist on the weekly assembly of the saints for preaching, prayer, fellowship, the giving of money and the singing of praises but not for observing the Lord's supper seems to demonstrate an inconsistency in one's methods of Bible interpretation. No respectable religious denomination would even consider giving their members any relief from the directive to assemble each first day of the week to fill the collection plates with money, and yet most of them will usually ignore the Lord's memorial feast. How inconsistent!

We will now go to the Scriptures in support of the arguments which are given above. We will examine all of the Scriptures in the New Testament that deal with the Lord's supper, or the breaking of bread, to show that the field can be narrowed down to only four which can be used to investigate the question of how often the ordinance should be observed. We will then examine these four passages to show how they establish our case in support of the weekly observance, on the first day of the week, of the Lord's supper.

We can first eliminate one class of passages which deal with the establishment of the Lord's supper, but which say absolutely nothing regarding the frequency of its observance. These are the three parallel passages in Matthew, Mark and Luke which describe the last passover meal which Jesus ate with his apostles. These passages record the first observance of the Lord's supper. Luke even quotes the Lord as saying "Do this in remembrance of me," but nothing specific is said regarding any periòdic repetition of this occasion. The passages referred to are Matthew 26:26-28, Mark 14:22-25 and Luke 22:14-20. Another group of verses which also fit in this category are to be found in 1 Corinthians 11, starting with verse 23 and going through verse 34. Here Paul first (verses 23-26) relates the story of the last supper in a manner similar to what we just observed in the three gospels. In addition verses 24, 25, 26, 27 and 33 make statements which seem to indicate that the Lord's supper is a thing that Christians should observe, with some regularity, but nothing is said that can be used to establish the frequency. In a similar manner 1 Corinthians 10:16 clearly indicates that the "cup of blessing which we bless" and the "bread which we break" constitute an ongoing institution, but the frequency with which it is to be observed is not specified.

There is a second class of passages which may be eliminated from the field. The New Testament uses the phrase "the breaking of bread" or "to break bread" in more than one connection. In some cases it is clear from the context that it refers to the memorial feast instituted by our Lord Jesus Christ as he observed the last passover supper with his apostles. In other cases, however, it is just as clear that the phrase refers simply to the eating of a normal meal, as food for the human body. The first example of this type which comes to mind is the situation where Paul was involved in a shipwreck. Paul and the others hadn't eaten for fourteen days. Then Acts 27:35 says, "Paul took bread and giving thanks to God in the presence of all he broke it and began to eat. This is obviously a case of eating just for sustenance. Paul's giving of thanks in this case is similar to our custom of giving thanks to God prior to eating a meal in our own homes today. This verse has nothing to do with the Lord's supper. Another example which clearly falls in this class is Acts 2:46. It refers to the Christians in Jerusalem. "And day by day, attending the temple together and breaking bread in their homes, they partook of food with glad and generous hearts." This "breaking bread" obviously refers to the eating of ordinary food and does not at all imply (as I have heard some people claim) that they partook of the Lord's supper daily. Another reference to breaking bread which we can rule out because it has nothing to do with the Lord's supper occurs during Paul's visit to Troas, after midnight on this occasion (not to be confused with the reference preceding it which was prior to midnight). Paul had talked until midnight, then he talked still longer, then a young man (Eutychus) fell from the window and died. Paul raised him from the dead and then Acts 20:11 says, "And when Paul had gone up and had broken bread and eaten. . . ." I am convinced that this specific reference to breaking bread and eating refers to Paul eating an ordinary meal. Thus we have eliminated three more passages from the field of interest in the present investigation.

The passage found in John 6:52-58 falls in yet a third category which may be eliminated from our study. This passage almost certainly has nothing to do with either the Lord's supper or with the eating of ordinary meals, but rather speaks figuratively of other things.

Thus we have narrowed the list of passages which are available for establishing the proper frequency for the observance of the Lord's supper down to four:

Acts 20:7	On the first day of the week, when we were gathered together to break bread....
Acts 2:42	And they devoted themselves to the apostles' teaching and fellowship, to the breaking of bread and the prayers.
1 Cor. 16:2	(16:1) Now concerning the contribution for the saints: as I directed the churches of Galatia, so you also are to do. (16:2) On the first day of every week, each of you is to put something aside and store it up....
1 Cor. 11:20	(11:18) ... when you assemble as a church, I hear there are divisions among you.... (11:20) When you meet together, it is not the Lord's supper that you eat. (11:21) For in eating, each one goes ahead with his own meal, and one is hungry and another is drunk.

I will summarize our arguments as clearly and concisely as possible:

Acts 20:7 tells us that the congregation at Troas partook of the Lord's supper on the first day of the week. We infer from the language that they were gathered together for this specific purpose. Furthermore we argue that since the text reads "the week" rather than "a week" that this implies that they did this thing regularly on the first day, rather than on only this one occasion; however, we do not depend on this inference for our complete support of this specific point.

Acts 2:42 tells us that whenever the Jerusalem Christians did meet, however frequent or infrequent this might have been, that the breaking of bread was one of the several things to which they devoted themselves, at least on an equal level with the apostles' teaching, fellowship and prayers.

First Corinthians 16:2 is the verse that all of Christendom has used throughout the centuries to prove that Christians should put money in the collection plate on each and every first day of the week. Thus all of Christendom has assumed that the giving of money to the church is to be placed on a par with teaching, fellowship, breaking of bread and prayer even though giving was not mentioned in Acts 2:42. Therefore if we are to give money "every" first day of the week we should also break the bread "every" first day of the week. This is a powerful argument in favor of our practice. Most of Christendom appears to have been inconsistent in their application of these verses. Any congregation of people who insist on the first day assembly every week for these other reasons would be well advised to also observe the Lord's supper on each such occasion. In fact I cannot see how they can justify its omission.

First Corinthians 11:20 provides additional support for the argument that when the first century Christians met, as a church, (however frequently or infrequently this might have been) the observance of the Lord's supper was one of the things that they were to do, by the authority of the inspired apostles. Since the text reads, "When you meet together, it is *not* the Lord's supper that you eat" we argue that it means that it *should be* the Lord's supper that you eat. This is not merely some weak, esoteric argument. The position we take here is consistent with all of the common usage of this type of grammatical structure. Thus from this verse we infer the sanction of the inspired apostles for the observance of the Lord's supper in congregations of Christians whenever they met as a church for teaching, fellowship, prayers, and for the giving of their means.

The above arguments constitute the sum total of our direct textual justification for the weekly observance of the Lord's supper. When we examine all of these passages together and apply them in concert it provides a powerful argument in favor of our practice. Does it provide an absolutely airtight proof, based on all accepted rules of logic and grammar, that we absolutely must observe the Lord's supper each and every week? I would answer the question with another question. How airtight is the case in support of the weekly observance of the first day of the week as a day to be set aside for the worship of God? As long as we, or any religious group, insist on the weekly assembly of the saints on the first day of the week we should observe the Lord's supper on each and every one of these occasions in order to be consistent in our methods of interpretation of Scripture. The reason that I say this is quite simple. Acts 20:7 and 1 Corinthians 16:2 are the two verses that all of Christendom uses to justify (to insist upon) the weekly assembly. These are two of the verses we just used to justify the weekly observance of the Lord's supper. Thus the arguments for the weekly observance of the Lord's supper are just as good (or as bad) as the arguments for the weekly assembly. The two stand or fall together. I believe that we in the Church of Christ can, without any reservations, say that Scripturally, grammatically and logically we stand on firm ground on this issue. I wonder, however, how many of our members in this generation really appreciate the strength of our position on this issue, or in fact how many of them would be able to adequately explain and justify our position to others. I know that I was not able to do this prior to my study of our history. Perhaps we need to re-evaluate whether or not our educational programs in some of the doctrinal areas have sufficient strength.

We will now examine some short articles written by our early restoration leaders as they defend our position along the same lines of argument as those used above. We will first examine two articles written by Alexander Campbell in 1825.

A Restoration of the Ancient Order of Things.
No. VII.
On the Breaking of Bread—No. II.
from
The *Christian Baptist,* No. I, Vol. III, 1825, p. 180.
by
Alexander Campbell

The apostles were commissioned by the Lord to teach the disciples to observe all things he had commanded them. Now we believe them to have been faithful to their master, and consequently he gave them to know his will. Whatever the disciples practised in their meetings with the approbation of the apostles, is equivalent to an apostolic command to us to do the same. To suppose the contrary, is to make the half of the New Testament of non-effect. For it does not altogether consist of commands, but of approved precedents. Apostolic example is justly esteemed of equal authority with an apostolic precept. Hence, say the Baptists, shew us where Paul or any apostle sprinkled an infant, and we will not ask you for a command to go and do likewise. It is no derogation from the authority for observing the first day of the week, to admit that christians are no where in this volume commanded to observe it. We are told that the disciples, with the countenance and presence of the apostles, met for worship on this day. And so long as we believe they were honest men, and taught all that was commanded them, so long we must admit that the Lord commanded it to be so done. For if they allowed, and by their presence authorized, the disciples to meet religiously on the first day, without any authority from their King, there is no confidence to be placed in them in other matters. Then it follows that they instituted a system of will-worship, and made themselves lords instead of servants. But the thought is inadmissible, consequently the order of worship they gave the churches was given them by their Lord, and their example is of the same force with a broad precept.

But we come directly to the ordinance of breaking bread, and to open the New Testament on this subject, we see (Matt. xxvi. 26.) that the Lord instituted bread and wine on a certain occasion, as emblematic of his body and of his blood, and as such, commanded his disciples to eat and drink them. This was done without any injunction as to the time when, or the place where, this was to be afterwards observed. Thus the four gospels, or the writings of Matthew, Mark, and John leave it. At this time the apostles were not fully instructed in the laws of his kingdom; and so they continued till he ascended up to his Father and sent them the Holy Spirit. After Pentecost, and the accession gained that day, the apostles proceeded to organize a congregation of disciples, and to set them in the order which the Lord had commanded and taught them by his Spirit. The historian tells us minutely that after they had baptized and received into their society three thousand souls, they continued steadfastly in a certain order of worship and edification. Now this congregation was intended to be a model, and did actually become such to Judea, Samaria, and to the uttermost parts of the earth. The question then is, What order of worship and of edification did the apostle give to the first congregation they organized? This must be learned from the narrative of the historian who records what they did. We shall now hear his testimony, (Acts ii. 41) "Then they who had gladly received his word were baptized, and about three thousand were that day added to them: and they continued steadfastly in the apostles' doctrine, and in the fellowship, and in breaking of bread, and in prayers." Other things are recorded of this congregation distinct from those cited, such as their having a community of goods, and for this purpose selling their possessions of houses and lands. But these are as peculiar to them and as distinct from the instituted order of worship, as was the case of Ananias and his wife Sapphira. Their being constantly in the Temple is also added as a peculiarity in their history. But it may be correctly inquired, How are we to distinguish between these things which are as peculiar to them as their vicinity to the Temple, and those things which were common to them with other christian congregations? This must be determined by a comparison of the practice of other congregations as recorded by the same historian, or as found in the letters to the churches written by the apostles. From these we see that no other christian congregation held a community of goods; no other sold their possessions as a necessary part of christian religion; no others met constantly in the Temple. Indeed, Luke, from his manner of relating the order of worship and means of edification practised by this congregation, evidently distinguishes what was essential from what was circumstantial. For after informing us, verses 41 and 42, of the distinct parts or

THE LORD'S SUPPER

acts of their social worship, he adds in a separate and detached paragraph the history of their peculiarities. "Now," adds he, "all they who believed were together and had all things in common, and they sold their possessions and goods," &c. This, too, is separated from the account of their social acts of worship by a statement of other circumstances, such as the fear that fell upon every soul, and the many wonders and signs which were done by the apostles. From a minute attention to the method of the historian, and from an examination of the historical notices of other congregations, it is easy to distinguish between what was their order of worship and manner of edification from what was circumstantial. And, indeed, their whole example is binding on all christians placed in circumstances similar to those in which they lived at that time. For though the selling of their possessions is mentioned as a part of the benevolent influences of the christian religion clearly understood and cordially embraced, as a voluntary act suggested by the circumstances of the times and of their brethren; yet were a society of christians absolutely so poor that they could live in no other way than by the selling of the possessions of some of the brethren, it would be an indispensable duty to do so, in imitation of him who, though he was rich, made himself poor, that the poor, through his impoverishing himself, might be made rich. But still it must be remarked that even in Jerusalem at this time the selling of houses and lands was a voluntary act of such disciples as were possessors of them, without any command from the apostles to do so. This is most apparent from the speech of Peter addressed to Ananias and his wife; who seem to have been actuated by a false ambition, or love of praise, in pretending to as high an exhibition of self denial and brotherly love as some others. Their sin was not in not selling their property, nor was it in only contributing a part; but it was in lying, and pretending to give the whole, when only a part was communicated. That they were under no obligation from any law or command to sell their property, Peter avows in addressing them, and for the purpose too of inculpating them more and more: "While it remained," says he, "was it not yours? It was still at your own disposal." You might give or withhold without sin. But the lie proved their ruin. Thus it is easy to discover what was essential to their worship and edification from what was circumstantial.

Their being baptized when they gladly received the word, was not a circumstance, neither was their continuing steadfastly in the apostles' docrine, in fellowship, in breaking of bread, and in prayers. This the order of all the congregations gathered and organized by the apostles, shows. With regard to our present purpose, enough is said on this testimony, when it is distinctly remarked and remembered that the first congregation organized after Pentecost by the apostles, now gifted with the Holy Spirit, CONTINUED AS STEADFASTLY IN BREAKING OF BREAD as in the apostles' doctrine, fellowship, or prayers. This is indisputably plain from the narrative, and it is all we want to adduce from it at present. It is bad logic to draw more from the premises than what is contained in them; and we can most scripturally and logically conclude from these premises, that the congregation of disciples in Jerusalem did as steadfastly, and as uniformly in their meetings, attend on the breaking of bread, as upon any other mean of edification or act of worship. It cannot, however, be shown from this passage how often that was, nor is it necessary for us to do so in this place. We shall find other evidences that will be express to this point. We dismiss this passage in the mean time, by repeating that the first congregation organized by the apostles after the ascension of the King, did as steadfastly attend on the breaking of bread in their religious meetings, as upon any act of worship or means of edification.

We shall again hear Luke narrating the practice of the disciples at Troas, (Acts xx.7.) "And on the first day of the week, when the disciples assembled to break bread, Paul, being about to depart on the morrow, discoursed with them, and lengthened out his discourse till midnight." From the manner in which this meeting of the disciples at Troas is mentioned by the historian, two things are very obvious: 1st. That it was an established custom or rule for the disciples to meet on the first day of the week. 2d. That the primary object of their meeting was to break bread. They who object to breaking bread on every first day of the week when the disciples are assembled, usually preface their objections by telling us that Luke does not say they broke bread every first day; and yet they contend against the Sabbatarians that they ought to observe every first day to the Lord in commemoration of his resurrection. The Sabbatarians raise the same objection to this passage when adduced by all professors of christianity to authorize the weekly observance of the first day. They say that Luke does not tell us that they met for any religious purpose on every first day. How inconsistent,

THE LORD'S SUPPER

then, are they who make this sentence an express precedent for observing every first day, when arguing against the Sabbatarians, and then turn round and tell us that it will not prove that they broke bread every first day! If it does not prove the one, it is most obvious it will not prove the other; for the weekly observance of this day, as a day of the meeting of the disciples, and the weekly breaking of bread in those meetings, stand or fall together. Hear it again: "And on the first day of the week, when the disciples assembled to break bread." Now all must confess, who regard the meaning of words, that the meeting of the disciples and the breaking of bread, as far as these words are concerned, are expressed in the same terms as respects the frequency. If the one were fifty-two times in a year, or only once, so was the other. If they met every first day, they brake bread every first day; and if they did not break bread every first day, they did not meet every first day. But we argue from the style of Luke, or from his manner of narrating the fact, that they did both. If he had said that on a first day the disciples assembled to break bread, then I would admit that both the Sabbatarians and the semiannual or septennial communicants might find some way of explaining this evidence away.

The definite article is, in the Greek and in the English tongue, prefixed to stated and fixed times, and its appearance here is not merely definitive of one day, but expressive of a stated or fixed day. This is so in all languages which have a definite article. Let us illustrate this by a very parallel and plain case. Suppose some five hundred or a thousand years hence, the annual observance of the 4th of July should have ceased for several centuries, and that some person or persons devoted to the primitive institutions of this mighty republic, were desirous of seeing every fourth of July observed as did the fathers and founders of the republic, during the hale and undegenerate days of primitive republican simplicity. Suppose that none of the records of the first century of this republic had expressly stated that it was a regular and fixed custom for a certain class of citizens to pay a particular regard to every fourth day of July—but that a few incidental expressions in the biography of the leading men in the republic spake of it as Luke has done of the meeting at Troas. How would it be managed? For instance, in the life of John Q. Adams, it is written, A.D. 1823, "And on the fourth day of July, when the republicans at the city of

Washington met to dine, John Q. Adams delivered an oration to them." Would not an American a thousand years hence, in circumstances such as have been stated, find in these words one evidence that it was an established usage during the first century of this republic to regard the fourth day of July as aforesaid. He would tell his opponents to mark that it was not said that on a fourth of July, as if it were a particular occurrence, but it was in the fixed meaning of the English language expressive of a fixed and stated day of peculiar observance. At all events he could not fail in convincing the most stupid that the primary intention of that meeting was to dine. Whatever might be the frequency or the intention of that dinner, it must be confessed, from the words above cited, that they met to dine.

Another circumstance that must somewhat confound the Sabbatarians and the lawless observers of breaking of bread, may be easily gathered from Luke's narrative. Paul and his company arrived at Troas either on the evening of the first day, or on Monday morning at an early hour; for he departed on Monday morning, as we term it, at an early hour; and we are positively told that he tarried just seven days at Troas. Now had the disciples been Sabbatarians or observed the seventh day as a Sabbath, and broke bread on it as the Sabbatarians do, they would not have deferred their meeting till the first day, and kept Paul and his company waiting, as he was evidently in a great haste at this time. But his tarrying seven days, and his early departure on Monday morning, corroborates the evidence adduced in proof that the first day of the week was the fixed and stated day for the disciples to meet for this purpose.

From the 2d of the Acts, then, we learn that the breaking of bread was a stated part of the worship of the disciples in their meetings; and from the 20th we learn that the first day of the week was the stated time for those meetings; and, above all, we ought to notice that the most prominent object of their meeting was to break bread. But this, we hope, will be made still more evident in our next. EDITOR.

A Restoration of the Ancient Order of Things.
No. VIII.
On the Breaking of Bread.—No. III.
The *Christian Baptist,* No. I, Vol. III, 1825, p. 188.
by
Alexander Campbell

We have proposed to make still farther apparent that the primary intention of the meeting of the disciples on the first day of the week, was to break bread. We concluded our last essay on this topic with a notice of Acts xx. 7. "And on the first day of the week when the disciples assembled to break bread." The design of this meeting, it is evident, was to break bread. But that this was the design of all their meetings for worship and edification, or that it was the primary object of the meetings of the disciples, is rendered very certain from Paul's first letter to the Corinthians, chapter xi. The apostle applauds and censures the church at Corinth with respect to their observance of the order he instituted among them. In the second verse he praises them for retaining the ordinances he delivered them, and in the conclusion of this chapter he censures them. They retained in their meetings the ordinance, but did abuse it. He specifies their abuses of it, and denounces their practice as worthy of chastisement. But in doing this, he incidentally informs us that it was for the purpose of breaking bread they assembled in one place. And the manner in which he does this is equivalent to an express command to assemble for the purpose. Indeed there is no form of speech more determinate in its meaning or more energetic in its force than that which he uses, verse 20. It is precisely the same as the two following examples. A man assembles laborers in his vineyard to cultivate it. He goes out and finds them either idle or destroying his vines. He reproves and commands them to business by addressing them thus—"Men, ye did not assemble to cultivate my vineyard." By the use of this negative he makes his command more imperative and their guilt more apparent. A teacher assembles his pupils to learn—he comes in and finds them idle or quarrelling. He addresses them thus—"Boys, ye did not assemble to learn." In this forcible style, he declares the object of their meeting was to learn, and thus commands and reproves them in the same words. So Paul addresses the disciples in Corinth—"When ye assemble, it is not to eat the Lord's supper;" or (Macknight,) "But your coming together into one place, is not to eat the Lord's supper," plainly and forcibly intimating that this was the design of their meeting or assembling in one place, commanding them to order, and reproving them for disorder. Now it must be admitted that Paul's style in this passage is exactly similar to the two examples given, and that the examples given mean what we have said of their import; consequently, by the same rule, Paul reminds the Corinthians, and informs all who ever read the epistle, that when the disciples assembled, or came together into one place, it was primarily for the purpose of breaking bread, and in effect most positively commands the practice. To this it has been objected that the 26th verse allows the liberty of dispensing with this ordinance as often as we please. In the improved translation of Macknight it reads thus: "Wherefore, as often as you eat this bread and drink this cup, you openly publish the death of the Lord till the time he come." Either these words, or those in the preceding verse, ("This do, as often as you drink it, in remembrance of me,") are said to give us the liberty of determining when we may break bread. If so, then the Lord's supper is an anomaly in revelation. It is an ordinance which may be kept once in seven months, or seven years, just as we please, for, remember, "where there is no law there is no transgression." But this application of the words is absurd, and perfectly similar to the papists' inference from these words; for they infer hence that "the cup may sometimes be omitted, and under this pretense have refused it altogether to the laity." And certainly if the phrase, "as often as you drink it," means that it may be omitted when any one please, it is good logic for the papists to argue that it may be omitted altogether by the laity, provided the priests please to drink it.

But neither the design of the apostle nor his words in this passage have respect to the frequency, but to the manner of observing the institution. If this is evident, that interpretation falls to the ground; and that it is evident, requires only to ask the question, What was the apostle's design in these words? Most certainly it was to reprove the Corinthians, not for the frequency nor unfrequency of their attending to it, but for the manner in which they did it. Now as this was the design, and as every writer's or speaker's words are to be interpreted according

THE LORD'S SUPPER

to his design, we are constrained to admit that the apostle meant no more than that christians should always, in observing this institution, observe it in the manner and for the reasons he assigns.

And last of all, on this passage, let it be remembered, that if the phrase, "as oft as," gives us liberty to observe it seldom, it also gives us liberty to observe it every day if we please.—And if it be a privilege, we are not straitened in the Lord, but in ourselves.

But, say some, "it will become too common and lose its solemnity." Well, then, the seldomer the better. If we observe it only once in twenty years, it will be the more uncommon and solemn. And, on the same principle, the seldomer we pray the better. We shall pray with more solemnity if we pray once in twenty years!

But "It is too expensive." How? Wherein? Is not the "earth the Lord's and the fulness thereof?" It costs us nothing. It is the Lord's property. He gives us his goods that we may enjoy ourselves. We never saw or read of a church so poor that could not, without a sacrifice, furnish the Lord's table. To make one "sacrament," requires more than to furnish the Lord's table three months. I hate this objection most cordially. It is antichristian—it is mean—it is base.

"It is unfashionable." So it is to speak truth, and fulfil contracts. So it is to obey God rather than man. And if you love the fashion, be consistent—don't associate with the Nazarenes—hold up the skirts of the high priest, and go to the temple. But all objections are as light as straws and as volatile as a feather.

To recapitulate the times adduced in favor of the ancient order of breaking bread, it was shewn, as we apprehend—

1. That there is a divinely instituted order of christian worship, in christian assemblies.

2. That this order of worship is uniformly the same.

3. That the nature and design of the breaking of bread are such as to make it an essential part of christian worship in christian assemblies.

4. That the first church set in order in Jerusalem, continued as stedfastly in breaking of bread, as in any other act of social worship or edification.

5. That the disciples statedly met on the first day of the week, primarily and emphatically for this purpose.

6. That the apostle declared it was the design or the primary object of the church to assemble in one place for this purpose, and so commanded it to the churches he had set in order.

7. That there is no law, rule, reason, or authority for the present manner of observing this institute quarterly, semi-annually, or at any other time than weekly.

8. We have considered some of the more prominent objections against the ancient practice, and are ready to hear any new ones that can be offered. Upon the whole, it may be said that we have express precedent and an express command to assemble in one place on the first day of the week to break bread. We shall reserve other evidences and considerations until some objections are offered by any correspondent who complies with our conditions. EDITOR.

In item 8, just above, Alexander Campbell says that we have an "express command" to assemble in one place on the first day of the week to break bread. I think he may have gotten a little carried away in this case, as he sometimes does in his efforts to use complicated logical developments to "prove" things. He is here claiming, I think, that the wording of 1 Corinthians 11:20 constitutes sort of a reverse "express command." I would not personally make such a claim. I agree with all of Campbell's conclusions relating to the weekly observance of the Lord's supper but I am not quite bold enough to claim an "express command" in this instance. It is also not necessary for us to make such a claim.

We will conclude our examination of Campbell's writings on this subject with two short quotes from the *Millennial Harbinger,* Extra No. II, "The Breaking of the Loaf," 1830.

(p. 71) Other corroborating evidences of the stated meeting of the disciples on the first day for religious purposes, are found in the fact that Paul says he had given orders to all the congregations in Galatia, as well as that in Corinth, to attend to the fellowship, or the laying up of contributions for the poor saints on the first day of every week. 1 Cor. xvi. 1. "On the first day of every week let each of you lay somewhat by itself, according as he may have prospered, putting it into the treasury, that when

THE LORD'S SUPPER

I come there may be no collections" for the saints. (Here Campbell is quoting a translation by Macknight). Kata mian Sabbaton Macknight justly renders, "the first day of every week;" for every linguist will admit that kata polin means every city; kata menan, every month; kata ecclesian, every church; and, therefore, in the same usage, kata mian Sabbaton means every first day of the week.

(p. 72) But when Acts 2.42, Acts 20.7, 1 Cor. 11.20 and 1 Cor. 16.1 & 2 are compared and added together, it appears that we act under the influence of apostolic teaching and precedent when we meet every Lord's day for the breaking of the loaf.

An article appears in the *Christian Messenger* in 1831, written by John Allen Gano, which is in support of the weekly observance of the Lord's supper. This article is a very good, concise summary of the restoration movement position on the subject. It has been suggested that this article may have been instrumental in convincing the followers of Barton W. Stone of the validity of the arguments for weekly communion. If this is true then Gano may have made a significant contribution toward effecting the union, one year later in 1832, between the congregations associated with Barton W. Stone and those associated with Alexander Campbell. This article follows:

The Lord's Supper
Christian Messenger, Vol. 5, No. 2, Feb. 1831, pp. 30-34.
by
John Allen Gano

The character and design of this blessed institution, are not the subjects proposed for investigation, at the present time.— The question to which I would particularly invite the attention of the brethren, is this: How often, is it the privilege and duty of the Christians, to attend to the Lord's Supper? I unhesitatingly answer; every first day of the week. In proof of which, I will now exhibit a considerable portion of that testimony, by which this conviction has been produced. And just here, may I not indulge the hope that prejudice, which ever acts on extremes, will have nothing to do with our minds in this examination; but that truth in the love of it may alone guide us. It is necessary then, first of all, that we glance at the origin of this Institution, and from thence closely trace, in the order in which they appear, all the intimations made of it in the New Testament. Our Saviour in instituting the Supper thus commands: "This do in remembrance of me." Luke 22-19. Notice here, not only the design of the institution brought to view; but also a positive command to do it. Were we to stop here, we might readily conclude, that the frequency of our attention to it, was a matter, the determination of which, was left entirely to the whim, the caprice, the zeal or the coldness, of an uninspired man, set of men, or congregation; but when we recollect, that the gospel system is perfect, that its laws and commands are perfect, and that herein we are thoroughly furnished, we feel disposed to examine farther, and if not from the lips of the Saviour, from the practice of his apostles at least, learn the proper understanding of this command, and the attention due to it. And indeed, nearly the whole order of the Christian Church, is thus to be learned. We find, then, on the day of Pentecost about three thousand inducted into the Church, and that "they continued steadfast in the apostles' doctrine and fellowship, and in breaking of bread, and in prayers." Acts ii.42. If the breaking of bread, does not here mean the emblem of the Lord's body; to what does it allude? The writer is evidently in this verse speaking of acts of public worship; this the connexion proves; on the one hand, the teaching of the apostles, and fellowship, are named; and on the other, prayer; and it seems, they continued publicly as steadfast in the one as in the other. Luke immediately connects with this, a short account of their temporal affairs. He adds, they were all together and had all things common; sold their property, and divided the proceeds with those that needed; they broke bread from house to house, and eat their meat with gladness, &c.—by which last expression, I merely understand an allusion to their manner of taking their daily food. Such a construction here does no violence to the context; in the former verse, it evidently would. But the xx.7, of Acts, will bring us at once much nearer the subject of inquiry: "And upon the first day of the week when the disciples came together to break bread, Paul preached unto them." Observe here the time of their assembling

THE LORD'S SUPPER

was, the first day; the principal object of their meeting was to break bread. Paul's preaching being adventitious. Suppose I should say, on the 22d of February, when the Lexingtonians assembled to celebrate the birth of Washington, Mr. Clay addressed them. Would not such an expression signalize that day of the year, (for it returns but once in a year,) as a day of assembling among that people, for that purpose? and does not the other equally signalize the first day of the week, (which returns every week,) as a day of assembling among Christians to break bread; and if the bread here, is not that of the Lord's supper; whence is it? Did they solemnly meet as a church at Troas, to eat a common meal one before the other? or for what purpose, if not the one proposed? In Hebrews x. 25, the apostle exhorts his brethren, not to forsake the assembling of themselves together; where the necessity of such an exhortation, if no regular time of assembling had been pointed out by inspired authority? Could there be a breach of such a command or exhortation, if it were as orderly to meet yearly, semi-annually, quarterly, or monthly, as weekly? And indeed the same uninspired authority, that says monthly, may say yearly or triennially. If then the first day be the day for christians regularly to assemble, it will appear from 1st Cor. 11. 20, 21, 33, that when they did assemble, it was to eat the Lord's Supper; for how could they abuse that, which they did not attend to? And the apostle here, after reproving them severely for its abuse, directs them how to attend to the institution when they did thus meet. Let us imagine one thus addresses his congregation, "Friends, when you come together, it is not to hear preaching, for one sleeps, another laughs, and another talks." Would not such a reproof or admonition plainly prove, that they did come, or ought to have come together to hear preaching? If so, the language in the passage just cited, being similar in form, this conclusion irresistibly follows; That they met every first day; when they did meet it was to eat the Lord's Supper; therefore they eat it every first day of the week.

But I would ask, by what authority is it, that the first, instead of the last day of the week, is so generally regarded as a day of worship? It will not do to say simply, because on that day the Lord arose. Have we apostolic example for its observance? If we have not, all our reasoning, good as it may be, must fail:— Were fallible reason alone the standard, innovations would never cease; but I contend, we have authority for its observance: and that in Acts xx. 7. already referred to. I know the women came to the sepulcre on the first day; but it seems, not to worship. The disciples on the same day assembled together; but it was for fear of the Jews. John xx.19. The same authority then we have for assembling on the Lord's day; the same we have for breaking bread when we do meet.

Having fairly arrived at the conclusion proposed, as I humbly conceive from scriptural authority, let me now turn your attention to another source of information on this subject, which, if it does not strengthen, cannot possibly weaken, the conviction produced by the authority already quoted; I mean the History of the Christian Church, for the first three centuries of its existence so far as it has come to us; I care not whether by Heathen or Christian writers, whether of this sect or that, all concur, (so far as I have read them) when speaking of the order of worship, practised in the primitive churches, in asserting that they assembled on the first day of the week, sung hymns, prayed, commemorated the death and resurrection of the Lord, &c.

This history, I am aware, is not inspired; but there is a degree of respect to which all history well authenticated is entitled.— Let this however go for what it is worth; to the Bible alone I appeal as sufficient on this point. How striking, then, the contrast between the order presented to view in the gospel, and that exhibited around us! In the former, each church had its Bishop chosen, and ordained to preside in its assemblies; and deacons, to provide necessaries or conveniences for worship. Like a family, its members were familiar, affectionate, and well acquainted; when one grieved, all were sorrowful; when one rejoiced, they all rejoiced; every Lord's day they assembled, they sung, they prayed, they broke bread, they read the scriptures, and exhorted, and encouraged each other as fellow labourers, heirs of the same glorious inheritance, and expectants of the same blissful immorality. In the order of the present day, if a church, perchance, have nominally a Bishop of her own, is he such as Paul would, were he on earth, approve? I think not, in most cases. If there are deacons, how seldom are they afforded the means of doing their whole duty!—What coldness and indifference! what a want of affection, sociability and fellow-feeling pervades society! and why? They seldom meet. What a shameful ignorance of the scriptures, compared with the intelligence attainable by every christian! and why? They seldom read. I may be told, they can do this at home. How many, I would ask, do it? He that neglects those religious duties which are social or public, is apt to neglect those that are private.

But it has been objected that by attending to the order proposed every week, there is danger of becoming mere formalists. I reply, there is danger of this in any order; every act of religious worship not attended to in the Spirit of Christ, is mere form; and surely, none will therefore contend for informality or disorder. It was for this cause Paul left Titus in Crete, that he might set things in order in the Churches; and the same apostle exhorts his Corinthian brethren to do all things decently, and in order, having previously declared that God was not the author of confusion. But it has also been objected that the Lord's Supper will thus become too common. Is it possible, that for the sake of ease, or from any other motive, a christian can object that any part of the religion of Heaven can become too common? Is prayer too common? Are praise, exhortation or reading too common? If not; let it not be said that the remembrance of the Lord can become too common. But should there be any other objections urged I would answer them all with this one sentence; If the Lord by his apostles has so ordered, assuredly it becomes us humbly to obey.

Dear brethren, I feel conscious I have not written one word of this in the spirit of contention: But, by Almighty aid, to elicit truth and promote practical religion as far as lies in my power: Farewell.—Yours in love:

Jan. 18, 1831.   JNO. ALLEN GANO.

6
SUMMARY OF OUR BEST ATTRIBUTES

The purpose of this chapter is to give a summary of the major points of doctrine which were a part of the 19th century Church of Christ and which have remained as hallmarks of the contemporary Church of Christ of the decade of the nineteen eighties. A list of the most significant items is given below:

1. The belief that Jesus Christ is the Son of God, and that man without Christ is eternally lost; however, because of the death of Christ on the cross as an expiation for our sins, man can have eternal life in heaven, by the grace of God, through faith in Jesus Christ and obedience to his teachings.
2. The belief in the weekly observance of the Lord's day, the first day of the week, as a day of worship to God.
3. The belief that the weekly Lord's day observance should include the following:
    a. The Lord's supper.

b. Teaching from the Bible.
   c. Singing praises to the Lord.
   d. Prayer
   e. Fellowship with other Christians; visiting, mutual encouragement, etc.
   f. The giving of money to the church.
4. Belief in the concept of baptism by immersion for the forgiveness of sins.
5. The stated belief that the Bible should be the only source of authority in the Christian religion.
6. The belief that God answers prayer.
7. A belief in the indwelling of the Holy Spirit in the Christian.
8. Opposition to pentecostal and charismatic teaching. Opposition to the idea of a second, separate baptism of the Holy Spirit subsequent to water baptism. Opposition to such mystical manifestations of the Holy Spirit as tongue speaking, faith healing and direct revelations from God to man, in the present age.
9. Opposition to all ecclesiastical organizations. The belief that each congregation should be completely autonomous, ministered to by its own elders and deacons.
10. A belief that there should be no distinction between the clergy and the laity, in other words no official clergy. A belief that any qualified man can teach or preach the gospel in any appropriate situation.

This an impressive list of beliefs for a group of people who claim to be New Testament Christians. In my limited study of our religious neighbors, I have seen no other major religious group (exclusive of the heirs of the Stone-Campbell restoration movement) that has a central doctrinal theme which is as reflective of what I believe to be sound New Testament teaching as is that represented by this list. These points of doctrine which have remained as part of our teaching for over 150 years serve to demonstrate that we have a strong Christian heritage, a

SUMMARY OF OUR BEST ATTRIBUTES

heritage of which we can all be proud. This list of beliefs, carried over from our 19th century Stone-Campbell restoration movement, carries a message that is badly needed by the divided religious world of the 20th century. However, the reader must realize that this list is only those items of doctrine which have survived from the 19th century. It is not a complete list of our current doctrine. Some important items of the 19th century doctrine have been deleted from the list (see Chapter Three). Also the first three items listed in Chapter Two (the three most well known points of contemporary Church of Christ doctrine) do not appear in this list. The remainder of this document will deal with the differences between the 19th century doctrine and the 20th century doctrine of the Church of Christ.

PART III

MAJOR ELEMENTS UNIQUE TO THE 20TH CENTURY CHURCH OF CHRIST TRADITION

7

THE PROBLEM CONCEPTS

In this document we will examine the three issues which have been the major source of problems for the 20th century Church of Christ. These are not the only issues, however, which have been a problem for the Church of Christ. We have been an issue oriented people and have divided many times over many issues. Other issues which did not quite cause division have nonetheless caused disharmony within the church.

Issues, however, are not our fundamental problem. The real problem lies with some problem "concepts" which we have allowed to misdirect much of our religious thinking. The misapplication of these problem "concepts" has given rise to many problem "issues." There are three of these concepts:

1. The Church of Christ has the perfect doctrine (i.e., we have perfectly restored the New Testament church).
2. There is Biblical authority in "silence."
3. There is Biblical authority in "necessary inference."

ENDANGERED HERITAGE

The early pioneer preachers had a lot to say about the importance of maintaining a proper respect for the silence of the Scriptures. They warned over and over again about the impropriety of placing too much emphasis on our own personal opinions or inferences regarding Scriptural teachings. We must be very careful about making laws or tests of fellowship based upon things of which the Bible says nothing. We certainly should not condemn people to hell over something of which the Scriptures do not even speak. Most of us (ranging from the most conservative to the most liberal) would probably agree with these general words of caution, as stated here. The problems sometimes arise over how to properly apply these guidelines to specific issues.

These problem concepts are introduced at this point in the document so that we can have them before us and make reference to them as we investigate the three problem issues of chapter two.

8

INSTRUMENTAL MUSIC USED IN WORSHIP IS A SIN

The subject which is introduced in this chapter, the use of instrumental music in Christian worship, has become a very prominent part of Church of Christ doctrine. Most serious Bible scholars, those of the Church of Christ included, would admit that a cappella singing is not an integral part of the atonement. It is not central to the theme of the gospel of Jesus Christ as revealed in the New Testament. We would admit this in response to a direct question. However our behavior has indicated something entirely different. It is not much of an overstatement to say that we in the 20th century Church of Christ have made the whole Christian economy to revolve around this one issue: a cappella singing. We have assumed that even if some other religious group believes and practices exactly as we do regarding all other issues (the atonement, the weekly assembly, the Lord's supper, baptism, etc.), but they sing with the accompaniment of mechanical instruments, that they are not true Christians and they have no hope of going to Heaven. Thus we will not fellowship with such a people in any way.

While many in the Church of Christ do not agree with the above statement it is by no means a dead issue among us. It is still the official doctrine. In February of 1983 I made a first visit to a medium sized main line Church of Christ in the Dallas-Fort Worth area. The regular pulpit minister, a well known man in the area, gave a 45 minute discourse on the evils of instrumental music. In this regular Sunday morning sermon he said, and I paraphrase, that "a cappella singing is just as important as baptism for the forgiveness of sins." The statement to this effect was made near the close of the sermon.

We cannot ignore an issue which we have elevated to a position of such prominence. Neither can we blindly accept the teaching of the previous generation. An issue of such importance merits a detailed and objective investigation by each generation. Our teaching must be very carefully measured against the Bible. Our battle cry is and has always been that we should not add to or take away from the Scriptures. I embrace this guideline with all of my heart and soul. But we might want to consider the possibility that it could be just as easy to add to the Scriptures by adding a "thou shalt not" where one never existed as it would be to add a practice or an act which was not explicitly enjoined.

A FRESH APPROACH

Several arguments have been used by Church of Christ people against the use of mechanical instruments of music when singing praises to our Lord and we will examine some of these in subsequent sections of this chapter. However, before looking at the standard arguments I would like to take what I believe to be a fresh approach to dealing with this problem. I have never seen a Church of Christ writer take this kind of a direct approach to the study of this subject. We discussed in an earlier chapter

INSTRUMENTAL MUSIC USED IN WORSHIP IS A SIN

the need to always be objective in our Bible study. With this thought in mind I would like to pretend that I am reading the Bible for the very first time, assuming only that for some reason I have enough interest in music to take special note of what the Bible says on this subject. I am assuming that I am going to read the Bible from cover to cover having no previous knowledge of the Church of Christ or even of the Christian religion. I believe that the process would go something like the following.

First I would read the Old Testament. Music in worship was commonly accompanied by the use of instruments. In some places the text refers to singing praises with instruments, in other places it merely says singing praises. There seems to be no significance attached to whether or not the instruments were specifically mentioned. In my notes I recorded 59 verses with these types of references (I make no claims as to the completeness or accuracy of that number). It seems that in the Old Testament the Lord loved beautiful music, both vocal and instrumental. Next I would read the New Testament and find seven references to singing praises without mention of instruments (Mark 14:26, Acts 16:25, Eph. 5:18, Col. 3:16, 1 Cor. 14:15, 1 Cor. 14:26 and James 5:13). I probably wouldn't notice the absence of the explicit reference to instruments in these verses, however, for several reasons:

a. There are at least 19 references to musical instruments not associated with worship interspersed throughout the New Testament, without one negative connotation attached to the instruments themselves in any of the non-worship contexts.
b. There are at least three references in Revelation to singing praises with instruments at the end of the age (Rev. 14:2, Rev. 15:2, Rev. 5:8).
c. There are two additional references to musical instruments being associated with the Lord and his angels at the second coming (Matt. 24:30, and 1 Thess. 4:16) although not declared in these cases to be associated with singing.

d. I have just finished reading the Old Testament where the two cases (singing praises with and without instruments) are so closely related, or at least where there is no distinction made between the two cases.

This all leads me to believe that if I had studied the Bible without my previous Church of Christ indoctrination it would never have occurred to me in any way whatsoever to forbid the use of musical instruments when singing praises to the Lord. I believe that this is the vantage point from which most people view this issue.

Even if the first time reader of the Bible in the hypothetical example that we used had had at his disposal the three ways that the 20th century Church of Christ teaches that one must use to establish Biblical authority (explicit command, approved example and necessary inference) I want to suggest to the reader that he would still have gotten no clue that there was anything wrong with instrumental music as used in worship. Please consider carefully the following:

a. EXPLICIT COMMAND - There is absolutely no command in the New Testament to "sing a cappella." It simply does not exist. Any attempt to claim that a command to "sing" is equivalent to a command to "sing a cappella" is a gross abuse of the English language. Even if you assume that the word sing itself only means to sing vocally, which might not be one hundred percent true, there is nothing inherent in the use of the word to imply either a cappella or accompanied.

b. APPROVED EXAMPLE - Our Church of Christ scholars have often claimed that the only examples of singing in the New Testament are without musical instruments. This is simply not true. There are no examples in the New Testament of singing with musical instruments or without them (excluding of course those related to the end of the age). There are only examples of singing. The use of the word sing alone tells the reader only that they "sang." It provides absolutely no information as to whether the singing was a cappella or whether it was accompanied by a mechanical instrument of music. One must look for other examples or pursue other arguments to establish a case for either. Consider even one of the most obvious cases (Acts 16:25) where Paul and Silas were praying and singing hymns in prison. I am absolutely sure that they were singing a cappella. I cannot even imagine any remote possibility that they just happened to have a musical instrument handy inside that prison. But the New Testament does not tell me that. In fact it does not even give me a clue. It is strictly a deduction or an inference on my part, a personal opinion of mine. The New Testament contains no "approved examples" of a cappella singing.

c. NECESSARY INFERENCE - Here is another place where a person with a Church of Christ background must proceed slowly and with care. Remember the hypothetical example with which we are dealing. Since musical instruments were used in the Old Testament, will be used when the Lord comes again, and since there is nothing in the New Testament to prohibit or even remotely caution against their use in the present age, the only logical conclusion to which one could come would be to say that if there is any inference at all to be drawn it would be to infer that their use would be approved in our time.

PATTERN, BLUEPRINT, LITURGY

It has been generally assumed within the 20th century Church of Christ, and often stated in many ways, that the New Testament provides a pattern or a blueprint for our corporate worship. This idea seems to go along well with some cliches which have been used quite freely in our time such as "We call Bible things by Bible names and do Bible things in Bible ways" and "We must have a thus saith the Lord for everything that we do." But this idea and these cliches have meant different things to different Church of Christ people. This idea of a literal, exact pattern or blueprint for every detail of Christian worship has caused much disharmony and division within the Churches of Christ. It is true that the leaders of the restoration movement did speak of the New Testament being a sufficient pattern for Christians in some of their early writing. Perhaps this is responsible for some of the later problems. But I believe that any early references to "pattern" were used in a special context related to their time and their situation. They were calling on Christians of all denominations to reject the "patterns" of Christianity dictated by their complex denominational systems and get back to a simple "pattern" of Christianity dictated only by the New Testament Scriptures. The word pattern used in this way could refer to a general doctrine or to the listing of a set of ordinances, rather than a detailed description of how to administer each ordinance. But even if there was, in their very early thinking, any tendency to assume that there must be a New Testament pattern given for every minute detail of Christian worship, they very soon realized their error. They taught that the New Testament pattern (if the word pattern is appropriate here) consisted of a "list" of the ordinances or items which were a part of or related to Christian worship. A fairly complete list of this type is as follows: the observance of the Lord's Day, the weekly observance of the Lord's supper, the concept of baptism by immersion for the forgiveness of sins, teaching, fellowship, prayers, singing and giving of their means. However, they taught that the exact, minute details of how these were to be carried out was not specified in the Bible but was left up to the discretion of the individual Christians. As early as 1828 Alexander Campbell writes of this subject in the *Christian Baptist*. In a lengthy article in which he is reviewing the history of churches in Europe and America he writes:

The New Testament contains no liturgy, no congregational service, as did the Old Testament. In the writings of the great Jewish apostle Moses, there is a ritual, a liturgy, a tabernacle or temple service laid down; but no such thing is found in the apostolic epistles. This point seems not to have been so clearly apprehended by some of these churches as was necessary to their consistency and comfort. Finding all the public, religious and social services of the Jews so clearly and emphatically laid down in the Jewish scriptures, many have expected and looked in vain to find similar regulations in the christian scriptures. And yet could such a ritual be found, or a liturgy made out for christian congregations, it would be a discrepancy not to be reconciled to the genius of the book. . . . Hence the New Testament after stating the ordinances and statutes of the kingdom of Jesus, prescribes no ritual or liturgy, but leaves the worshippers to act from that holy spirit which the gospel inspires. Being adopted into the family of God, they are to be treated as sons of God, and are to act as the children of God. Hence none of the circumstantials of the christian worship are laid down in the New Testament, as were all the circumstantials of the Jewish worship in the Old Testament. Take, for instance, the Lord's supper. The weekly and joint participation of the loaf and of the cup are clearly propounded and commanded, in commemoration of the Lord's death. But no rules are appended thereto regulating the sitting, standing, kneeling, or reclining of the members; no time of the day set apart; no particular form of a table or the furniture thereof; no arrangement of the seats; no collocation of the disciples; no prescriptions concerning the quantity of either element to be used, nor advices concerning what remains, etc. All of these items would have merited attention under the old economy; but for the reasons assigned would be incompatible with the genius of the new. These or similar observations might be made concerning every item of the christian worship; but this sufficiently illustrates our meaning, and demonstrates the weakness of those who would lay down rules binding upon individuals, prescribing forms of these points which are left to the discretion of christians. Every attempt, therefore, on the part of any christian society to institute forms or models of the circumstantials, and to bind these upon individuals, or to require them in other societies before they can fraternize with them, is an attempt to judaize, or, what is the same thing in this connexion of ideas, to bring into bondage to the spirit of the elements of the world.

An attempt to find a liturgy in the New Testament, under the terms of "express precept or precedent for every thing," is what subjected those called Sandemanians and Haldanians to so much censure from many good men. How far they carried this attempt it matters not, or whether they deserved so much reproach of this account is not the question; the principle itself, if at all admitted, must lead to a stiff, unnatural, and formal profession of the christian religion, and to a spirit and temper not exactly in accordance with the spirit of adoption, and of high-born sons of God. Most of those congregations which commenced their career with a good share of this spirit, and with the expectation of finding as much precision in the New Testament in laying down express commands or precedents for every thing, as was exhibited during the non-age of the religious world, have since found their mistake, and have accordingly changed their course, and found a different spirit resulting from a change of sentiment on this important point. While they have found all the instituted acts of social worship and of the discipline of the church clearly laid down, they have found also that the absence of that minutia of prescription as to time, place, and circumstances, which characterized the Jewish age, has left it necessary for them to possess and exhibit a tolerant, forbearing, and condescending spirit, and to make love the bond of perfection.[1]

Campbell writes on this subject again in December of the same year under the title of "A Restoration of the Ancient Order of Things, 'On the Discipline of the Church' ":

They greatly mistake who expect to find a liturgy, or a code of laws in the New Institution, designed to govern christians either in their private or public relations and character. . . . The former institution was an institution of law—the new an institution of favor. Christians are not now, nor were they ever, under law, but under favor. . . . Many christians have read and rummaged the apostolic writings with the spirit and expectations of a Jew in perusing the writings of Moses—Jews in heart, but

---

1. Alexander Campbell, "Review of the History of Churches.-No. II.," the *Christian Baptist*, June 2, 1828, Vol. V, No. 11, p. 449.

christians in profession. They have sought, but sought in vain, for an express command or precedent for matters as minute as the seams in the sacerdotal robes, or the pins and pilasters of the tabernacle.[2]

Again in 1835, in an article in the *Millennial Harbinger* entitled "Co-operation," p. 121, Alexander Campbell writes:

> There is too much squeamishness about the manner of co-operation. Some are looking for a model similar to that which Moses gave for building the tabernacle. These seem not to understand that this is as impossible as it would be incompatible with the genius of the gospel. A model for translating the Scriptures from Greek into Latin, and from Latin into the English, French, and Spanish tongues; a model for making types, paper, ink, and for printing the Bible, might be as rationally expected, as a model for the co-operation of churches on the banks of the Ohio for republishing the gospel in the valley of the Mississippi.

I do not intend to make any lengthy application of this concept at this time; however, one thought flows so logically from this discussion that I cannot help but present it. In the first quote just above, from June 2, Mr. Campbell picks the Lord's supper as an example and goes on to explain that the particulars associated with its observance are not specified in the Scriptures. What if Mr. Campbell had picked a different example, such as singing? Alexander Campbell is so consistent in his methods of interpreting the Bible, across a broad spectrum of subjects, that I would suggest to the reader that he might have written as follows:

> Take, for instance, singing. Singing and making melody are clearly propounded and commanded. But no rules are appended thereto regulating the sitting, standing, kneeling, or reclining of the members; no time of the day set apart; no particular form of singing, solo, small chorus, large choir, or the entire congregation; nothing to specify monophonic chanting or polyphonic four part harmony; nothing to specify the use or non use of

---

2. Alexander Campbell, "A Restoration of the Ancient Order of Things No. XXVIII, 'On the Discipline of the Church No. V,'" The *Chrisitan Baptist*, Dec. 1, 1828, Vol. VI, No. 5, p. 500.

song books, song leaders, electronic microphones for the song leader, or the accompaniment of mechanical instruments of music. All of these items would have merited attention under the old economy; but for the reasons assigned would be incompatible with the genius of the new.

AUTHORITY IN SILENCE

The reason most often given nowadays (and it has been used since the middle 1880s) to justify the Church of Christ's doctrine that the use of instrumental music in the Lord's worship is wholly corrupt and sinful is that there is no Biblical authority for it. Our people will apply this phrase whenever the situation calls for it and then smugly assume that the issue has been adequately settled to the total satisfaction of all reasonable persons within earshot. This phrase does, I must admit, have somewhat of a wholesome, righteous ring about it. But what our brethren really mean when they say this is that the Bible is silent on the subject. Hence the concept of the authority of silence.

One thing which we must always keep foremost in our minds when we are studying the Bible is that we must be consistent in our methods of interpretation. If we are inconsistent, our methods will be questioned and our message mistrusted. What many of our brethren in the main line Church of Christ apparently fail to realize is that they are extremely inconsistent in their application of this principle of the "authority in silence." What this concept says, precisely, is that anything not expressly commanded (authorized) is absolutely prohibited. That is exactly how, for all of these years, we have prohibited instrumental music. Let's examine together the ramifications and the sphere of influence of a consistent application of this principle (or concept) to several issues with which we may be familiar. If Biblical silence absolutely prohibits a thing then the following is a partial list of the things which the Church of Christ must absolutely prohibit: Sunday schools, multiple communion cups, church support for orphan homes and homes for the elderly, support of the Herald of Truth and Christian colleges, song books, song leaders, microphones for song leaders, polyphonic (4 part harmony) singing, paid preachers located permanently at a church which has elders, literature other than the Bible used in Sunday schools, partaking of the Lord's supper at any place except an upper room (upstairs), partaking of the Lord's supper in the morning, baptizing in anything except natural bodies of water, youth meetings, ownership of church buildings, educational directors, using unfermented grape juice in place of the wine specified in Scriptures and congregational singing (the whole congregation singing at once). And the list could probably be extended considerably.

I wish that we in the Church of Christ could look at ourselves objectively and contemplate the ramifications of this list. If instrumental music is wrong then all of these other things are also wrong, for exactly the same reason, and we would be hard pressed to find a Church of Christ with enough forbidden practices to claim the name Christian. We in the main line Church of Christ have criticized our brethren in the more conservative congregations. We do consider them brethren, but we sometimes seem to consider them inferior to us in Bible knowledge, wisdom, understanding and probably in intelligence. However, an objective evaluation of the facts would indicate the following: If instrumental music is wrong then what some may have considered as the most narrowminded, self-righteous Church of Christ to be found among us is actually the most enlightened, intelligent, Scriptural, Godly congregation among us, and perhaps the only one whose members have any hope at all of spending eternity with the Father in heaven (unless, of course, they too forgot to prohibit something).

The most famous statement in the history of our restoration movement speaks of this subject of the silence of Scriptures. After Thomas Campbell was forced to withdraw from the Presbyterian Seceder synod he continued in his ministerial labors. He

ENDANGERED HERITAGE

preached wherever he could, sometimes in homes and sometimes in the outdoors. Sometime in 1807 or 1808 he called a special meeting of those who, like himself, were interested in Christian freedom and Christian union based upon the Bible. They met at the home of one Abraham Altars, who lived between Mount Pleasant and Washington, Pennsylvania. It was during the course of this meeting that Thomas Campbell is said to have made his oft-quoted statement:

> Where the Scriptures speak, we speak; and where the Scriptures are silent, we are silent.[3]

This phrase has been widely acclaimed by all of the heirs of the restoration movement. We in the Churches of Christ have been very good at speaking where the Bible speaks, but we seem to have had more trouble in the areas where the Bible is silent on some particular subject. Several years later, in the fall of 1838, Alexander Campbell stated a slightly amplified version of this same sentiment:

> Where the Bible is silent we ought to be as silent as the grave; and when it speaks often and clear, we ought to speak with corresponding clearness and frequency.[4]

Robert Richardson describes some of the attitudes of Thomas Campbell and the men with whom he was associated at the time when he made his now famous statement:

> They sought, therefore, for some common ground upon which all could unite without any sacrifice of truth; and having decided that the Scriptures alone, without note or comment, furnished such a basis, they felt it their duty to urge this truth upon the religious communities, proposing that all matters not distinctly revealed in the Bible should be held as matters of opinion and of mutual forbearance.[5]

---

3. Thomas Campbell, as quoted by Robert Richardson, *Memoirs of Alexander Campbell,* Vol. I, p. 236.

4. Alexander Campbell, as quoted by Robert Richardson, *Memoirs of Alexander Campbell,* Vol. II, p. 449.

5. Robert Richardson, *Memoirs of Alexander Campbell,* Vol. I, p. 234.

No remote inferences, no fanciful interpretations, no religious theories of any kind were to be allowed to alter or pervert its (the Bible's) obvious meaning. . . . Whatever private opinions might be entertained upon matters not clearly revealed must be retained in silence, and no effort must be made to impose them upon others. Thus the silence of the Bible was to be respected equally with its revelations.[6]

In the year 1809, Thomas Campbell wrote a document called the "Declaration and Address." Proposition 5 of this document relates directly to our present subject:

That with respect to the commands and ordinances of our Lord Jesus Christ, where the Scriptures are silent as to the express time or manner of performance, if any such there be, no human authority has power to interfere, in order to supply the supposed deficiency by making laws for the Church; nor can anything more be required of Christians in such cases, but only that they do observe these commands and ordinances as will evidently answer the declared and obvious end of their institution. Much less has any human authority power to impose new commands or ordinances upon the Church, which our Lord Jesus Christ has not enjoined. Nothing ought to be received into the faith or worship of the Church, or be made a term of communion among Christians, that is not as old as the New Testament.[7]

He continues later in the same document in a related vein:

Many of the opinions which are now dividing the Church, had they been let alone, would have been long since dead and gone; but the constant insisting upon them, as articles of faith and terms of salvation, have so beaten them into the minds of men, that, in many instances, they would as soon deny the Bible itself as give up one of those opinions.[8]

Working under the assumption that the New Testament is silent regarding the use of musical instruments in Christian

---

6. Ibid., p. 67.
7. Thomas Campbell, "Declaration and Address," St. Louis: Mission Messenger, p. 45.
8. Ibid., p. 67.

worship, the Church of Christ doctrine has been that this silence somehow carries with it an "authority in silence" which absolutely prohibits the use of the instrument. I would like to suggest that this is not a clear perspective of the issue. In an honest but misdirected effort not to add a practice to their worship service some of our second generation leaders committed the much more flagrant offense of actually adding a command to the sacred Scriptures. They in effect added the command "thou shalt not sing praises to the Lord thy God with the accompaniment of a mechanical instrument of music." They replaced the silence of Scripture with a command. An objective examination of the issue from this perspective will show that in each of the previous six quotes from our early restoration leaders they are condemning our continuation of this abuse of the silence of Scriptures. Looking at the six quotes respectively:

a. We have not been silent where the Scriptures are silent.

b. We certainly have not been as silent as the grave.

c. This matter (instrumental music), which we say is not distinctly revealed in the Scriptures, has not "been held as a matter of opinion and of mutual forbearance."

d. We have dealt in "remote inferences," "fanciful interpretations," and "religious theories," which in and of itself would have been permissible; however we erred because these opinions were not "retained in silence," and we attempted "to impose them upon others." Thus the silence of the Bible was not respected equally with its revelations.

e. We attempted to supply the supposed deficiency in the Scriptures by making laws for the church.

f. I am afraid that some of our people give the impression that "they would as soon deny the Bible itself as give up one of those opinions" regarding the evils of instrumental music.

NECESSARY INFERENCE

One of the lines of reasoning used by people in the Church of Christ to explain why we absolutely prohibit the use of mechanical instruments of music in worship is the following. We say that since it is not specifically mentioned in relation to New Testament worship this "necessarily implies" that it is absolutely forbidden. This concept of necesary inference has become a very integral part of our theology and it deserves our careful attention and study. It constitutes the third part of the three-pronged approach which we utilize in the 20th century Church of Christ for establishing Biblical authority. These three elements are: explicit command, approved example and necessary inference. This third method of establishing Biblical authority, necessary inference, is conspicuously missing from the writings of all of the major leaders of the first generation of the restoration movement. I first find historical reference to it during the period when the opposition to instrumental music was becoming prominent. I believe that it was probably invented in an attempt to give some credibility to the position of those who were opposed to such things as instrumental music and located preachers. We will examine some of this historical background.

Thomas and Alexander Campbell had read and were to some degree influenced by the English religious philosopher John Locke. Alexander Campbell was sufficiently impressed by Locke's writing that he reprinted "A Letter Concerning Toleration," written by Locke over a century earlier, in the 1844 edition of the *Millennial Harbinger*. The following is an excerpt from that document:

> But since men are solicitous about the true church, I would only ask them here, by the way, if it be not more agreeable to the church of Christ to make the conditions of her communion to consist on such things, and such things only as the Holy Spirit has in the holy scriptures declared, in express words, to be necessary for salvation; I ask, I say, whether this be not more agreeable to the church of Christ, than for men to impose their own inventions and interpretations upon others, as if they were of divine authority; and to establish by ecclesiastical laws, as absolutely necessary to the profession of Christianity, such things as the holy scriptures do either not mention, or at least not

expressly command. Whosoever requires those things in order to ecclesiastical communion, which Christ does not require in order to life eternal, he may perhaps indeed constitute a society accommodated to his own opinion and his own advantage; but how that can be called the church of Christ, which is established upon laws that are not his, and which excludes such persons from its communion as he will one day receive into the kingdom of heaven, I understand not.[9]

Notice that Locke here mentions one and only one of our three criteria for establishing Biblical authority, "such things only as the Holy Spirit has declared, in express words, to be necessary for salvation." Thus Locke seems to be suggesting that only "explicit command" should be used to establish biblical authority.

Thomas Campbell expands somewhat on the thinking of Locke in the "Declaration and Address" in 1809.

> (He speaks of their desire to) . . . reduce to practice that simple original form of Christianity, expressly exhibited upon the sacred page; without attempting to inculcate anything of human authority, of private opinion, or inventions of men, as having any place in the constitution, faith, or worship, of the Christian Church, or anything as matter of Christian faith or duty, for which there can not be expressly produced a "Thus saith the Lord, either in express terms, or by approved precedent."[10]

(A few pages later in propositions 3, 6, and 7 he says:)

> (Prop. 3) . . . nothing ought to be inculcated upon Christians as articles of faith; nor required of them as terms of communion, but what is expressly taught and enjoined upon them in the word of God. Nor ought anything to be admitted, as of Divine obligation, in their Church constitution and managements, but what is expressly enjoined by the authority of our Lord Jesus Christ and his apostles upon the New Testament Church; either in express terms or by approved precedent.

---

9. John Locke, "A Letter Concerning Toleration," *Millennial Harbinger*, 1844, p. 56.
10. Thomas Campbell, "Declaration and Address," St. Louis: Mission Messenger, pp. 25-26.

(Prop. 6) That although inferences and deductions from Scripture premises, when fairly inferred, may be truly called the doctrine of God's holy word, yet are they not formally binding upon the consciences of Christians farther than they perceive the connection, and evidently see that they are so; for their faith must not stand in the wisdom of men, but in the power and veracity of God. Therefore, no such deductions can be made terms of communion, but do properly belong to the after and progressive edification of the Church. Hence, it is evident that no such deductions or inferential truths ought to have any place in the Church's confession.

(Prop. 7) That although doctrinal exhibitions of the great system of Divine truths, and defensive testimonies on opposition to prevailing errors, be highly expedient, and the more full and explicit they be for those purposes, the better; yet, as these must be in a great measure the effect of human reasoning, and of course must contain many inferential truths, they ought not to be made terms of Christian communion; unless we suppose, what is contrary to fact, that none have a right to the communion of the Church, but such as possess a very clear and decisive judgment, or are come to a very high degree of doctrinal information; whereas the Church from the beginning did, and ever will, consist of little children and young men, as well as fathers.[11]

Here Thomas Campbell proposes the second of our three criteria for establishing biblical authority, express terms (i.e., explicit command) and approved precedent (i.e., approved example). These are the "two" criteria that are discussed and used throughout the first generation of the restoration movement. Necessary inference is conspicuously missing from these passages and from all of the major writings of the first generation of the restoration movement. Not only did the early writers omit it from the list of criteria for establishing biblical authority but they argued that inferences should specifically "not" be used to establish doctrine because human inference is equivalent to human opinion and human opinion was not to be elevated to be equivalent to an express command. I will provide some further references relating to this idea later in this section, but

---

11. Ibid., pp. 45, 46.

first some interesting historical references regarding approved precedent. In 1848 Alexander Campbell was responding in the *Millennial Harbinger* to a query as to how he was led to interpret the Scriptures differently, and to teach and practice differently from what he had once thought, believed and practiced. He responded as follows:

> The first proof sheet that I ever read was a form of my father's Declaration and Address, in press in Washington, Pennsylvania, on my arrival there in October, 1809. There were in it the following sentences: "Nothing ought to be received into the faith or worship of the Church, or be made a term of communion amongst Christians, that is not as old as the New Testament. Nor ought any thing to be admitted as of divine obligation, in the church constitution and management, but what is expressly enjoined by the authority of our Lord Jesus Christ and his Apostles upon the New Testament church; EITHER IN EXPRESS TERMS OR BY APPROVED PRECEDENT." These last words "express terms" and "approved precedent" made a deep impression on my mind, then well furnished with the popular doctrines of the Presbyterian church in all its branches. While there was some ambiguity about this "approved precedent," there was none about "express terms."[12]

Apparently Alexander Campbell realized that there could be some disagreement as to which examples were approved and which were just incidental. He was right, and this did cause some problems. However, with the exception of the issues which are examined in our present document, the restoration movement seems to have handled this concept of approved precedent in a generally realistic and acceptable manner. Sixteen years after he first read the Declaration and Address Alexander Campbell, in a series entitled "A Restoration of the Ancient Order of Things," explains his thinking on this concept of approved precedent. I believe this well represents the position of the early restoration movement leaders on this subject.

> The Apostles were commissioned by the Lord to teach the disciples to observe all things he had commanded them. Now

---

12. Alexander Campbell, "Anecdotes, Incidents and Facts No. 1," *Millennial Harbinger,* 1848, p. 280.

we believe them to have been faithful to their master, and consequently he gave them to know his will. Whatever the disciples practised in their meetings with the approbation of the apostles, is equivalent to an apostolic command to us to do the same. To suppose the contrary, is to make the half of the New Testament of non-effect. For it does not altogether consist of commands, but of approved precedents. Apostolic example is justly esteemed of equal authority with an apostolic precept. Hence, say the Baptists, shew us where Paul or any apostle sprinkled an infant, and we will not ask you for a command to go and do likewise. It is no derogation from the authority for observing the first day of the week, to admit that christians are no where in this volume commanded to observe it. We are told that the disciples, with the countenance and presence of the apostles, met for worship on this day. And so long as we believe they were honest men, and taught all that was commanded them, so long we must admit that the Lord commanded it to be so done. For if they allowed, and by their presence authorized, the disciples to meet religiously on the first day, without any authority from their King, there is no confidence to be placed in them in other matters. Then it follows that they instituted a system of will-worship, and made themselves lords instead of servants. But the thought is inadmissable, consequently the order of worship they gave the churches was given them by their Lord, and their example is of the same force with a broad precept.[13]

But now to continue with our historical references regarding human inference. Thomas Campbell issues some specific warnings in the "Declaration and Address":

> There is a manifest distinction between an express Scripture declaration, and the conclusion or inference which may be deduced from it;[14]
>
> We dare not, therefore, patronize the rejection of God's dear children, because they may not be able to see alike in matters of

---

13. Alexander Campbell, "A Restoration of the Ancient Order of Things, No. VII, On the Breaking of Bread, No. II," the *Christian Baptist*, Vol. III, 1825, p. 180.

14. Thomas Campbell, "Declaration and Address," St. Louis: Mission Messenger, p. 60.

human inference—of private opinion; and such we esteem all things not expressly revealed and enjoined in the word of God. If other wise, we know not what private opinion means.[15]

We would then no longer exalt our own opinions and inferences to an equality with express revelation, by condemning and rejecting our brother for differing with us in those things.[16]

Alexander Campbell also mentions inferences in an article in the *Millennial Harbinger* in 1845.

> Amongst the peculiarities of our profession there is a prominent one—that we are not allowed to make our own private judgment, interpretation, or opinion, a ground of admission into, or of exclusion from, the Christian church. The faith, the precepts, the ordinances, and the promises of the gospel, are public property; while our own reasonings, inferences, and opinions are private property, and are so to be regarded by all. The precepts of the gospel are to be obeyed, its models to be imitated, its spirit to be cherished, cultivated, and displayed in all the acts of justice, brotherly kindness, and charity. Opinions as to the policy or impolicy, the prudence or the imprudence of any set of measures, or of what other persons ought to do in certain circumstances, whether similar or dissimilar to our own, not being matters of revelation, or of express precept, are not to be causes of alienation and schism among the members of the household of faith.[17]

There seems to have been universal agreement among the first generation leaders of the restoration movement that lines of fellowship were not to be drawn on matters involving human inference. Among what I refer to as the second generation leaders, the situation was somewhat different. There arose a small group of men who were much more narrow in their methods of interpretation. They lumped together several activities which they considered as sinful. Among these offenses were such

---

15. Ibid., p. 61.
16. Ibid., p. 82.
17. Alexander Campbell, "Our Position to American Slavery, No. V," *Millennial Harbinger,* 1845, p. 233.

things as pew renting, dancing, theatre going and the use of instrumental music in worship. Within this group are such well known names as Moses E. Lard, J. W. McGarvey, and Benjamin Franklin.

The first reference that I have found to necessary inference in our restoration history literature is one by Moses E. Lard in his periodical, *Lard's Quarterly,* in 1864. The article is condemning instrumental music and dancing and he says:

> Either it must be actually asserted or necessarily implied, or it must be positively backed by some divinely approved precedent, otherwise it is not even an item in Christianity, and is therefore, when it is attempted to be made a part of it, criminal and wrong.[18]

Here we have for the first time (to my knowledge) all three of the 20th century criteria for determining Biblical authority listed together; "actually asserted" (explicit command), "divinely approved precedent" (approved example) and "necessarily implied" (necessary inference). I believe Lard needed this third method (necessary inference) as support for some of his personal opinions.

A second early reference to necessary inference is given by J. W. McGarvey in the *Millennial Harbinger* in 1868:

> The loudest call that comes from heaven to the men of this generation is for warfare, stern, relentless, merciless, exterminating, against everything not expressly or by necessary implication authorized in the New Testament. Such is my unwavering conviction; and my only regret is, that I cannot fight this fight as it should be fought.[19]

Notice the zealous determination with which these men have begun to classify matters which are derived from inference as basic requirements of Christian doctrine. The first generation leaders had considered matters derived from inference to be

---

18. Moses E. Lard, "Instrumental Music in Churches and Dancing," *Lard's Quarterly,* March, 1864, Vol. 1, p. 330.
19. J. W. McGarvey, *Millennial Harbinger,* 1868, p. 219.

human opinion and they thus considered such items to be matters of forbearance. This demonstrates the contrast between the zeal for the superfluous which came to be characteristic of some of the second generation leaders and the zeal for the essential which was the hallmark of the great Bible scholars of the first generation.

I think it quite appropriate to end this section on necessary inference (i.e., human opinion or human presumption) with a quote from Thomas Campbell:

> Upon the whole, we see one thing is evident; the Lord will bear with the weaknesses, the involuntary ignorances, and mistakes of his people, though not with their presumption.[20]

For many Church of Christ members this should be a very sobering thought indeed. May God bless our continuing feeble efforts to reflect the true spirit of Jesus Christ in our lives.

THE AUTHOR'S STUDY REGARDING MUSIC

I have yet to read a book written from the point of view favoring the use of instrumental music in worship. This is not by accident. I searched for, bought and read only books written by Church of Christ men who opposed the use of the instrument. I proceeded in this manner on purpose. I did not want some other religious philosophy to corrupt my mind. I wanted Church of Christ authors to have every opportunity to convince me that instrumental music in worship is sinful.

As far back as I can remember I have suspected that we might be wrong in our opposition to instruments. I had suspected, as I am convinced that the majority of Church of Christ members of today suspect, that we might not have solid Scriptural support for our position. However, I was not really sure until I

---

20. Thomas Campbell, "Declaration and Address," St. Louis: Mission Messenger, p. 65.

had undertaken my own personal study of the subject. The Church of Christ books written against instrumental music convinced me beyond any doubt that instrumental music was perfectly acceptable to our Lord. Their arguments against the instrument were so weak, illogical and obviously in error that I was ashamed to admit that these kinds of books were written by my brethren. By contrast the arguments of the opposition which they presented, supposedly to support and reinforce our position, appeared strikingly clear, accurate and true.

SUMMARY OF THE ARGUMENTS AGAINST INSTRUMENTAL MUSIC

I will now present a summary of the major arguments which have been advanced in opposition to the use of instrumental music in worship. Some of the points have been addressed in previous sections.

1. IT IS NOT AUTHORIZED. This point was shown to be invalid in the "Authority in Silence" section of this chapter.

2. IT IS NECESSARILY INFERRED TO BE WRONG. We have just shown in the section on "Necessary Inference" that this should not be used to establish Biblical authority. At least it should not be used to draw lines of fellowship.

3. IT WAS NOT USED BY THE CHURCH FOR THE FIRST SEVERAL CENTURIES. This is a good argument, and if true it is probably the best argument that the Church of Christ could advance in support of its position. Unfortunately, it is also totally invalid. We claim that we go back to the Bible for all of our rules of faith and duty. We will not let other religious groups quote secular historians of the first few centuries in their arguments for infant baptism, sprinkling, ecclesiastical organizations, etc. Therefore, we cannot quote secular historians

of the first few centuries in our support of a cappella singing. We can only draw our evidence from the Bible. Our people often seem to have conveniently forgotten this fact when arguing against instrumental music. Robert Richardson quotes Alexander Campbell on this subject:

> The Bible alone must always decide every question involving the nature, the character or the designs of the Christian institution. Outside of the apostolic canon, there is not, as it appears to me, one solid foot of terra firma on which to raise the superstructure ecclesiastic. The foundation of apostles and prophets is that projected and ordained by the Lawgiver of the universe. On this, and on this only, can we safely found the Church of Jesus Christ, whether we contemplate its doctrine, its discipline or its government. Nothing less authoritative and divine can fully satisfy the conscientious of all parties, or withstand the assaults of the adversaries of our most holy faith. Whenever we close the apostolic records and open the volumes of the "primitive Fathers," the converts and successors of the apostles, as they are reverentially designated, we find ourselves on a sea of uncertainties, without a single haven on our horizon or in our chart.[21]

4. IT WOULD BE ADDING A SEPARATE ELEMENT OF WORSHIP. This is simply not true. We are commanded to sing. How we are to sing is not specified. There are probably both reverent and irreverent ways to sing a cappella and likewise both reverent and irreverent ways to sing with an instrument. It has been said that if we allow the instrument we must allow such things in worship as the lighting of candles, burning of incense, use of the rosary in prayer and auricular confession. This also is just not true. The use of the instrument in singing is not in the same class with these other items. The use of an instrument is a very closely related and a very natural part of singing, and we already have a command to sing. We do not

---

21. Alexander Campbell, as quoted by Robert Richardson, *Memoirs of Alexander Campbell,* Vol. II, p. 495.

have commands or examples to support the addition of these other things. I have also been told that playing an instrument is a thing of "like kind" with singing. Again, this is simply not true. It is not a thing of like kind with singing in this context, it is rather something which can be just a very natural part of, or accompaniment to, singing.

5. THE GREEK WORD FOR SING (*PSALLO*) SPECIFICALLY EXCLUDES INSTRUMENTAL MUSIC. A man named M.C. Kurfees wrote what seems to be accepted as the premier Church of Christ reference work on instrumental music. It is entitled "Instrumental Music in the Worship."[22] The author's preface is dated 1911. This book purportedly proves that in New Testament times the definition of the Greek word *psallo* specifically excluded instrumental accompaniment. In chapter two the author lists definitions of the word *psallo* from seventeen different Greek lexicons. However, in all except two of the seventeen definitions, major portions of the definitions are related to instrumental music. It would seem that an objective reader would consider this to invalidate Mr. Kurfee's claim. Two other of the lexicons say, in addition to their references to instrumental music, that in the New Testament the word meant to sing praises, sacred songs, and psalms. They don't say with or without an instrument in their references to the New Testament. If one wanted to infer "a cappella" from this (pure conjecture) this would be offset by yet a fifth lexicon which states, in addition to its reference to the instrument, the following: "In Septuagint and New Testament to sing, to chant, properly as accompanying stringed instruments." Mr. Kurfees then has the audacity to proceed, in the face of this obvious refutation of his premise, to use various esoteric arguments in an attempt to discredit all of the lexicons except the ones which say what he wants to hear. This book probably does more to

---

22. M.C. Kurfees, *Instrumental Music in the Worship,* Nashville: Gospel Advocate Company (My copy dated 1975).

damage the case of the Church of Christ against the instrument than any other single document. I cannot imagine any non Church of Christ person ever reading past chapter two of this book.

I am willing to approach this entire subject under the basic assumption that when the New Testament says "sing" that it means just what it says, to sing, not implying either a cappella or instrumental. All of our discussions in this chapter are based on this assumption. However, the definitions from the Greek lexicons which Mr. Kurfees presents in his book might indicate to the objective observer that there may actually be some Biblical authority for the use of the instrument built into the use of the word *psallo* in the Greek New Testament. At a very minimum, Mr. Kurfees misleads the reader by suggesting the existence of Biblical evidence against the use of instrumental music in New Testament worship when, in fact, it does not exist.

6. TO ALLOW ONLY A CAPPELLA SINGING IS THE SAFE APPROACH. This argument has often been used by our people in situations where it might appear that our other arguments have not been totally convincing, as a sort of last resort. How can it be a "safe approach" to add a command to God's holy Scriptures? When we in effect (and in a very literal way) add the command "thou shalt not sing praises to the Lord thy God with the accompaniment of a mechanical instrument of music," this is not a safe approach. In doing this we endanger the very essence of our restoration movement heritage which is exemplified in that famous quote which we have already referenced from Thomas Campbell "Where the Scriptures speak, we speak; and where the Scriptures are silent, we are silent."[3] And all in the Church of Christ do readily admit that the verses relating to singing to which we often refer in the English New Testament (Eph. 5:19, Col. 3:16, James 5:13, Acts 16:25, 1 Cor. 14:15, 1 Cor. 14:26, Mark 14:26) are silent as to how we are to sing.

It is perfectly proper and acceptable for us to conclude, for whatever reason, based on our own background and study, that a cappella singing is what we think, in our own opinion, that God prefers. And it is just as proper for us to practice a cappella singing exclusively in our worship, to never use an instrument in any way. What is not proper and acceptable is for us to draw lines of fellowship based on our opinion and to condemn others to hell because they happen not to have arrived at the same conclusion that we did about a subject on which the Scriptures are silent.

7. A MAJORITY OF CHRISTIANS HAVE SUNG A CAPPELLA. It is truly amazing that this argument has actually been used. For us in the Church of Christ it is completely invalid. We claim that we go back to the Bible for all of our doctrine. We claim not to rely on the traditions of men. The majority of Christians have also practiced infant baptism. Should we do the same? The majority of Christians have also practiced sprinkling. Should we do the same? It is truly amazing to what extremes we can go in trying to justify a personal opinion.

8. IT HAS BEEN DIVISIVE. I would almost like to refrain from dignifying this argument with a response. But what I will do is point out that what has actually been divisive, and horribly so, is the sectarian spirit of such men as Moses E. Lard who have taught, since at least the year 1864, that we should withdraw all fellowship whatsoever from those who use instruments.[18] The instrumental group never displayed such a divisive attitude toward us.

IS CONGREGATIONAL SINGING AUTHORIZED?

It may be a shock to many Church of Christ people that this question even be asked. But it has been asked in years past and it is still being asked today. We need to examine this question very carefully. I was taught in the Church of Christ that choirs, solo singing and musical instruments were strictly forbidden but that congregational singing (the whole congregation singing at once) was absolutely authorized and commanded in the New Testament. A careful examination of Scriptures will show that this is simply not true. If we insist on an explicit command for, or an example of, congregational singing in a New Testament congregation of Christians in order to justify our practice, we are in for a real shock. There is neither. This puts us on very shaky ground when we realize that we try to forbid the instrument because of no explicit command or approved example, but we insist on congregational singing and, for it, we have neither. We will now examine all relevant New Testament passages in order to justify the above conclusion. All quotes of Scripture are from the Revised Standard Version. First we will look at six of the familiar passages.

> (Eph. 5:19) . . . addressing one another in psalms and hymns and spiritual songs, singing and making melody to the Lord with all your heart.
>
> (Col. 3:16) . . . teach and admonish one another in all wisdom, and sing psalms and hymns and spiritual songs with thankfulness in your hearts to God.
>
> (James 5:13) Is any cheerful? Let him sing praise.
>
> (Acts 16:25) . . . about midnight, Paul and Silas were praying and singing hymns to God. . . . (in prison)
>
> (1 Cor. 14:15) I will sing with the spirit and I will sing with the mind also.
>
> (1 Cor. 14:26) . . . when you come together, each one has a hymn, a lesson, a revelation, a tongue, or an interpretation. Let all things be done for edification.

None of the above passages explicitly authorizes, by command or example, an entire congregation singing at once. In all cases the reference is most likely to one person or at most two persons singing at once. James 5:13, 1 Corinthians 14:15, and 1 Corinthians 14:26 all obviously refer to one person only. Acts 16:25

refers to two people either singing a duet or taking turns singing solos. Even Ephesians 5:19 and Colossians 3:16 are most likely referring to singing in a one on one situation. They refer to addressing, teaching and admonishing "one another." Can one prove this assumption? No, probably not. I suppose that you could address, teach and admonish one another in congregational singing, although it would not seem in general to be very easy to do without considerable confusion. But these are certainly not proof texts for congregational singing. Congregational singing is not specifically mentioned. One might infer congregational singing, but the inference certainly would not be "necessary" (i.e., not the only possible inference). Continuing now with other verses:

> (Heb. 2:12) (The writer quotes from Psalm 22:22.) I will proclaim thy name to my brethren, in the midst of the congregation I will praise thee. (The King James and NIV translations say "sing praises.") (This certainly does not support congregational singing because it says "I," not "we" or "they.")
>
> (Heb. 13:15) . . . through him then let us continually offer up a sacrifice of praise to God, that is, the fruit of lips that acknowledge his name. (This probably does not even refer to singing, just praise. No version in the *Eight Translation New Testament* which I have mentions singing.)
>
> (Mark 14:26) And when they had sung a hymn, they went out to the Mount of Olives.

The last verse referenced above, Mark 14:26, is the only one which unequivocally refers to corporate singing. But this was just after the Lord's supper was instituted, and before the death of Christ on the cross. Thus it could not be an example of congregational singing in a New Testament church, not if you assume that the Church of Christ was initiated on the day of Pentecost. Also, one must realize that if it is acceptable to go back prior to the death of Christ to establish the authority for congregational singing then it is just as acceptable to go back prior to this event for authority for the use of instrumental music in worship.

All in all, we have a very, very weak case if we try to insist that we in the Church of Christ have explicit authorization for everything that we do. I am comfortable with congregational singing, not because it is specifically directed in Scripture, but because it is intuitively obvious to even the most casual observer that if it is good and proper for one person to sing praises to God alone then it is just as good and proper for several persons to sing praises to God together. In the same vein, it is just as obvious (to all except those of us who are steeped in Church of Christ tradition) that if it is good to sing praises to God then it is good to sing praises to God with or without the accompaniment of a musical instrument. We need no "specific" authority for a musical instrument because its use is not an addition to Scripture at all, its use is very simply a natural part of singing; so closely related so as to not require any specific mention in the text.

SOLO SINGING IN A CONGREGATIONAL SETTING

This is just an interesting point to note for those of us in the Church of Christ. We have insisted on Congregational singing, which we have just shown to not be specifically authorized. We have just as strongly forbidden the singing of solos in our congregational worship. But notice 1 Corinthians 14:26: "When you come together, each one has a hymn, a lesson, a revelation, a tongue, or an interpretation. Let all things be done for edification." The text says that "each one" has a hymn, not that "everyone all together and at once" has a hymn. This example is in a corporate setting and hence would seem to be explicit authorization for the singing of a solo in the presence of the congregation.

JUDGING

It is entirely proper and appropriate, and even necessary, for all who profess the name of Christ to study the Bible and to determine for themselves what is, in their opinion, true and what is false on every issue of interest. It is then just as appropriate and necessary that they practice these beliefs in their own lives and that they teach what they believe to be true to all who will listen. However, it is not as proper and appropriate to immediately declare that all who have somewhat different beliefs or who practice Christianity in a slightly different manner are condemned to spend eternity in hell. Even if the different beliefs and practices are indeed wrong, God never established, as one of the duties of every Christian, the job of deciding who is going to heaven and who is going to hell. Especially in areas where the Scriptures do not specifically address a subject, such as the use or nonuse of mechanical instruments of music in New Testament congregational worship, one should be very cautious in passing judgment. The New Testament addresses this topic in several passages:

> (James 4:11) Do not speak evil against one another, brethren. He that speaks evil against a brother or judges his brother, speaks evil against the law and judges the law. But if you judge the law, you are not a doer of the law but a judge. There is one lawgiver and judge, he who is able to save and to destroy. But who are you that you judge your neighbor?

> (1 Cor. 4:3-5) But with me it is a very small thing that I should be judged by you or by any human court. I do not even judge myself. I am not aware of anything against myself, but I am not thereby acquitted. It is the Lord who judges me. Therefore do not pronounce judgment before the time, before the Lord comes, who will bring to light the things now hidden in darkness and will disclose the purposes of the heart. Then every man will receive his commendation from God.

> (Romans 2:1) Therefore you have no excuse, O man, whoever you are, when you judge another; for in passing judgment upon

him you condemn yourself, because you, the judge, are doing the very same things. We know that the judgment of God rightly falls upon those who do such things. Do you suppose, O man, that when you judge those who do such things and yet do them yourself, you will escape the judgment of God? Or do you presume upon the riches of his kindness and forbearance and patience?

(Romans 14:1-13) As for the man who is weak in faith, welcome him, but not for disputes over opinions. One believes he may eat anything, while the weak man eats only vegetables. Let not him who eats despise him who abstains, and let not him who abstains pass judgment on him who eats; for God has welcomed him. Who are you to pass judgment on the servant of another? It is before his own master that he stands or falls. And he will be upheld, for the Master is able to make him stand. One man esteems one day as better than another, while another man esteems all days alike. Let every one be fully convinced in his own mind. He who observes the day, observes it in honor of the Lord. He also who eats, eats in honor of the Lord, since he gives thanks to God; while he who abstains, abstains in honor of the Lord and gives thanks to God. None of us lives to himself, and none of us dies to himself. If we live, we live to the Lord, and if we die, we die to the Lord; so then, whether we live or whether we die, we are the Lord's. For to this end Christ died and lived again, that he might be Lord both of the dead and of the living. Why do you pass judgment on your brother? Or you, why do you despise your brother? For we shall all stand before the judgment seat of God; for it is written, "As I live, says the Lord, each of us shall give account of himself to God. Then let us no more pass judgment on one another, but rather decide never to put a stumbling block or hindrance in the way of a brother."

(James 2:13) For judgment is without mercy to one who has shown no mercy; yet mercy triumphs over judgment.

The reason for including the verses on judging was to make the following observation. If we are so quick to deliver a wholesale condemnation of all other religious groups because they may have an opinion which differs from one of ours or because they may have some doctrinal errors in their beliefs, how can we expect the Lord to be merciful in regards to any of our possible misjudgments or our possible doctrinal errors? The Bible tells us, as we saw in James 2:13, that "judgment is without mercy to one who has shown no mercy." It is a fearful thing to think that we might be depriving ourselves of the mercy which we all, as mere mortal sinners, will most certainly need when we face our maker, because of our harsh judgment and lack of mercy in our dealings with other religious groups.

Thomas Campbell, in his Declaration and Address, has some sobering words on this subject. He speaks of three great evils:

First
To determine expressly, in the name of the Lord, when the Lord has not expressly determined, appears to us a very great evil. (see Deut. 18:20) "But the prophet who presumes to speak a word in my name which I have not commanded him to speak, . . . that same prophet shall die."

Second
A second evil is, not only judging our brother to be absolutely wrong, because he differs from our opinions, but more especially, our judging him to be a transgressor of the law in so doing, and, of course, treating him as such by censuring or otherwise exposing him to contempt, or, at least, preferring ourselves before him in our own judgment, saying, as it were, Stand by, I am holier than thou.

Third
A third and still more dreadful evil is, when we not only, in this kind of way judge and set at nought our brother, but, moreover, proceed as a Church, acting and judging in the name of Christ, not only to determine that our brother is wrong because he differs from our determinations, but also, in connection with this, proceed so far as to determine the merits of the cause by rejecting him, or casting him out of the Church, as unworthy of a place in her communion, and thus, as far as in our power, cutting him off from the kingdom of heaven. In proceeding thus, we not only declare, that, in our judgment, our brother is in an error, which we may sometimes do in a perfect consistence with charity, but we also take upon us to judge, as acting in the name

ENDANGERED HERITAGE

and by the authority of Christ that his error cuts him off from salvation; that continuing such, he has no inheritance in the kingdom of Christ and of God.[23]

In the same document Thomas Campbell makes a one sentence summary of his feelings in this regard:

> As for our part, we dare no longer give our assent to such proceedings; we dare no longer concur in expressly asserting or declaring anything in the name of the Lord, that he has not expressly declared in his holy word.[24]

There is one phrase in the Bible which I think we in the Church of Christ should keep in mind when we attempt to establish our own opinion, on a subject on which the Scriptures are not explicit, as an absolute rule for all of Christendom. Romans 4:15 says, "... where there is no law there is no transgression."

SUMMARY

There is one thing which I need to make very clear as I begin this summary of our examination of the instrumental music issue. I am not proposing that, and I have no desire for, the Churches of Christ to institute the use of instrumental music in their congregational singing. Most of the Church of Christ members with whom I have discussed this topic are of the opinion that there would be absolutely nothing wrong with the use of mechanical instruments of music in the Lord's worship. However, I know of absolutely no one who is suggesting that the Church of Christ begin to use instruments. There are two reasons why I believe that we should continue to sing a cappella in our congregational singing.

The first reason is simply that I think a cappella singing is the best method to use when the whole congregation is singing

---

23. Thomas Campbell, "Declaration and Address," St. Louis: Mission Messenger, pp. 72-73.
24. Ibid., p. 71.

INSTRUMENTAL MUSIC USED IN WORSHIP IS A SIN

together. I don't know how much my Church of Christ background is influencing me here, but, nevertheless, that is the way I feel. Even forgetting religion for a moment, when I hear a group like the Vocal Majority from Dallas, wherein 100-150 men are singing barbershop quartet style four part harmony (a cappella) I feel that an organ could not add to the music; it probably would even detract from it. In fact, I don't even like organ music. I remember the first time that I walked into a church which used an organ. It was turned up so loud that it hurt my ears. It drowned out the few people who were trying to sing along. But I must remember that just because I personally dislike something does not make it wrong, does not make it a sin. It is only a sin if it violates some Biblical injunction. In fact, I feel that a cappella singing is so clearly superior in a setting where a large crowd of people are singing together that I think we might possibly have some success at convincing some of the other denominations to use this method if we promoted it in a different manner; if we suggested that they sing a cappella because it sounds better or seems more natural, rather than telling them that they are going to hell if they use instruments. An approach is always better than a reproach.

The second reason is probably more important. This document is intended to be a harbinger of pacification, reunion and reconciliation and not to be a cause of division. I couldn't cause division over this issue if I wanted to, however, because the division was caused over 100 years ago by those with the spirit of men like Moses E. Lard. Still, we must always proceed with caution and with consideration in mind for the feelings of our fellow Christians. Sometimes those who discover a new freedom in Christ seem bound and determined to immediately push this freedom to the limits as if to prove something to the world. I think that this demonstrates an attitude of arrogance and haughtiness that is not very indicative of a Christian spirit. We must realize that among our brethren in the Church of Christ there is a significant percentage who are in the latter portion of their walk through this life. They have spent many, many years singing a cappella with many of them being taught that this is the only Scriptural way. Even if they could all now be convinced intellectually that instrumental music is not a sin (and I think this would be impossible) it would still not "feel" right to them. A mind set which has been acquired and nurtured over many years cannot be changed easily, especially in those of an advanced age. It still doesn't even "feel" completely right to me and I completely resolved all of the intellectual questions on this issue some years ago. For this reason alone, if for no other, I think we should not introduce instrumental music into our congregational singing in our generation, if indeed ever.

We must, however, make some changes in our teaching, our preaching and in our writing. We have taken a personal opinion, an inference regarding something of which the Scriptures do not speak, and we have tried to make it a condition of salvation. We have committed the grave sin of adding to the Word of God. We have in a very real way added the command "thou shalt not sing praises to thy Lord with the accompaniment of a mechanical instrument of music." And as if this weren't enough, we have compounded the offense by adding the condition that "if thou doest this thing thou shalt spend eternity in hell." It is time that we swallow our pride and in the most humble way we know how ask our Lord and our fellow Christians for their forgiveness. We could have held our personal opinion and maintained our practice with all propriety, but we tried to force it on others as a condition of Christian fellowship and eternal salvation. In doing this we have endangered the heritage of our restoration movement, the very thing that we have accused others of doing.

At this point someone may say, "Wait a minute sir, I am opposed to instruments but my doctrine is not quite that harsh." In some individual cases this is true; however, I think that I have accurately described the Church of Christ's doctrinal position. It is a doctrine which has been explicitly taught for several generations. If it is currently any less explicitly taught in some areas, it is still implicit in our attitude and in our behavior. This is how we are perceived by the general public. No leader of any consequence dares to publicly challenge the status quo. The music issue is a sacred cow which cannot be approached. A preacher could get blacklisted very quickly and ruin his career for not being "sound" in this area. We seem to have largely accepted the doctrine of a previous generation without any serious question. We have "taken as our doctrine the traditions of men," the very thing that we love to accuse the rest of the entire religious world of doing.

Our position on the music issue has probably done more to damage our reputation than has any other single thing. By taking a position which is so obviously false (to everyone but ourselves) we have destroyed the credibility of our whole approach to Bible study. It has ruined our reputation throughout Christendom. We have much Bible truth to offer to the world, such as the importance of baptism, in connection with faith and repentance, for the forgiveness of sins, but people won't take us seriously; largely, I think, because we have destroyed our credibility with the music issue.

Many of our preachers don't talk about the music issue anymore. Now, one way or another we have a problem. If the use of instruments is a sin, then we owe it to our Lord to teach about it regularly, to train our young people and to try to save the rest of the world. If this is the case, then our preachers who don't teach it have a real problem. On the other hand, if we have been wrong, and we most certainly have, then we must start to teach the truth. My experience tells me that the vast majority of the Church of Christ lay people, the members out in the pews, do not believe that instrumental music is a sin. But no one speaks up publicly. A few of the leaders still preach this doctrine and the rest of us just sit and listen. We dare not, we must not, we can not, remain silent any longer. Thomas Campbell, when speaking of another topic in the Declaration and Address, made a statement which I believe to be very applicable to our present situation. He said, in 1809:

You will not, you cannot, therefore, be silent upon a subject of such vast importance to his personal glory and the happiness of his people—consistently you cannot; for silence gives consent.[25]

To remain silent on this subject, which has caused so much division among God's people, is to agree (by default) with the official doctrine and makes us just as guilty as anyone for falsely condemning and judging on the grandest scale.

---

25. Ibid., pp. 39-40.

9

THE CHURCH OF CHRIST IS NOT A DENOMINATION

It would not really be necessary to quote any Bible verses or study any of our history to thoroughly investigate the claim that the Church of Christ is not a denomination. It is not a matter of Scriptural interpretation or of historical perspective. It does not relate to a proper respect for Biblical authority or rightly dividing the Word. It even has very little to do with the difference between ourselves on one end of the spectrum (having each congregation completely autonomous) and a group like the Roman Catholic Church on the other end of the spectrum (with its gigantic world-wide organization). This is not an issue of right vs. wrong, truth vs. falsehood or the Lord vs. the devil. It is very simply a matter of the proper understanding and use of one word. It is a matter that deals with the proper use of our language regarding the definition of a single word, "denomination." For two or more people to communicate via either the spoken or written word they must not only use a common

ENDANGERED HERITAGE

language with all of its associated structures and nuances, but they must also maintain one other absolutely critical area of commonality. They must each, the communicator and the communicatee, use the same definitions for the words. If they do not use consistent definitions for words then no matter how accurate both the sender and the receiver share a common grammar and syntax, the meaning of the original thought will be lost, or worse yet, misinterpreted. It is this that we are dealing with here, the definition of a single word, "denomination."

All of the English speaking world uses a fairly standard and widely accepted definition for the word denomination except the Church of Christ. We reject the definition which is in common usage and try to use one of our own. This has resulted in much confusion, much of the bad feelings of others for the Church of Christ, and has contributed measurably to our bad reputation. The commonly accepted definition of the word denomination, as it relates to religion, is that it is a word which denotes a particular religious group, distinguishable from other religious groups by various characteristics. Among these characteristics would be the following: its own separate name, its own buildings, its own schools and colleges, its own preachers, its own preacher training centers, its own literature, its own separate listing in the telephone yellow pages, its own separate radio or television programs, its own foreign missionaries and its own particular set of religious beliefs. We have all of these. By most, if not all, of the commonly accepted aspects of the definition of the word "denomination" the Church of Christ obviously is one. It is as plain and simple as that. Absolutely nothing could be more obvious. When we proceed, in direct opposition to this plain and simple fact, to claim that we are not a denomination, it makes us look totally ridiculous to anyone who can read or hear. The results of this situation are catastrophic. When people can see that our reasoning is so obviously faulty when dealing with a concept as simple as this, there is no way that they will risk listening to us propound on subjects requiring more study and thought, such as the atonement, baptism, the Lord's supper, the Holy Spirit, etc. They think that we will probably try to lead them astray even further on these more complex issues. And, unfortunately, I must admit that this is a logical and safe conclusion from their vantage point. If I were looking in from the outside, I would come to the same conclusion. We have much that is good, true and valuable to offer to the world, but we have damaged our credibility to the point where people often will not listen to us.

There is one fine point (one technicality) of the definition of the word denomination to which the Church of Christ does not conform. It is the one reason that we could say that we are not a denomination and have the statement (to that limited extent) be true. Our congregations are not officially connected to each other by a hierarchial structure. In my opinion this congregational autonomy is an extremely good and important thing about us. It is not to be slighted or diminished in importance in any way. However, this is a Church of Christ characteristic which is not communicated by the "we are not a denomination" doctrine. We have a good characteristic which is not being effectively advertised. When a person can see that there are a large number of plain and obvious reasons why we should be called a denomination and we are trying to tell them that we are not a denomination because of one fine point (a technicality which may well appear obscure and unimportant to them at the time) then we are failing to communicate. We are grossly abusing the English language. If we would tell them that we are a denomination which is absolutely opposed to any ecclesiastical organization, this would make sense; then we would be communicating effectively. Then we would be using the English language properly. Then we would have a common framework within which to work and we would have the opportunity of perhaps convincing them that our point of view is worth their consideration.

In order to support my claims regarding the definition of the word denomination I will present, for the reader's examination, the definitions from several English dictionaries. First for the three major unabridged English dictionaries.

Webster's Third New International Dictionary, Copyright 1973.

Denomination

1. the act of denominating or naming.
2. that by which something is denominated or styled; appellation, name, designation, title; esp: a general name for a class of like individuals: category
3. a class or society of individuals called by the same name; esp; a religious group or a community of believers called by the same name (i.e. Presbyterians form one denomination of Christians)
4. a value or size naming one of a particular series of values or sizes (as of monetary issues, stamps, units of weight or measure) (bills in $5 and $10 denominations) (liter is a metric denomination)
5. the suit or no-trump named in a bridge bid.

The Oxford English Dictionary, reprinted 1978—the 12 volume set, Clarendon Press.

Denomination

1. the action of naming from or after something: giving a name to, calling by a name. b. A mentioning or specifying by name.
2. a characteristic or qualifying name given to a thing or class of things; that which anything is called; an appellation, designation, title.
3. Arith. A class of one kind of unit in any system of numbers, measures, weights, money, etc., distinguished by a specific name.
4. a class, sort, or kind (of things or persons) distinguished or distinguishable by a specific name.
5. a collection of individuals classed together under the same name; now almost always spec. a religious sect or body having a common faith and organization, and designated by a distinctive name.

The Random House College Dictionary, revised edition, copyright 1980.

Denomination

1. a name or designation, esp. one for a class of things.
2. a class or kind of persons or things having a specific name.

3. a religious group, usually including many local churches.
4. the act of naming or designating a person or thing.
5. one of the grades or degrees in a series of values, measures, weights, etc.: bills of small denomination.

These certainly should constitute a sufficient group of authorities. Webster's Third New International Dictionary (unabridged) is probably considered the single most authoritative source in the United States. Notice that the Church of Christ completely fits the definitions from all three sources. Webster says "a religious group or a community of believers called by the same name." We certainly are that. Oxford says "a religious sect or body having a common faith and organization, and designated by a distinctive name." We are that. Our common organization is that we have elders and deacons in local congregations and these congregations are completely autonomous. Nothing in the definition specifies an intercongregational organization. One could possibly read this into the definition but it would be an inference. It certainly is not explicit in this regard. And Random House simply says "a religious group, usually including many local churches." We obviously fit that definition. And so it is clear that according to the most complete and unabridged authorities the Church of Christ is a denomination.

However in an attempt to be thorough I was able to find, in some smaller desk top dictionaries, the other more subtle aspect of the definition of the word denomination, that relating to an intercongregational organization.

The American Heritage Dictionary, copyright 1980 and the Second College Ed. 1982.
Denomination

1. the act of naming
2. a name; designation.
3. the name of a class or group; classification.
4. a class of units having specified values, as in a system of currency or weights.
5. an organized group of religious congregations.

ENDANGERED HERITAGE

Webster's Ninth New Collegiate Dictionary, copyright 1985.
Denomination.
1. an act of denominating.
2. a value or size of a series of values or sizes (as of money)
3. name, designation; esp: a general name for a category.
4. a religious organization uniting in a single legal and administrative body a number of local congregations.

Here at last we find a nuance in the definition which does not apply to the Church of Christ. It is interesting that it appears only in the small desk sized volumes and not in the large unabridged editions.

Another tack which many of our people have taken in the past is to say something like the following: "We are the one and only true church, therefore we are not a denomination." Again this is an abuse of the English language. If someone feels that this is a true concept and he wishes to communicate it to others he should say something such as: "We are the only present-day denomination which constitutes the one and only true church—all other denominations today are false churches." Now at least he is using the English language properly; whether or not his contention is true.

This problem, our abuse of the word denomination, is a very serious problem and it is very much alive and well in our writing and in our rhetoric even today. There is hardly a sermon or an article or a chapter in one of our books which does not contain at least one reference to "the denominations" or "denominationalism" in some way. The use of such phrasing has become so much an integral part of our being that even many of our more moderate and enlightened leaders, who through prayer, study and personal reflection seem to have relieved themselves of some of the attitudes that have plagued us in the past, still use this anti-denominationalism approach in much of their writing. It seems to be like cursing. Once a person gets into the habit, it sort of feels good and, thus, it is very hard to quit; and it is probably just as detrimental to our efforts to communicate with the rest of the religious world.

THE CHURCH OF CHRIST IS NOT A DENOMINATION

We have, in our own minds, become very adept at making use of this dirty word, denomination, and we use it in several ways. When we say that some other religious group is a denomination and we are not a denomination we have said that we are better than they. We have not said that we are better because we are more pious, or have more of the truth or for any other tangible reason. We are just better than they are for the simple, intangible reason that we are not what they are, we are not a denomination. We can cut people down with one swift and deadly slash of the tongue. We speak of two regimes; the "true church," which is us, and the "denominational world," which is all of the other religious groups, and we certainly make the implication (if not the explicit statement) that this other world, this realm of which we are not a part, is completely lost and going to hell. This is a style or mode of speaking and writing which may sound and feel good to us, but to others it sounds presumptuous to the ultimate degree. It does not convert anyone to Christ or teach anyone the truth. It only closes doors and makes enemies. Even if it were perfectly and completely true, it would probably not be in the interest of good public relations to speak in this manner. However, once we realize that, based on a proper use of the English language, it is actually false, and obviously so to all but ourselves, it becomes a source of shame. It is a gross exhibition of vain self-righteousness.

We have resorted to euphemisms to keep from using the word denomination. We speak of the Church of Christ denomination as either the "brotherhood" or the "fellowship." This sounds a little quaint and odd to other people but when one has heard these terms used since childhood they don't sound too bad. They work quite nicely when we are talking among ourselves. We just plug in "brotherhood" or "fellowship" where others would use the word denomination.

The restoration movement began partly as a Christian unity movement and had as one of its ideals the achievement of non-denominational Christianity. The achievement of New Testament non-denominational Christianity is still and should always remain as our ideal objective. The problem is that we in the Church of Christ seem to have lost the ability to distinguish between having non-denominational Christianity as a goal which we are working toward on the one hand, and as something that we have already achieved on the other. We certainly have not achieved it at this time. The early restoration movement leaders really believed that their concept of getting back to the Bible would be swiftly accepted by all of the denominations of their day and cause them all to start believing and teaching the same things. Hence all of the denominations would melt into one, thus, in effect, bringing about a non-denominational Christian world. One hundred and eighty years of history tells us that this did not happen. The religious world is still divided into various groups, sects, parties, brotherhoods, fellowships, or denominations (whichever you choose to call them). We in the Church of Christ are one of these many groups, sects, parties, brotherhoods, fellowships, or denominations (whichever label you want to assign to us). The label in most common use in our English language of today is "denomination." We are one, so why not admit it? We should start using the name so we can better communicate with the people around us. We might be the best, the purest, the most Scriptural, the most like the New Testament, the most righteous or even the only one with people in it who will get to heaven, but we are still a denomination.

Any religious movement may, like our own restoration movement, be truly non-denominational in its early stages. This is during the formative stages before it has developed a unique character of its own. But unless this new movement completely conquers the religious world almost immediately, it will soon add exactly one to the list of existing denominations. As soon as it develops any significant number of the attributes in the list which we discussed above (name, buildings, books, etc.) it becomes, in a very real way, a denomination. This is not in and of itself good or bad. It is just a fact of life.

THE CHURCH OF CHRIST IS NOT A DENOMINATION

I have heard our people say (and seen it in print) that denominationalism itself is wrong and sinful. At first glance this may read well to those with our background, but we should reevaluate this thought very carefully. It is true that division in the Christian world has been throughout history, and still is, very detrimental to the cause of Christ. The division and fighting among those who claim to be Christians is, I truly believe, the devil's most effective tool; and he has used it to good advantage throughout the ages. But we should be careful about just how and what we criticize. As long as we live in a world where everyone else does not agree with each and every one of our religious views, we had better be thankful for denominationalism. To criticize denominationalism is the same thing as criticizing religious freedom. It is our beloved American religious freedom (denominationalism) which gives us the freedom to form an association with others of like mind and to practice and promote that form of doctrine which we believe to be so precious and true. We should thank the Lord for denominationalism. Instead of criticizing denominationalism itself, we should criticize the errors that the devil has caused in the other denominations (and also acknowledge any errors that the devil might have caused in our own denomination) and rather than making the absolutely ridiculous claim that we are not a denomination, try instead with the help and grace of God to be the best one.

So I would like to suggest to all of our brethren that we perhaps begin to phase out the use of those two odd terms that we use (brotherhood and fellowship) and start to call ourselves what we really are, a denomination. Try it. It hurts a little at first, I'll admit. But before long, with diligent practice, the pain starts to subside. And then, lo and behold, after a while it even starts to feel good. And it starts to feel good for a very noble and Godly reason. It starts to feel good when we realize that we have torn down yet another man-made wall that has divided us from other professors of the name of Christ. And in doing this, ironically, we have come one step closer to our ideal—our goal of not being a denomination.

10

ONLY CHURCH OF CHRIST MEMBERS CAN GO TO HEAVEN

INTRODUCTION

This is, without a doubt, the most difficult chapter of this document. It deals with a concept which has been a problem for many groups of Christians, to varying degrees, since the time of Christ. The Churches of Christ, in their attempts to restore the ancient order of things, seem to have experienced more difficulties than most groups in this area.

I want to say a few words, by way of introduction to this chapter, which will perhaps alleviate the apprehension of some Church of Christ readers. For some who have never had the occasion to discuss these concepts with people outside of their Church of Christ sphere, or for those who have had no exposure to the historical development of the Church of Christ over the last 200 years, there may be some new ideas or some new thoughts presented. I ask that you give this chapter your most careful consideration. I believe that it represents sound, solid and conservative New Testament theology. There is absolutely no attempt toward, and no tendency to, water down New Testament Christianity. This chapter will deal with such issues as baptism for the remission of sins and the weekly observance of the Lord's supper. I believe that Church of Christ teaching in these areas has been essentially correct. The pioneer preachers of our restoration movement were very strong in their support of these concepts. In fact, we must remember that it was these early leaders of our own restoration movement who reestablished believers' baptism for the remission of sins and the weekly observance of the Lord's supper as prominent elements of the Christian economy. They not only believed these things themselves, but they rediscovered them and presented them to the religious world in the face of strong opposition. The chapters on baptism and the Lord's supper in this document are presented primarily to establish beyond any doubt that these early restoration movement leaders were, as we would say, "sound" in these areas that we consider to be so fundamental and important.

I will continue for a moment, still by way of introduction, specifically regarding the concept of baptism for the forgiveness of sins. This subject will, of necessity, be discussed at great length throughout this chapter. I personally believe that baptism is for the forgiveness of sins. I do not consider this to be some sort of religious theory. I consider it to be an established fact. The New Testament explicitly makes this statement on several occasions. The Church of Christ has always considered this to be true. I also believe that the only mode of baptism used in the New Testament was immersion. Although this is not explicitly stated in the New Testament the circumstances surrounding the examples of baptism are such as to, in my opinion, establish this also as a fact not to be disputed. The Church of Christ has also always believed this to be true. I am not now willing, the Church of Christ has never in the past been willing, and we should never in the future be willing to compromise on these basic fundamental beliefs in any way in our practice or in our teaching. Furthermore, I believe that we should never accept a person as a member of one of our congregations who has not been immersed into the Lord Jesus. I will even go a little farther and state that I do not believe we should welcome as members any who do not understand that baptism is for the forgiveness of sins. To do so would be to either be lax in our teaching or to admit that this is not really very important after all. The Church of Christ has stood firm in its support of the New Testament teachings and examples in these areas in both the 19th and 20th centuries and I hope and pray that we continue to do so until the Lord comes again. I also believe that to talk of unity with any other religious group or denomination that does not believe and practice as we do in these areas is meaningless. This also is consistent with the historical Church of Christ position.

The question under investigation throughout this chapter is not, then, whether or not the Church of Christ doctrine on such issues is correct. It is assumed to be completely correct. The question deals with how we should relate to, or what our attitude should be toward, other conscientious professors of the name of Christ who have either never heard our doctrine taught or who have not yet been convinced of its validity.

The concept under investigation is one of "our presumed perfection of doctrine" or our "exclusivism." We can introduce it into this discussion by asking an old familiar question. Is it absolutely necessary to be a member of the Church of Christ in order to go to heaven? The standard 20th century Church of Christ answer to that question has been a resounding "Yes, you must." It might be argued by someone that not everyone believes that, however at least for the last 30 to 50 years most have believed this, or at least most teaching has been to this effect. In fact, this is the one attribute by which we are most widely known.

I would like to ask this question in another way which I think more clearly states the issue at hand. In fact, I think that this restatement will not only more clearly define the concept under consideration but will also help to suggest an answer to the question. The restatement is as follows: Is it necessary for one to be absolutely perfect regarding all doctrinal issues in order to go to heaven? Must one have a perfect understanding of the Bible, a perfect understanding of all doctrinal issues and be perfect in his execution of all the ordinances in order to go to heaven?

The contemporary Church of Christ position amounts to an answer of "Yes" to all of these questions. This position has far reaching implications. It has become in vogue in the Church of Christ in recent years to teach about grace, but only relating to moral issues. Does grace not apply in areas relating to doctrine? Does the grace of God, made available through the blood of our Lord and Saviour Jesus Christ by his death on the cross, serve as an expiation for our sins regarding moral issues, but have no effect in areas relating to doctrine? Can this be? What Scripture would indicate that grace could be effective in one area and not in the other?

We have in effect said to the world, "We are perfect in doctrine. If you want to go to heaven come over and be perfect with us." This is a most precarious position to occupy. What if we are yet found to be lacking in some area? What if we are told on the judgment day, much to our dismay, that since the Bible did not mention Sunday school classes we were not permitted to have them? Then we in the main line Church of Christ will all go to hell and some of our more conservative brethren will still have a chance at salvation. But they still might not make it because, perhaps, they practiced multi-cup communion as we do, but it turns out that using a single cup is the only acceptable method. This example could go on ad infinitum. If perfection is required in doctrine then somewhere there is one very small, conservative, sectarian Church of Christ with a few people in it who will get to heaven—unless they too have neglected something.

It therefore begins to appear, based on this very cursory examination of the situation, that any group that assumes that they alone have any chance at all of going to heaven might occupy a very untenable position. The New Testament writers gave us some very ominous warnings in this area in the Scriptures which we examined earlier relating to judging. We also want to look at what our heritage in the restoration movement teaches us regarding this subject. We will see what the first and second generation restoration leaders believed and taught on this subject. Alexander Campbell and Walter Scott taught the importance and significance of immersion for the forgiveness of sins with more fervor and success than probably any other men since the New Testament times. We will examine their feelings about this exclusivistic attitude. Thomas Campbell, Alexander Campbell, Walter Scott and Barton W. Stone are sometimes called the big four of the restoration movement. Each of them had something to say on this subject, most of them had a lot to say on this subject. Then also we can look at some of the second generation leaders; what might be called the main line Church of Christ leaders of the second generation, those who continued after the big four had died or become too old to be major participants in any debates. The early restoration literature is rich with material on this subject. We will examine some of the more important articles in this chapter.

THE DEFINITION OF A CHRISTIAN

It will be interesting to compare the definitions of a Christian which have been in common use in the 20th century with those definitions which we see in the literature from the 19th century. Since we have no official church definition of what constitutes a Christian, the best I can do for a 20th century definition is to list several phrases which I have seen used in this regard.
1. A baptized believer.
2. One who is baptized for the forgiveness of sins.
3. One who is baptized for the forgiveness of sins and who lives faithfully thereafter.

4. A member of the Church of Christ who is baptized by immersion, who has the words "for the forgiveness of sins" uttered over him just prior to immersion, who fully understands at the time that the baptism about to be performed on him is specifically for the forgiveness of sins, and who remains a faithful member of the Church of Christ thereafter.

These are a few of the ideas that I have heard expressed. Notice that the word baptized appears in each of the definitions and "for the forgiveness of sins" appears in most. These are references to compliance with specific doctrinal teachings.

Let us now look at some definitions which were used by the early leaders of the restoration movement. Alexander Campbell gives an example in the *Millennial Harbinger* in 1837.

> But who is a Christian? I answer, Every one that believes in his heart that Jesus of Nazareth is the Messiah, the Son of God; repents of his sins, and obeys him in all things according to his measure of knowledge of his will.[1]

Later in the same series of articles Campbell gives another definition.

> A Christian is one that habitually believes all that Christ says, and habitually does all that he bids him.[2]

Barton W. Stone gives a definition in the *Christian Messenger* in 1831.

> Let us still acknowledge all to be brethren, who believe in the Lord Jesus, and humbly and honestly obey him, as far as they know his will, and their duty.[3]

Robert Richardson quotes Alexander Campbell in his *Memoirs*.

> So long as any man, woman or child declares his confidence in Jesus of Nazareth as God's own Son, that he was delivered for

---
1. Alexander Campbell, *Millennial Harbinger,* 1837, p. 411.
2. Ibid., p. 566.
3. Barton W. Stone, *Christian Messenger,* 1831, p. 21.

our offences and raised again for our justification—or, in other words, that Jesus is the Messiah, the Saviour of men—and so long as he exhibits a willingness to obey him in all things so far as his knowledge extends, so long will I receive him as a Christian brother and treat him as such.[4]

I present these definitions only to make an overall comparison of the two groups. The present day definitions give the most emphasis to obedience to a specific command or understanding of a specific point of doctrine. The definitions given by our pioneer ancestors, on the other hand, seem to speak of an overall compliance with the gospel (as understood by each individual) coupled with a Christlike lifestyle.

OPINION

One of the major points emphasized by the leaders of the restoration movement was the need to recognize the difference between faith and opinion, or the difference between an explicit Biblical directive and a personal opinion on some particular issue. The dividing line between the two sometimes seems somewhat blurred because men have differing opinions as to what constitutes an opinion. The early leaders minimized the problems in this area by keeping the list of issues or items classified as faith (or doctrine) very small and the list classified as opinion relatively large. In the 20th century Church of Christ the relative size of these two lists seems to be reversed. Many of our people have left very little except the trivia to be classified as opinion. The result is that whenever two people disagree on some subject it is assumed that they have conflicting doctrines and a split in the body of Christ is the result. I will present at this time a collection of quotes relating to this subject of opinion. The

---

4. Robert Richardson, quoting Alexander Campbell, *Memoirs of Alexander Campbell,* Vol. 2, p. 134.

first group of quotes are by Thomas Campbell from the Declaration and Address.[5]

(From the opening paragraph:) We are also persuaded that as no man can be judged for his brother, so no man can judge for his brother; every man must be allowed to judge for himself, as every man must bear his own judgment—must give account of himself to God. We are also of opinion that as the Divine word is equally binding upon all, so all lie under an equal obligation to be bound by it, and it alone; and not by any human interpretation of it; and that, therefore, no man has a right to judge his brother, except in so far as he manifestly violates the express letter of the law. That every such judgment is an express violation of the law of Christ, a daring usurpation of his throne, and a gross intrusion upon the rights and liberties of his subjects. We are, therefore, of opinion that we should beware of such things; that we should keep at the utmost distance from everything of this nature; and that, knowing the judgment of God against them that commit such things, we should neither do the same ourselves, nor take pleasure in them that do them.

(On page 53, speaking to lovers of Jesus everywhere he says:) You believe that the word itself ought to be our rule, and not any human explication of it; so do we. You believe that no man has a right to judge, to exclude, or reject his professing Christian brother, except in so far as he stands condemned or rejected by the express letter of the law; so do we. You believe that the great fundamental law of unity and love ought not to be violated to make way for exalting human opinions to an equality with express revelation, by making them articles of faith and terms of communion; so do we.

(Page 61) . . . thus we conclude, to make no conclusion of our own, nor of any other fallible fellow-creature, a rule of faith or duty to our brother.

(Page 65) . . . for no man can relinquish his opinions or practices till once convinced that they are wrong; and this he may not be immediately, even supposing they were so. One thing, however, he may do: when not bound by an express command, he need not impose them upon others, by anywise

---

5. Thomas Campbell, "Declaration and Address," St. Louis: Mission Messenger.

requiring their approbation; and when this is done, the things, to them, are as good as dead, yea, as good as buried, too, being thus removed out of the way.

(Page 66) And here let it be noted, that it is not the renunciation of an opinion or practice as sinful that is proposed or intended, but merely a cessation from the publishing or practicing it, so as to give offense;

(Page 71) Which of them takes the greatest latitude? Whether those that expressly judge and condemn where they have no express warrant for so doing, or those that absolutely refuse so to do?

(Page 67, quoted earlier) Many of the opinions which are now dividing the Church, had they been let alone, would have been long since dead and gone; but the constant insisting upon them, as articles of faith and terms of salvation, have so beaten them into the minds of men, that, in many instances, they would as soon deny the Bible itself as give up one of those opinions.

(Page 81) . . . nor, indeed, is there anything either in scripture or the nature of things that should induce us to expect an entire unity of sentiment in the present imperfect state. . . . But that all the members should have the same identical views of all divinely revealed truths, or that there should be no difference of opinion among them, appears to us morally impossible, all things considered. Nor can we conceive what desirable purpose such a unity of sentiment would serve, except to render useless some of those gracious, self-denying, and compassionate precepts of mutual sympathy and forbearance which the word of God enjoins upon his people.

(Page 82) We would then no longer exalt our own opinions and inferences to an equality with express revelation, by condemning and rejecting our brother for differing with us in those things.

(Page 85) . . . an express violation of the expressly revealed will of God—to a manifest transgression of the express letter of the law; for we have declared, that except in such a case, no man, in our judgment, has a right to judge, that is, to condemn or reject his professing brother.

Alexander Campbell disagreed with Barton W. Stone regarding some of Stone's teachings on Biblical subjects. Robert Richardson quotes Campbell on this subject.

> For my part, I can and do make great allowance for early and long-established habits of thinking and speaking on all religious questions, and therefore regard Brother Stone as confiding in the sacrifice and death of Christ as indispensable to salvation, and though by no means asquiescing in some of his interpretations of the meaning and designs of the Messiah's death, I can bear with a difference of opinion on a subject so vital, which many would regard as an insuperable obstacle to Christian communion.
>
> Men may and do hold the Head, Christ, and his death and mediation indispensable to salvation, who, nevertheless, have very inadequate conceptions of some of the aspects of these transcendent subjects. And as we are not saved by the strength and comprehension of our views, but from obeying from the heart the apostolic mould of doctrine, more stress ought to be laid upon moral excellence than upon abstract orthodoxy, especially when all the facts and documents of Christianity are cordially believed and cherished. Our bond of union is one Lord, one faith, one baptism, one body, one spirit, one hope, one God and Father of all. And as many as walk by this rule, peace be on them and mercy, and upon the whole Israel of God![6]

Earlier in the same book Richardson himself describes Alexander Campbell's attitude regarding the distinction between faith and opinion.

> Especially did he mark out clearly the important distinction between faith and opinion, previously but dimly perceived, showing that men's conjectures and theories respecting matters of which the Bible does not speak should never be made terms of communion or be allowed to create religious differences.[7]

---

6. Alexander Campbell, quoted by Robert Richardson, *Memoirs of Alexander Campbell,* Vol. 2, pp. 483, 484.
7. Ibid., p. 47.

In order to provide substantiation for Richardson's description of Campbell's attitude in this area we quote Campbell himself from the pages of the *Millennial Harbinger*.

> I beg leave to state emphatically, that I do not make my own opinion a prominent part of the system of truth.[8]

Robert Richardson provides an appropriate close to this series of quotes with the following statement:

> ... entire unanimity in opinion is neither possible nor desirable in this imperfect state, nor was it indeed ever contemplated by the Author of Christianity, as the exhortations to mutual forbearance in the Scriptures themselves attest.[9]

ARE THERE ANY CHRISTIANS IN THE OTHER DENOMINATIONS?

To a person who has grown up in or been associated for many years with the Church of Christ this question may almost seem to be taboo. The generally accepted answer in the 20th century Church of Christ tradition has been that there are not any Christians in the "denominations." There has not been much objective, critical, discussion of this topic in our sermons or our Bible study classes. This was not true in the 19th century Church of Christ. The literature available to us from that period is rich with short quotes and entire articles on topics that relate to this question. In the pages which follow I will let the first and second generation leaders of the restoration movement speak for themselves, without comment or editorial, first in a collection of short quotes followed by some more comprehensive and lengthy articles. I think that it would be appropriate to begin this section by reading Mark 9:38-41.

---

8. Alexander Campbell, *Millennial Harbinger*, 1837, p. 292.
9. Robert Richardson, *Memoirs of Alexander Campbell*, Vol. 1, p. 268.

> John said to him, "Teacher, we saw a man casting out demons in your name, and we forbade him, because he was not following us." But Jesus said, "Do not forbid him; for no one who does a mighty work in my name will be able soon after to speak evil of me. For he that is not against us is for us. For truly, I say to you, whoever gives you a cup of water to drink because you bear the name of Christ, will by no means lose his reward."

A Collection of Short Quotes

As Barton W. Stone and others were breaking away from the Presbyterian Church in 1804 they wrote "The Last Will and Testament of the Springfield Presbytery." In the last paragraph of the document they say:

> We candidly acknowledge, that in some things we may err, through human infirmity; but he will correct our wanderings, and preserve his church. Let all Christians join with us, in crying to God day and night, to remove the obstacles which stand in the way of this work, and give him no rest till he make Jerusalem a praise in the earth. We heartily unite with our Christian brethren of every name, in thanksgiving to God for the display of his goodness in the glorious work he is carrying on in our Western country, which we hope will terminate in the universal spread of the gospel, and the unity of the church.[10]

In his autobiography Barton W. Stone speaks of two fellow reformers who defected back to the Presbyterian church. He says, "These two brothers were great and good men. Their memory is dear to me, and their fellowship I hope to enjoy in a better world."[11] In this same book Stone speaks of the union of the Stoneites (Christians) and the Campbellites (Reformers). This is the union between the two groups of reformers which took place in 1832.

---

10. Barton W. Stone and others, "Last Will and Testament of the Springfield Presbytery," St. Louis: *Mission Messenger,* p. 22.
11. Barton W. Stone, *A Short History of the Life of Barton W. Stone,* reprinted in the Cane Reader, Cane Ridge, Kentucky, July 6, 1972, p. 66.

This union, I have no doubt, would have been as easily effected in other States as in Kentucky, had there not been a few ignorant, headstrong bigots on both sides, who were more influenced to retain and augment their party, than to save the world by uniting according to the prayer of Jesus. Some irresponsible zealots among the Reformers, so called, would publicly and zealously contend against sinners praying, or that professors should pray for them—they spurned the idea that preachers should pray that God would assist them in declaring his truth to the people— they rejected from Christianity all who were not baptized for the remission of sins, and who did not observe the weekly communion, and many such doctrines they preached. The old Christians, who were unacquainted with the preachers of information amongst us, would naturally conclude these to be the doctrines of us all; and they rose up in opposition to us all, representing our religion as a spiritless, prayerless religion, and dangerous to the souls of men.[12]

The next three quotes are by Thomas Campbell from the "Declaration and Address." He speaks of having brethren in all of the denominations and refers to the various denominations as the Churches of Christ.

The cause that we advocate is not our own peculiar cause, nor the cause of any party, considered as such; it is a common cause, the cause of Christ and our brethren of all denominations.[13]

Our dear brethren of all denominations will please to consider that we have our educational prejudices and particular customs to struggle against as well as they. But this we do sincerely declare, that there is nothing we have hitherto received as matter of faith or practice which is not expressly taught and enjoined in the word of God, either in express terms or approved precedent, that we would not heartily relinquish, that so we might return to the original constitutional unity of the Christian Church; and, in this happy unity, enjoy full communion with all our

---

12. Ibid., p. 78.
13. Thomas Campbell, "Declaration and Address," St. Louis: Mission Messenger, p. 34.

brethren, in peace and charity. . . . To this we call, we invite, our brethren of all denominations. . . .[14]

As to creeds and confessions, although we may appear to our brethren to oppose them, yet this is to be understood only in so far as they oppose the unity of the Church, by containing sentiments not expressly revealed in the word of God; or, by the way of using them, become the instruments of a human or implicit faith, or oppress the weak of God's heritage. Where they are liable to none of those objections, we have nothing against them. It is the abuse and not the lawful use of such compilations that we oppose. Our intention, therefore, with respect to all the Churches of Christ is perfectly amicable. We heartily wish their reformation, but by no means their hurt or confusion. Should any affect to say that our coming forward as we have done, in advancing and publishing such things, has a manifest tendency to distract and divide the Churches, or to make a new party, we treat it as a confident and groundless assertion, and must suppose they have not duly considered, or, at least, not well understood the subject.[15]

Thomas Campbell wrote a letter to his son Alexander in March of 1811 in which he discussed religious fellowship. Richardson presents excerpts from this letter in the *Memoirs of Alexander Campbell*. The first paragraph to follow is from this letter and the second paragraph is Richardson's comments:

"In order, then, to direct and determine our practice in existing circumstances, when all the world are called Christians, and the great majority seem to persuade themselves that they are so in some sense, and therefore are in a condition with respect to Christ and salvation vastly different from the heathen world, both as to persons and circumstances, we believe, as we have a right to hope, that there are Christians in all the denominations of professors where the great fundamental truths of the gospel are acknowledged, although we have no reason to believe that the majority of professors are such. Therefore, when any number of persons assemble on the Lord's day for the avowed purpose

---

14. Ibid., p. 35.
15. Ibid., p. 59.

of public worship, there we may reasonably hope that there are some believers, and however this be, the persons thus assembling, in so far avow themselves to be voluntary subjects of the gospel dispensation; nor is it our place to determine, what in many cases we cannot, who of them are or are not Christians, or whether or not they may not be all so, seeing that in the point of view in which they present themselves to our considerations, as also in the course of the service, they manifest themselves to partake with us in the acts of religious worship. There can be no doubt, then, in such a case, but we are to consider and address them as the professed worshipers of the true God through Jesus Christ. I do not say as unfeigned and believing worshipers, for, even in the most perfect Church, we would scarcely be justifiable in considering all as such. This conclusion proceeds upon the supposition that Christ has a people amongst the visible professors of his name, and that these may be expected to be found where the great fundamental truths of the gospel are publicly professed; nay, that wheresoever this is the case, there the professors, if sincere, of course must be his people. But this, as I said above, is scarcely to be expected in the most perfect Church that ever did or shall exist. See the seven Epistles to the seven Asiatic Churches. Moreover, every irregularity, error or mistake does not unpeople a professing people. Therefore I conclude that where we bear an open faithful testimony against the existing evils of a professing people who acknowledge the great fundamental truths of the gospel, we are warranted to join in all public acts of religious worship with such of them as voluntarily attend upon our ministrations, and thus countenance our instructions both by their voluntary attendance and manifest concurrence with us in those religious acts."

Such were the sentiments of Thomas Campbell upon the subject of religious fellowship in March, 1811, and in these his son Alexander substantially agreed. When, about three months after the above correspondence, the church at Brush Run became a body of immersed believers, these views became more clearly and sharply defined, no one being afterward recognized as duly prepared to partake in religious services, except those who had professed to put on Christ in baptism. From his lively sense of the prevalent corruptions of the gospel and its institutions, and his conscientious scruples in regard to yielding to these any countenance or toleration, Mr. Campbell, even down to his later years, would occasionally, amongst private friends, contend strenuously for principles almost as exclusive and rigid as those of Walker. His benevolent feelings, however; his Christian courtesy and his sympathy for those whom he regarded as sincere but mistaken, did not permit him to carry out such principles. Both he and his father had great consideration for the unintentional mistakes and errors in which religious society had become involved, and in this feeling, the members of the church at Brush Run, for the most part, participated. However clear their convictions had become as to the primitive method of confessing Christ, and the primitive faith and order of the Church, they had too fresh a recollection of their own struggles and difficulties in attaining to the views they held, and too deep a sympathy with the pious but priest-ridden members of other communities, to refuse to recognize them as being intentionally at least, followers of Christ. As they could not, however, make any compromise with the corrupt systems and practices of the day, and were prevented by their principles from recognizing fraternally any one who had not publicly complied with the requisitions of the gospel, they were necessarily inhibited from inviting any except the actual members of the church to take a part in religious exercises. This was specially true with regard to the Lord's Supper, which they continued to celebrate weekly, and of which none but baptized believers were invited to partake. It was not, however, the custom of the Church, nor has it ever been that of any of the Churches of the Reformation, to "fence the tables," as sectarians express and practice it; or to withhold the symbols from any pious person who might be present and feel disposed to unite in commemorating the death of Christ.[16]

Richardson quotes Alexander Campbell in a passage taken from the *Christian Baptist* where he is referring to the more rigid views to which he previously ascribed (in 1811) on the subject of religious fellowship.

> I have tried the pharisaic plan and the monastic. I was once so straight that, like the Indian's tree, 'I leaned a little the other way.' And however much I may be slandered now as seeking

---

16. Thomas Campbell and Robert Richardson, *Memoirs of Alexander Campbell,* Vol. 1, pp. 452-454.

popularity or a popular course, I have to rejoice that to my own satisfaction, as well as to others, I proved that truth and not popularity was my object; for I was once so strict a separatist that I would neither pray nor sing praises with any one who was not as perfect as I supposed myself. In this most unpopular course I persisted until I discovered the mistake, and saw that on the principle embraced in my conduct there never could be a congregation or church upon the earth.[17]

In March of 1826 a letter to the editor of the *Christian Baptist,* signed W----Co. Ind. Dec. 12, 1825, was published under "A Restoration of the Ancient Order of Things No. XI" and was answered by Alexander Campbell in this same article. The author of the letter expressed his belief in six items which are not in line with Church of Christ doctrine: (1) the washing of feet is a plain commandment, (2) the kiss of charity is a plain commandment, (3) he was not convinced of the necessity of weekly communion, (4) that whenever communion was observed that the night was the time, yea, the only time, according to Christ's institution and the practice of the apostles to observe this ordinance, (5) that baptism should be trine, i.e., triple, immersion; once each for the Father, the Son, and the Holy Spirit. (6) that baptism should not be performed transversely, but forwards, in the most humble manner of obedience. Mr. Campbell began and ended his reply as follows:

> Dear Brother—For such I recognized you, notwithstanding the varieties of opinion which you express on some topics, on which we might never agree. But if we should not, as not unity of opinion, but unity of faith, is the only true bond of christian union, I will esteem and love you, as I do every man, of whatever name, who believes sincerely that Jesus is the Messiah, and hopes in his salvation. . . . Wishing you favor, mercy and peace, from our Lord and Saviour, and glad to hear from you at any time, I subscribe myself your brother in the hope of immortality. A.C. February 25, 1826.[18]

---

17. Alexander Campbell, quoted by Robert Richardson, *Memoirs of Alexander Campbell,* Vol. 2, p. 137.
18. Alexander Campbell, *Christian Baptist,* Vol. III, March 6, 1826, pp. 222-225.

Again in the *Christian Baptist* in 1826 Alexander Campbell writes while responding to letters from students of theology in the Hamilton Seminary, New York.

> And while I write and labor as I do, he that knows the hearts of all flesh knows that I do it from the fullest conviction from his oracles that the christianity of our day is a corrupt christianity, and that the ancient order of things is lost sight of in almost all denominations of professing christians. I do consider that there are many, very many christians, in the present day, greatly out of the way, and that they are suffering famine and disease in their souls because of it.[19]

Two years later in the same periodical, in a "Letter to Bishop Semple.-No. I." Alexander Campbell writes:

> I love all christians, of whatever name; and if there is any diversity in my affection, it is predicated upon, or rather graduated by, the scale of their comparative conformity to the will of my Sovereign. I do profess, before heaven and earth, to be a christian. I will claim this title, and defend it by that course of behaviour which I think my Master requires. This is the sole cause of my departure from the customs of my baptist brethren in those items, whenever they have departed from the customs of those elder brethren, the primitive christians.[20]

Walter Scott, writing in *The Evangelist* in 1833, expressed the opinion that congregations do not have to be perfect in order to contain Christians.

> But it is on christianity we are writing. Now, then, our holy religion, when contemplated as a unique and distinct institution, resolves itself ultimately into this fact, and is based upon it, viz: 'Jesus of Nazareth is the Son of God.' If this be false, christianity is false; if this be true, christianity must prevail, and earth and hell in vain assail it: for great is truth and mighty above all things, and must prevail. 'Upon this rock,' said Jesus to Peter when he publickly confessed this truth—'Upon this rock will I build my church, and the gates of hell shall not

---

19. Ibid., Vol. IV, No. 4, p. 285.
20. Ibid., Vol. V, p. 425.

prevail against it.' It was for confessing this truth that Jesus was condemned by the Jewish Sanhedrin—he died for this, and was the first martyr to it. The Apostles died for confessing this—men were pardoned of God for confessing it—and congregations which held it were styled the church of Christ, whether they were in order or no; whether they had ordinances, oracles, or officers, or no; and it is on the confession of this fact that the church, within these few years, has begun, according to the ancient gospel, again to admit sinners to baptism for the remission of their sins. Glory to God and to Jesus Christ![21]

The next six quotes relate in one way or another to baptism. The early reformers were not as strict in requiring reimmersion for those entering their ranks from other denominations as many of our brethren have been in this century. One incident which points out the degree of tolerance and forbearance which was characteristic of our movement in the early days is the case involving an Englishman, a physician, named John Thomas who was baptized by Walter Scott. Robert Richardson describes the incident:

> Ambitious of distinction, fluent and captivating as a public speaker, and manifesting, especially in his writings, a bold spirit of independence, (he commenced the publication of the "Apostolic Advocate") he soon acquired a considerable degree of popularity. Being unfortunately, however, self-confident in his disposition, and having imperfectly comprehended the principles of the Reformation, he soon began to evince a spirit of dogmatism and of opinionativeness wholly inconsistent with them. This was first shown in his refusing to recognize religiously or even pray with any who had not submitted to the gospel as he understood it, and in his bold advocacy of the doctrine that immersion, as practiced by the Baptists, was invalid. By his specious reasonings several who had been Baptists became unsettled in regard to their baptism, and Albert Anderson and a few others were induced to submit to reimmersion. It was the Baptists themselves, indeed, who, some time before, had originated the practice

---

21. Walter Scott, *The Evangelist,* No. 2, Vol. 2, "The Holy Spirit, A Discourse," Feb. 4, 1833, p. 33.

of reimmersion, having required it of some who had been baptized by the Reformers and who wished afterward to unite with the Baptist church. Mr. Campbell had, however, always been entirely opposed to the practice of reimmersion upon such trivial grounds as were alleged in favor of it, believing it to be in all cases valid where there was a sincere belief in Christ, however uninformed the baptized person might be at the time with regard to the nature or design of the institution. Nothing, he justly thought, could ever justify reimmersion, except a consciousness on the part of the individual that at his first baptism he was destitute of faith in Christ.[22]

John Thomas was not successful in promoting his theories and he soon left the movement. Barton W. Stone makes a comment on immersion in the *Christian Messenger* in 1831.

My opinion is that immersion only is baptism. But shall I therefore make my opinion a term of Christian fellowship? If in this case I thus act, where shall I cease from making my opinions terms of fellowship?[23]

Alexander Campbell made a somewhat similar statement in the *Millennial Harbinger* in 1837.

I cannot, therefore, make any one duty the standard of the Christian state or character, not even immersion into the name of the Father, of the Son, and of the Holy Spirit, and in my heart regard all that have been sprinkled in infancy without their knowledge and consent, as aliens from Christ and the well-grounded hope of heaven.[24]

We have occasionally, in recent years, given a considerable amount of attention to the specifying of the exact words to be uttered over a person at the time of his baptism. In the early part of the restoration movement there was not universal agreement among the leaders that this was of extreme importance. Robert Richardson describes Alexander Campbell's attitude in this regard.

---

22. Robert Richardson, *Memoirs of Alexander Campbell,* Vol. 2, p. 443.
23. Barton W. Stone, *Christian Messenger,* Vol. 5, 1831, p. 19.
24. Alexander Campbell, *Millennial Harbinger,* 1837, p. 412.

> Mr. Campbell greatly disapproved the practice of making such issues, and of using such strong and unguarded expressions as the "power of remitting sins" and "washing away sins in baptism." "These," said he, "have been most prejudical to the cause of truth, and have given a pretext to the opposition for their hard speeches against the pleadings of Reformers." The habitual use of such expressions he thought also calculated to lead men to overlook or disparage that faith in the sacrifice of Christ from which alone baptism derived its efficacy. On this account, in baptizing persons, he used only the simple formula, "Into the name of the Father and of the Son and of the Holy Spirit," and forebore adding to it, like Mr. Scott and others, the expression "for the remission of sins." "When any doctrine," said he (Mill. Harb. for 1832, p. 299), "is professed and taught by many, when any matter gets into many hands, some will misuse, abuse and pervert it. This is unavoidable. We have always feared abuses and extremes."[25]

Later in the same book Richardson again comments on Alexander Campbell's attitude toward baptism.

> The occasion of these remarks was a tendency for a time, on the part of Walter Scott, to exalt beyond measure the importance of the practical restoration of the design of baptism, and to claim that this was in reality the restoration of the gospel. Mr. Campbell could not, with his more enlarged views, regard this, or any other particular development of truth in the progress of the Reformation, as the restoration of the gospel—an honor which he urged might, with even more propriety, be claimed for the restoration of the primitive confession of faith in Christ.[26]

It was never Alexander Campbell's desire to separate from the Baptists, with whom he had been associated for many years during the early years of his efforts at restoring the New Testament gospel. Richardson describes an incident from the year 1866 when Alexander Campbell was on his death bed.

---

25. Robert Richardson, *Memoirs of Alexander Campbell,* Vol. 2, p. 288.
26. Ibid., p. 442.

When, in conversation, Dr. Richardson spoke to him of the proposed meeting of the Baptists and Reformers at Richmond, Va., to confer upon the subject of union, he expressed great satisfaction in hearing of it. "There was never any sufficient reason," said he, "for a separation between us and the Baptists. We ought to have remained one people, and to have labored together to restore the primitive faith and practice." He hoped that much good would result from the proposed meeting, and spoke with animation of the glorious results which would ensue if the divisions of religious society were healed and the people of God were striving unitedly for the conversion of the world.[27]

These remarks, of course, were made in the years before the Church of Christ's stand against the use of instrumental music became an additional dividing wedge between the two religious groups.

The Lunenburg Letters

In the year 1837 a lady from the town of Lunenburg wrote a letter to the editor of the *Millennial Harbinger*. She asked a question relating to exactly how and when anyone becomes a Christian. Her inquiry resulted in the publishing of a series of three articles by Alexander Campbell in the *Millennial Harbinger* of that year. These three articles have been often referred to as the Lunenburg Letters. These articles relate very directly to the question which has been raised, i.e., "Are there any Christians in the other denominations?" The first two of the letters are included here in their entirety along with excerpts from the third.

---

27. Ibid., p. 675.

ONLY CHURCH OF CHRIST MEMBERS CAN GO TO HEAVEN

THE LUNENBURG LETTERS

Three separate articles in the *Millennial Harbinger,* 1837, p. 411, 506, 561.

ANY CHRISTIANS AMONG PROTESTANT PARTIES. Page 411.

"Lunenburg, July 8th, 1837.

"Dear brother Campbell—I was much surprised today, while reading the Harbinger, to see that you recognize the Protestant parties as Christian. You say, you 'find in all Protestant parties Christians.'

"Dear brother, my surprise and ardent desire to do what is right, prompt me to write to you at this time. I feel well assured, from the estimate you place on the female character, that you will attend to my feeble questions in search of knowledge."

"Will you be so good as to let me know how any one becomes a Christian? At what time had Paul the name of Christ called on him? At what time did Cornelius have Christ named on him? Is it not through this name we obtain eternal life? Does the name of Christ or Christian belong to any but those who believe the gospel, repent, and are buried by baptism into the death of Christ?"

In reply to this conscientious sister, I observe, that if there be no Christians in the Protestant sects, there are certainly none among the Romanists, none among the Jews, Turks, Pagans; and therefore no Christians in the world except ourselves, or such of us as keep, or strive to keep, all the commandments of Jesus. Therefore, for many centuries there has been no church of Christ, no Christians in the world; and the promises concerning the everlasting kingdom of Messiah have failed, and the gates of hell have prevailed against his church! This cannot be; and therefore there are Christians among the sects.

But who is a Christian? I answer, Every one that believes in his heart that Jesus of Nazareth is the Messiah, the Son of God; repents of his sins, and obeys him in all things according to his measure of knowledge of his will. A perfect man in Christ, or a perfect Christian, is one thing; and "a babe in Christ," a stripling in the faith, or an imperfect Christian, is another. The New Testament recognizes both the perfect man and the imperfect man in Christ. The former, indeed, implies the latter. Paul commands the imperfect Christians to "be perfect," (2 Cor. 3.11) and says he wishes the perfection of Christians. "And this also we wish" for you saints in Corinth, "even your perfection:" and again he says, "We speak wisdom among the perfect," (1 Cor. 2.6) and he commands them to be "perfect in understanding," (1 Cor. 14.20) and in many other places implies or speaks the same things. Now there is perfection of will, of temper, and of behaviour. There is a perfect state and a perfect character. And hence it is possible for Christians to be imperfect in some respects without an absolute forfeiture of the Christian state and character. Paul speaks of "carnal" Christians, of "weak" and "strong" Christians; and the Lord Jesus admits that some of the good and honest-hearted bring forth only thirty fold, while others bring forth sixty, and some a hundred fold increase of the fruits of righteousness.

But every one is wont to condemn others in that in which he is more intelligent than they; while, on the other hand, he is condemned for his Pharisaism or his immodesty and rash judgment of others, by those that excel in the things in which he is deficient. I cannot, therefore, make any one duty the standard of Christian state or character, not even immersion into the name of the Father, of the Son, and of the Holy Spirit, and in my heart regard all that have been sprinkled in infancy without their own knowledge and consent, as aliens from Christ and the well-grounded hope of heaven. "Salvation was of the Jews, acknowleged the Messiah; and yet he said of a foreigner, an alien from the commonwealth of Israel, a Syro-Phenician, "I have not found so great faith—no, not in Israel."

Should I find a Pedobaptist more intelligent in the Christian Scriptures, more spiritually-minded and more devoted to the Lord than a Baptist, or one immersed on a profession of the ancient faith, I could not hesitate a moment in giving the preference of my heart to him that loveth most. Did I act otherwise, I would be a pure sectarian, a Pharisee among Christians. Still I will be asked, How do I know that any one loves my Master but by his obedience to his commandments? I answer, in no other way. But mark, I do not substitute obedience to one commandment, for universal or even for general obedience. And should I see a sectarian Baptist or a Pedobaptist more spiritually-minded, more generally conformed to the requisitions of the Messiah, than one who precisely acquiesces with me in the theory or practice of immersion as I teach, doubtless the former rather than the latter, would have my cordial approbation and love as a Christian. So I judge, and so I feel. It is the image of Christ the Christian looks for and loves; and this does not consist in being exact in a few items, but in general devotion to the whole truth as far as known.

With me mistakes of the understanding and errors of the affections are not to be confounded. They are as distant as the poles. An angel may mistake the meaning of a commandment, but he will obey it in the sense in which he understands it. John Bunyan and John Newton were very different persons, and had very different views of baptism, and of some other things; yet they were both disposed to obey, and to the extent of their knowledge did obey the Lord in every thing.

There are mistakes with, and without depravity. There are wilful errors which all the world must condemn, and unavoidable mistakes which every one will pity. The Apostles mistook the Saviour when he said concerning John, "What if I will that John tarry till I come;" but the Jews perverted his words when they alleged that Abraham had died, in proof that he spake falsely when he said, "if a man keep my word he shall never see death."

Many a good man has been mistaken. Mistakes are to be regarded as culpable and as declarative of a corrupt heart only when they proceed from a wilful neglect of the means of knowing what is commanded. Ignorance is always a crime when it is voluntary; and innocent when it is involuntary. Now, unless I could prove that all who neglect the positive institutions of Christ and have substituted for them something else of human authority, do it knowingly, or, if not knowingly, are voluntarily ignorant of what is written, I could not, I dare not say that their mistakes are such as unchristianize all their professions.

True, indeed, that it is always a misfortune to be ignorant of any thing in the Bible, and very generally it is criminal. But how many are there who cannot read; and of those who can read, how many are so deficient in education; and of those educated, how many are ruled by the authority of those whom they regard as superiors in knowledge and piety, that they never can escape out of the dust and smoke of their own chimney, where they happened to be born and educated! These all suffer many privations and many perplexities, from which the more intelligent are exempt.

The preachers of "essentials," as well as the preachers of "non-essentials," frequently err. The Essentialist may disparage the heart, while the Non-essentialist despises the institution. The latter makes void the institutions of Heaven, while the former appreciates not the mental bias on which God looketh most. My correspondent may belong to a class who think that we detract from the authority and value of an institution the moment we admit the bare possibility of any one being saved without it. But we choose rather to associate with those who think that they do not undervalue either seeing or hearing, by affirming that neither of them, nor both of them together, are essential to life. I would not sell one of my eyes for all the gold on earth; yet I could live without it.

There is no occasion, then, for making immersion, on a professing of the faith, absolutely essential to a Christian—though it may be greatly essential to his sanctification and comfort. My right hand and my right eye are greatly essential to my usefulness and happiness, but not to my life; and as I could not be a perfect man without them, so I cannot be a perfect Christian without a right understanding and a cordial reception of immersion in its true and scriptural meaning and design. But he that thence infers that none are Christians but the immersed, as greatly errs as he who affirms that none are alive but those of clear and full vision.

I do not formally answer all the queries proposed, knowing the one point to which they all aim. To that point only I direct these remarks. And while I would unhesitatingly say, that I think that every man who despises any ordinance of Christ, or who is willingly ignorant of it, cannot be a Christian; still I should sin against my own convictions, should I teach any one to think that if he mistook the meaning of any institution, while in his soul he desired to know the whole will of God, he must perish forever. But to conclude for the present—he that claims for himself a license to neglect the least of all the commandments of Jesus, because it is possible for some to be saved, who, through insuperable ignorance or involuntary mistake, do neglect or transgress it; or he that wilfully neglects to ascertain the will of the Lord to the whole extent of his means and opportunities, because some who are defective in that knowledge may be Christians, is not possessed of the spirit of Christ, and cannot be registered among the Lord's people. So I reason; and I think in so reasoning I am sustained by all the Prophets and Apostles of both Testaments. (A.C.)

CHRISTIANS AMONG THE SECTS.

page 506—the 2nd article

In an article on a query from Lunenburg, which appeared in the September number, certain sentences have been objected to by some two or three intelligent and much esteemed correspondents. We gave it as our opinion that there were Christians among the Protestant sects; an opinion, indeed, which we have always expressed when called upon. If I mistake not, it is distinctly avowed in our first Extra on Remission; yet is now supposed by these brethren that I have conceded a point of which I have hitherto been tenacious, and that I have misapplied certain portions of scripture in supporting said opinion. In the article alluded to, we have said that we "cannot make any one duty the standard of Christian state or character, not even Christian immersion," &c. Again, we have said that "there is no occasion for making immersion on a profession of the faith absolutely essential to a Christian, though it may be greatly essential to his sanctification and comfort." These two sentences contain the pith and marrow of the objectionable portion of said article, to which we again refer the reader.

Much depends upon the known temper and views of a querist in shaping an answer to his questions. This was the case in this instance. We apprehended that the propounder of the queries that called for these remarks, was rather an ultraist on the subject of Christian baptism; so far at least as not to allow that the name Christian is at all applicable to one unimmersed, or even to one immersed, without the true intent and meaning of baptism in his understanding previous to his burial in water. This we gathered from her epistle; and of course gave as bold an answer as we ever gave—perhaps more bold than on any former occasion, yet nothing differing from our former expressed views on that subject.

My high regard for these correspondents, however, calls for a few remarks on those sentences, as farther explanatory of our views. We cheerfully agree with them, as well as with our sister of Lunenburg, that the term Christian was given first to immersed believers and to none else; but we do not think that it was given to them because they were immersed, but because they had put on Christ; and therefore we presume to opine, that, like every other word in universal language, even this term may be used as Paul sometimes uses the words saint and sinner, Jew and Gentile—in a part of their signification.

We have, in Paul's style, the inward and the outward Jews; and may we not have the inward and the outward Christians? for true it is, that he is not always a Christian who is one outwardly: and one of my correspondents will say, 'Neither is he a Christian who is one inwardly.' But all agree that he is, in the full sense of the word, a Christian who is one inwardly and outwardly.

As the same Apostle reasons on circumcision, so we would reason on baptism:—"Circumcision," says the learned Apostle, "is not that which is outward in the flesh;" that is, as we apprehend the Apostle, it is not that which is outward in the flesh; but "circumcision is that of the heart, in the spirit, and not in the letter (only) whose praise is of God, and not of man." So is baptism. It is not outward in the flesh only, but in the spirit also. We argue for the outward and the inward—the outward for men, including ourselves—the inward for God; but both the outward and the inward for the praise both of God and of men.

Now the nice point of opinion on which some brethren differ, is this: Can a person who simply, not perversely, mistakes the outward baptism, have the inward? We all agree that he who wilfully or negligently perverts the outward, cannot have the inward. But can he who, through a simple mistake, involving no perversity of mind, has misapprehended the outward baptism, yet submitting to it according to his view of it, have the inward baptism which changes his state and has praise of God, though not of all men? is the precise question. To which I answer, that, in my opinion, it is possible. Farther than this I do not affirm.

My reasons for this opinion are various; two of which we have only time and space to offer at this time. Of seven difficulties it is the least; two of these seven, which, on a contrary hypothesis would occur, are insuperable:—The promises concerning an everlasting Christian church have failed; and then it would follow that not a few of the brightest names on earth of the last three hundred years should have to be regarded as subjects of the kingdom of Satan!!

ONLY CHURCH OF CHRIST MEMBERS CAN GO TO HEAVEN

None of our brethren regard baptism as only outward. They all believe that in the outward submersion of the body in the water, there is at the same time the inward submersion on the mind and heart into Christ. They do moreover suppose that the former may be without the latter. They have only to add that it is possible for the latter to be not without the former in some sense, but without it in the sense which Christ ordained.

Still my opinion is no rule of action to my brethren, nor would I offer it unsolicited to any man. But while we inculcate faith, repentance, and baptism upon all, as essential to their constitutional citizenship in the Messiah's kingdom, and to their sanctification and comfort as Christians, no person has a right to demand our opinions on all the differences of this generation, except for his private gratification. He is certainly safer who obeys from the heart "that mould of doctrine" delivered to us by the Apostles; and he only has praise of God and man, and of himself as a Christian, who believes, repents, is baptized, and keeps all the ordinances, positive and moral, as delivered to us by the holy Apostles.

The scriptures quoted in the essay complained of, are all applied to the Christian character, and not to the Christian state, as contemplated by one of our correspondents. They are therefore not misapplied. It is hoped these general remarks will be satisfactory on this point. (A.C. Sept. 28th, 1837)

ANY CHRISTIANS AMONG THE SECTS?

page 561—the 3rd article

(Only excerpts from this article will be included.)

(A.C. quotes from the *Christian Baptist,* 1828, p. 140) I have no idea of seeing, nor one wish to see, the sects unite in one grand army. This would be dangerous to our liberties and laws. For this the Saviour did not pray. It is only the disciples of Christ dispersed among them, that reason and benevolence would call out of them. Let them unite who love the Lord, and then we shall soon see the hireling priesthood and their worldly establishments prostrate in the dust.

But we had still more urgent reasons than the difficulties of this sister to express such an opinion:—Some of our brethren were too much addicted to denouncing the sects and representing them in masse as wholly aliens from the possibility of salvation—as wholly antichristian and corrupt. Now as the Lord says of Babylon, "Come out of her, my people," I felt constrained to rebuke them over the shoulders of this inquisitive lady. These very zealous brethren gave countenance to the popular clamor that we make baptism a saviour, or a passport to heaven, disparaging all the private and social virtues of the professing public. Now as they were propounding opinions to others, I intended to bring them to the proper medium by propounding an opinion to them in terms as strong and as pungent as their own.

The case is this: When I see a person who would die for Christ; whose brotherly kindness, sympathy, and active benevolence know no bounds but his circumstances; whose seat in the Christian assembly is never empty; whose inward piety and devotion are attested by punctual obedience to every known duty; whose family is educated in the fear of the Lord; whose constant companion is the Bible: I say, when I see such a one ranked amongst heathen men and publicans, because he never happened to inquire, but always took it for granted that he had been scripturally baptized; and that, too, by one greatly destitute of all these public and private virtues, whose chief or exclusive recommendation is that he has been immersed, and that he holds a scriptural theory of the gospel: I feel no disposition to flatter such a one; but rather to disabuse him of his error. And while I would not lead the most excellent professor in any sect to disparage the least of all the commandments of Jesus, I would say to my immersed brother as Paul said to his Jewish brother who gloried in a system which he did not adorn: 'Sir, will not his uncircumcision, or unbaptism, be counted to him for baptism? and will he not condemn you, who, though having the literal and true baptism, yet dost transgress or neglect the statutes of your King?'

We have a third reason: We have been always accused of aspiring to build up and head a party, while in truth we have always been forced to occupy the ground on which we now stand. I have for one or two years past labored to annul this impression, which I know is more secretly and generally bandied about than one in a hundred of our brethren may suspect. On this account I consented the more readily to defend Protestantism: and I have, in ways more than I shall now state, endeavored to show the Protestant public that it is with the greatest reluctance we are compelled to stand aloof from them—that they are the cause of this great "schism," as they call it, and not we.

ONLY CHURCH OF CHRIST MEMBERS CAN GO TO HEAVEN

Some of our fellow-laborers seem to forget that approaches are more in the spirit and style of the Saviour, than reproaches. We have proved to our entire satisfaction, that having obtained a favorable hearing, a conciliatory, meek, and benevolent attitude is not only the most comely and Christian-like, but the most successful. Many of the Protestant teachers and their communities are much better disposed to us than formerly; and I calculate the day is not far distant when many of them will unite with us. They must certainly come over to us whenever they come to the Bible alone. Baptists and Pedobaptists are daily feeling more and more the need of reform, and our views are certainly imbuing the public mind more and more every year.

(regarding brethren of Eastern Virginia) . . . Had not some of them greatly and unreasonably abused the sects, or countenanced, aided, and abetted them that did so, and had not a few in some other regions made Christianity to turn more upon immersion than upon universal holiness, in all probability I would have answered the sister from Lunenburg in the following manner and style:

The name Christian is now current in four significations;—

1. The ancient primitive and apostolic import simply indicates follower of Christ. With a strict regard to its original and scriptural meaning, my favorite and oft-repeated definition is, "A Christian is one that habitually believes all that Christ says, and habitually does all that he bids him."

2. But its national and very popular sense implies no more than a professor of Christianity. Thus we have the Christian nations, as well as the Pagan and Mahometan nations; the Christian sects as well as the sects political and philosophical.

3. But as soon as Controversies arose about the ways and means of putting on Christ or of making a profession of his religion, in a new and special or appropriated sense, ' a Christian' means one who first believes that Jesus is the Christ, repents of his sins, is then immersed on confession into Christ's death, and thenceforth continues in the Christian faith and practice.

4. But there yet remains the sense in which I used the term in the obnoxious phrase first quoted by our sister of Lunenburg. As in the judgment of many, some make the profession right and live wrong; while others make the profession wrong, but live right; so they have adopted this style—"I don't know what

he believes, nor how he was baptized, but I know he is a Christian." Thus Adam Clarke quotes some poet—

> "You different sects who all declare,
> Lo! Christ is here, and Christ is there!
> Your stronger proofs divinely give,
> And show me where the Christians live!"

Now in this acceptation of the word, I think there are many, in most Protestant parties, whose errors and mistakes I hope the Lord will forgive; and although they should not enter into all the blessings of the kingdom on earth, I do fondly expect they may participate in the resurrection of the just.

The Limits of Religious Fellowship - Isaac Errett

In the *Millennial Harbinger,* 1862, p. 39, Geo. W. Elley has an article relating to the Lord's Supper entitled "Communion with the 'Sects'" in which he takes the position that only the immersed in the Church of Christ have any chance of going to heaven. This is in opposition to the co-editors of the *Millennial Harbinger,* (Dr. Robert Richardson, W. K. Pendleton, and Isaac Errett) who are all on record as favoring fellowship with "Christians" (even Christians in error) in the sects, even with some of the unimmersed.

Isaac Errett is the first to reply with his article "The Limits of Religious Fellowship," *Millennial Harbinger,* 1862, p. 120. Excerpts from this article follow:

> (p. 123) We have no thought of impeaching the candor of the brethren in their mistaken utterances; but we cannot help saying that if we had no more charity for them in their blunders, than they seem to have for pious Pedobaptists in blunders not more gross; if we would allow a certain narrow kind of logic to get the better of our hearts, they would soon be to us as 'heathen men and publicans.'
>
> They are discussing the question of communion, as between the church and the world. Bro. Elley's questions would be pertinent in such a controversy; but this is a question arising out of the apostasy, and relates to parties not known in the

ONLY CHURCH OF CHRIST MEMBERS CAN GO TO HEAVEN

Scriptures. It relates to a condition of things known only in prophecy, in the Scriptures—in which the people of God should be found scattered, bewildered, and erring, but still fearing God and working righteousness; loving Christ, and as far as known to them, earnestly and joyfully walking in His ways. There are myriads of godly people, who are in error on baptism, of whom, nevertheless, we are compelled to say, "They are not of the world." To urge against these a strict and literal application of passages which are meant to mark the distinction between the church and the world, and thus to attempt to thrust them out from our Christian love, among heathens and reprobates, is, in our view, a grievous wrong. As it is a question growing out of the times—a question not directly known in form in the Scriptures, it must be settled in the light of well-established Christian principles, and not by a severely literal construction of Scripture language, spoken with reference to other classes of persons, and another condition of things.

(p. 126) It has now become a question, growing out of the peculiar logic employed by these brethren, whether we shall have any religious fellowship whatever with any outside of our own churches? Whether we shall not outvie the Old Landmark Baptists themselves in exclusiveness, and make ourselves ridiculous before the whole religious world by the monstrous extravagance of our assumptions?

(p. 127) Let us see, now, if there is not a better way of approaching this question, and disposing of the difficulty before us. We view it in the light of Scripture and of History.

The saints were carried captive into Babylon, and remained there a long time. The church lost her primitive purity and excellency.—The truth was in chains. Yet God had a people in Babylon—for when the time came for reformation, the proclamation was to be, "Come out of her, MY PEOPLE," etc. (Rev. 18.4). Now our good brethren may be able to prove to their own satisfaction that all these people of God in Babylon were immersed believers; and they may point, here and there, to bands of religionists, who kept up a protest against the corruptions of Rome. But it strikes us that a people could not come out of Babylon who were not in Babylon; and immersed believers, walking in the light, would have been hard to find within Babylon's limits! But there was a people of God in Babylon. We incline to the opinion that most of them were unimmersed. They were in many respects an erring people—in regard to baptism they certainly were in great error; but they "feared God and wrought righteousness;" and,—what seems as great a stumbling block to many good men now as it was to Peter, until the trammels of sectarianism were knocked off—"in every nation, he that feareth God and worketh righteousness is accepted with him." At one and another trumpet call of Reformation, multitudes came forth from Babylon.—They did not reach Jerusalem. But they wrought great deeds for God and for his word. They talked much and suffered much for the name of Christ. We inherit the blessed fruits of their labors. We follow them through the scenes of their superhuman toil, to the dungeons where they suffered, and to the stakes where they won the glories of martyrdom, and whence they ascended in chariots of fire to the heavens; and as we embrace the chains they wore, and take up the ashes from the altar-fires of spiritual freedom, we ask not whether these lofty heroes of the church militant, to whom we owe our heritage of spiritual freedom, may commune with us—but rather, if we are at all worthy to commune with them! We feel honored in being permitted to call them brethren. Our reformation movement is the legitimate offspring of theirs. Neither in Pennsylvania, where the Campbells and Scott began, nor in Kentucky, where Stone and others led the van of reformation, did this movement spring from Baptist, but from Pedobaptist influences. It is the legitimate result of Pedobaptist learning, piety and devotion. Unless we can recognize a people of God among these heroical, struggling, sacrificing hosts of Protestants, from whom we have legitimately sprung, then the promise of Christ in regard to his church has failed: since, if we insist on the rigid test of the letter of gospel conditions, no such people as the Disciples can be found for many centuries. But of this people of God of whom we speak, we affirm that they loved the Lord Jesus Christ in sincerity. They loved and magnified his word. They possessed his Spirit—manifesting it in very precious fruits of righteousness and holiness. The spirit of obedience dwelt not less in them than in us.—They erred in regard to the letter of baptism, even as it may yet be found that we have erred in regard to the letter of other requirements. We felt the necessity of further reformation. We have seen the mischievous and wicked tendencies of the sect-spirit and life.—We have eschewed it. We invite all who love the Savior to a scriptural basis of union. We do not, meanwhile, deny nor refuse their prayers, their songs, their exhortations, nor their sympathy with truth and goodness. Whilst we cannot endorse their position nor their practice, as lacking immersion, and as practising infant baptism, but lift up a loud and constant voice against it,—we must still deal with them as Christians in error, and seek to right them. To ignore their faith and obedience, and to deal with them as heathen men and publicans, will be indeed to "weaken the hands" of the pleaders for reformation, and expose ourselves, by a judgment of extreme narrowness and harshness, to the pity, if not the scorn, of good men everywhere.

(p. 128) The question is not, Can an unbelieving, impenitent, unbaptized person be recognized as a Christian? or, can a believer who refuses baptism be thus recognized? But, must a believer in Christ who, in the spirit of obedience is seeking faithfully to serve him, be rejected from fellowship and from Christian recognition, because of an error in regard to the letter of baptism?

(p. 129) To our mind, there are three items of Bible teaching which seem equally clear and indisputable.

1. That where a spirit of unbelief and disobedience shows itself, even in the rejection of the least commandment, there the disapprobation and curse of God will rest. Adam and Eve in the garden, Cain at the altar, the sons of Aaron with strange fire, and Saul in his dealings with Amalek, are clear instances of this. In the light of such awful facts, we dare not make it a light thing to disobey God.

2. That a mere compliance with the letter of a commandment, while the spirit of it is rejected, cannot be pleasing to God. Such was Balaam's case. In the light of such facts, to invite all immersed persons to the Lord's table, and make welcome there, as Christians, many unworthy persons, merely because they have complied with the letter of the law of baptism, is to take a fearful responsibility.

3. That where the spirit of faith and obedience is found, a person is accepted with God, even when failing to obey positive commands, because it was not in his heart to disobey.

(p. 130) "Why talk of unimmersed Christians?" We answer, for the same reason that Paul talks of uncircumcised Jews.

b. The covenant of circumcision was strictly binding; the law of baptism is not uttered in language more imperative than the law of circumcision—"The uncircumcised man child shall be cut off from his people; he hath broken my covenant." Yet, in millions of instances, the letter of this law was violated without the visitation of the penalty. See Josh. 5.1-9.

c. The passover was kept "otherwise than it was written," without forfeiting the approbation of God. See 2 Chron. 30.1-20. It was kept in the second month instead of the first. And "a multitude of people, even many of Ephraim and Manasseh, Issachar and Zebulun, had not cleansed themselves, yet did they eat the Passover otherwise than it was written. But Hezekiah prayed for them, saying, the good Lord pardon every one that prepareth his heart to seek God, though he be not cleansed according to the purification of the sanctuary. And the Lord hearkened to Hezekiah, and healed the people."

d. Not to multiply instances from the Old Testament, we observe that the Savior also overstepped the letter of his mission, to satisfy the spirit of it. He did so in healing sickness and in plucking ears of corn on the Sabbath day; and in extending religious recognition to Gentiles and Samaritans, although he declares he was not sent but to the lost sheep of the house of Israel.

In the light of these facts and teachings, we feel authorized to affirm that it is not always a sin to approach an ordinance of God without a literal compliance with its antecedents; and that where people "prepare their heart to seek God," an error in regard to the letter of the law does not thrust them out from divine fellowship, and cannot authorize us to drive them from ours.

. . . we trust Bro. Franklin will allow us to counsel him not to damage their great plea for Christian union by a spirit of exclusiveness which will only allow of "supposed piety and Christianity" in neighboring denominations, which refuses to recognize as Christians all the unimmersed, and claims for ourselves to be Christians par excellence, because of a bit of accuracy on the question of baptism;—lest it should place us in a position so ridiculous or so odious, as to close the avenues of approach to multitudes of godly people—our equals in faith, our superiors in piety and humanity—whom we wish to enlighten on the evils of sectarianism. A denominationalism more intense and more intolerant it would be difficult to conceive, than that in which we must land, if this kind of argument is to prevail among us. We are not yet prepared to repudiate Bro. Campbell's defense of Protestantism, nor ignore the noble plea of the leaders of this movement, for the "union of Christians on Christian principles."

What Has Been the Custom Among Us?
— W. K. Pendleton.

The second reply to Elley's letter is by W. K. Pendleton in his article "What has been the custom among us?" *Millennial Harbinger.* 1862, p. 132. This article is discussing who should be allowed to partake of the Lord's Supper (i.e., commune). Only excerpts from this article will be included. First Pendleton quotes large extracts from the Lunenburg Letters, then he refers to such as follows:

> This, I believe, has been the uniform teaching of the author (Alexander Campbell) from the earliest numbers of the Christian Baptist. A part of the foregoing article was quoted by Dr. Rice in the Lexington debate, (p. 517) and the response which was made is a full re-iteration of the opinion.—On page 556 of the Debate, we find the following noble words, worthy of the triumphant defender of Protestantism against the learned and subtle Purcell:
>
>> "No good—no religious, moral, or virtuous man, can perish through our views or principles. Our theory thunders terrors to none but the self-condemned. Human responsibility, in my views and doctrines, always depends upon, and is measured by, human ability. It is so, certainly, under the gospel. The man born blind will not be condemned for not seeing, nor the deaf for not hearing. The man who never heard the gospel, cannot disobey it; and he who, through any physical impossibility, is prevented from any ordinance, is no transgressor. It is only he who knows, and has power to do, his Mater's will, that shall be punished for disobedience. None suffer, in our views, but those who are willfully ignorant, or negligent of their duty. Natural ability, time, place, and circumstances, are all to be taken into the account; and none but those who sin against these, are, on our theory, to perish with an everlasting destruction, 'from the presence of the Lord, and from the glory of his power.'"

Again, on page 559, he says:

> "I circumscribe not the Divine philanthrophy—the Divine grace. I dare not say that there is no salvation in the church of Rome, or in that of Constantinople; though, certainly, Protestants do not regard them as churches builded upon the foundation of apostles and prophets, Jesus Christ being the chief corner-stone. In all the Protestant parties there are many excellent spirits, that mourn over the desolations of Zion—that love the gospel and its Author most sincerely. My soul rejoices in the assurance that there are very many excellent spirits groaning under the weight of human tradition and error, who are looking for redemption from these misfortunes before a long time."

From these opinions as to the essential character of many among the various religious organizations of this and other days, we could readily infer what would be the custom that would grow up amongst those who entertained them, as to communion with such. This rule has been frequently announced by Father Campbell and others—not simply as to what we ought to do, but as to what we really do practice. In the Debate with Dr. Rice on Human Creeds, p. 785, Father Campbell, than whom none, surely, ought better to know the practice of the churches, says:

> "We find much philosophy in one of Paul's precepts, somewhat mistranslated, 'Receive one another without regard to differences of opinion.' We, indeed, receive to our communion persons of other denominations who will take upon them the responsibility of their participating with us. We do, indeed, in our affections and in our practice, receive all Christians, all who give evidence of their faith in the Messiah, and of their attachment to his person, character and will."

Dr. Rice, in harmony with his method of cavilling, expressed his surprise to hear this declaration, and quoted, as inconsistent with it, a passage from Father Campbell's correspondence with W. Jones, of London, in reply to the question, "Do any of your churches admit unbaptized persons to communion?" In reply to this cavil, Father Campbell showed that Dr. Rice had fallen into the very same confusion which seems to bewilder some of our own brethren, on this subject—the confusion of not distinguishing between our custom, and what is commonly known as "Free or Open Communion." This is made very clear on page 798:

> "The gentleman has introduced an extract from my correspondence with Mr. Jones, of London, touching upon communion, which demands an observation or two. I have more respect for his understanding than to think that Mr. Rice does not comprehend this subject better. The English Baptists very generally practice open communion, as they call it.— They invite persons unbapitized to participate with them at the Lord's table. Now, the difference between them and our brethren, in cases where such persons occasionally commune with them, is this: They do not invite them, as such, to commune in the supper; but some of them sometimes say, that 'the table is the Lord's, and not theirs;' and that, though they cannot invite any to partake of it, but those visibly and ostensibly, by their own baptism, the Lord's people, in this day of division, we debar no consistent professor of the faith, or any party, who, upon his own responsibility, chooses to partake with us. Thus we throw the responsibility upon him, while the English Baptists, in many instances, take it upon themselves. I argue not the merits of this question here. I only exhibit it, in evidence that our liberality, as it is called, goes beyond the most strict sects of the Pedobaptists—beyond the party represented by my opponent."
>
> . . . Surely there is a broad distinction between declining to decide, in an untaught case, against the communion of one who gives many and convincing proofs of his love of the Saviour, and exercising the right of authoritatively inviting indiscriminately all professors;—between examining our neighbor, and urging and allowing him to examine himself.

Do the Unimmersed Commune? — *Moses E. Lard*

An article by Moses E. Lard entitled "Do the Unimmersed Commune?" appeared in *Lard's Quarterly,* Sept. 1863, p. 41. In this article Lard attacks Richardson, Pendleton, and Errett for their position as declared in their 1862 *Millennial Harbinger* articles (pp. 120, 132, and 256) regarding fellowship with Christians in error. Throughout this twelve page article Lard maintains that the unimmersed cannot be Christians. This would sound like the contemporary Church of Christ position except that he uses a very interesting definition for the word Christian. On the tenth page of his article he states positively that the Lord saves many who are not Christians. Somewhere between 1863 and the mid-20th century the definitions changed such that only the immersed Church of Christ people can be Christians and only Christians can go to heaven. Some excerpts from his article follow:

> With the right spirit, without the right acts, a man may be eminently good and pious, but he is not a Christian. . . . God may esteem him very highly, much more so than many of the immersed, and even very certainly save him; still, with becoming decency be it said, he is not a Christian.
> I mean to say distinctly and emphatically that Martin Luther, if not immersed, was not a Christian—this is what I mean to say. I do not mean to deny that Martin Luther was eminently a good and pious man; neither do I mean to deny that God took him when he died—I deny that he was a Christian.
> If a man can be a Christian without immersion, let the fact be shown; or if a man can or may commune without being a Christian, let the fact be shown. I deny both. Immovably I stand here. But I shall be told that this is Phariseeism, that it is exclusivism. Be it so; so it be true, and this is the only question with me respecting it, then am I so far the defendant of Phariseeism and exclusivism.
> . . . but then no one will contend that a man may do the things which the Bible does not prohibit, merely because it does not prohibit them. That the foregoing positions are offensive to the pious unimmersed, that they render it the more difficult for us to come into profitable contact with them, I well know, and that they even seem to imply a feeling of self superiority on our part, I shall not deny.
> . . . But that these brethren have, in claiming for these pious unimmersed the right to commune, put forth a position deeply injurious to the truth of Christ, I cannot but think. . . . Brother Pendleton is my steadfast friend, but that he has stained the

pages of the Harbinger with an error, I as conscientiously believe as I believe him to be my friend.

. . . Since they are a pious people, God accepts them as His, not because they are indeed Christians, but because they would be had they a chance. . . . On this ground alone have I hope for many of the pious whom I am still compelled in pain to regard as not Christians.

Here doubtless I shall be met with the assertion, that it is inconsistent to admit that a man may be saved, and yet deny that he can commune. I shall not deny a seeming inconsistency; but a real one I must certainly deny. If God saved none but Christians, the inconsistency would be real. But this is not the case. He saves many who are not Christians—saves them because they do the best they can in the circumstances which surround them.

Our churches in the West, I am sorry to say, without an exception known to me, permit the unimmersed to commune.

These quotations are given to show that even as the thinking began to get more exclusivistic, Lard, one of the leaders in the newer narrow thinking (see his article against instrumental music and dancing on page 330 of his same Quarterly) still acknowledged that some outside of the Church of Christ fellowship (even some of the unimmersed) would be saved and hence would go to heaven.

Opinion — Barton W. Stone

This article by Barton Stone appears in the *Christian Messenger,* Vol. 5, Jan. 1831, p. 19.

We have long believed, and have long expressed our belief, that opinions of truth, and not the truth itself, have so distracted and divided the church of God into contending, jarring sects.— All Christians of every order, honestly believe the Bible, the sum of all truth; but with regard to many truths in that book, they have formed different opinions. For this they cannot be blamed, when they have honestly searched for the right understanding of the truth. That which is blamable in them, is, that they attach such importance to their opinions, as to reject from their communion all, who reject those opinions, and receive different ones. This is the haughty spirit of infallibility.

To one subject particularly I wish to direct the attention of my brethren at this time, I mean, the subject of baptism. This has long been the cause of sore contention, and unnatural division among Christians. We have looked and hoped for an end, but it now appears farther off then ever. All but the Quakers, believe in water baptism as a solemn ordinance of the Lord Jesus Christ, by which we are inducted into the church, or become members of the kingdom of heaven.—Some think that water poured or sprinkled on a believer is baptism, and is what the Lord required; others think that immersion is the only baptism required by the Lord. Therefore they cannot believe that those who have been only sprinkled are baptized; and consequently have not been inducted into the church or kingdom of God on earth. They have therefore denied them the privileges of the kingdom. Here is a great diversity of opinions. One or the other must be wrong. Who shall determine the point? The Christian world is too much interested in this matter to judge impartially. My opinion is that immersion is only baptism.— But shall I therefore make my opinion a term of Christian fellowship? If in this case I thus act, where shall I cease from making my opinions terms of fellowship? I confess I see no end. But you may say, that immersion is so plainly the meaning of Christian Baptism, you know not how any honest man can be ignorant of it. This is the very language of all opinionists; says one, the doctrine of trinity is so plainly taught, I cannot think an honest man can deny it. So speak all Sectarians respecting their opinions. Shall we reason with them of the impropriety of making their opinions tests of Christianity, and terms of fellowship, and do the same? Is this consistency? Is this the spirit of reformation? You may say, my idea of baptism as meaning immersion is not an opinion, but a fact. So say the orthodox respecting many of their unscriptural opinions, and are as firmly persuaded of them, as you can be respecting immersion not being an opinion of baptism. Here again a disinterested umpire is needed. The case I shall leave sub judice, till a satisfactory determination of the matter be made. Till then would it not be better, and would not the cause of Christianity more gloriously advance, if all would cultivate brotherly affections towards each other, and bear with each other's weakness and errors, which affect not their pious and holy life? Forbearance would more speedily effect a reformation from those errors, than an intemperate zeal, and rigid course. These more generally confirm in error, than produce a reformation from it. We remember what effects this course produced in us, when we lived in the error. We were honest; but never were we moved to relinquish the error but by the mild persuasive and forcible arguments of the gospel.

But the great objection is, the unimmersed are not in the kingdom, therefore should not be admitted to the privileges of those in the kingdom. The objection is plausible. But I would ask, can Sectarians be members of the kingdom, or of the body of Christ? There can be but one opinion of this point; all who know the meaning of the word Sectarian must answer, no. If Sectarians are not members of the kingdom or body of Christ, how can they be admitted to the privileges of it? Is not the Baptist church itself, though immersed, Sectarian? How can they then be admitted to the privileges of the kingdom? If then, the privileges of the kingdom are not to be granted to the unimmersed, because they are not in the kingdom; with what consistency shall they be granted to others not in the kingdom, though they have been immersed? It is equally clear to my mind that a Sectarian is as far from being a member of the kingdom or body of Christ, as an unimmersed person is—Therefore if one be rejected the other should.

How many honest, pious, godly souls are there among the different sects, who have not, till lately, ever thought seriously on these subjects: of this we are assured, because we speak from experience. But the time is come, when the minds of all the sects are roused to inquiry. Let truth be exhibited in all its clearness in the wisdom of the serpent and harmlessness of the dove—let tenderness, brotherly love, and forbearance be exercised one towards the other—let piety, justice and mercy be cultivated by us all. Then will be effected the union of Christians in the truth—then will be answered the prayers of all the saints. Let us all remember, that we all have long been in the apostacy, nor have we yet escaped out of the dark mists of Babylon.

But says one, I cannot have communion with an unimmersed person; because he is not a member of the church of Christ, however pious and holy he may be. I ask, is he a heathen, or publican? for such is the character of those excluded from the church, Matt. 18. All are either for or against Christ the Lord. "He that is not with me is against me." Shall we say, all are the enemies of Christ who are not immersed? We dare not. If they are not enemies, or if they are not against him, they are for him and with him; shall we reject those who are with Jesus, from us? Shall we refuse communion with those, with whom the Lord communes? Shall we reject those who follow not with us in opinion? Shall we make immersion the test of religion? and shall we centre all religion in this one point? Shall we more insist on this point, than on faith, repentance and the love of God, connected with a life of holiness, mercy and self denial. Cornelius was a devout or pious man, who feared God with all his house, who gave much alms to the people, and prayed always; of him and such as him Peter said, "Of a truth I perceive that God is no respecter of persons; but in every nation he that feareth him, and worketh righteousness is accepted with him." God had accepted him before his baptism; Cornelius had the kingdom of righteousness in him; but not the fulness of it. Peter was sent to him that he might be fully inducted into the kingdom. Does God accept such pious souls, and shall we reject them? Let us be followers (imitators) of God as dear children.

Do they really distinguish themselves above all others in piety and holiness, who reject from fellowship all the unimmersed? If this were a fact, it would be a prevailing argument indeed. I advise the Christians not to be too solicitous to enquire, "What shall this man, or those men do." Let them attend to their own duty. Let us still acknowledge all to be our brethren, who believe in the Lord Jesus, and humbly and honestly obey him, as far as they know his will, and their duty. Let us not reject whom the Lord has received. "By their fruits shall ye know them." Let us not reject experience, as good evidence of our acceptance with God. We know we have passed from death unto life, because we love the brethren, etc. Religion without experience is nothing better than a body without the spirit.

Union — Barton W. Stone

The following article by Barton W. Stone appears in the August 1831 (p. 180) edition of the *Christian Messenger*. Approximately one-half of the article is presented at this time.

ONLY CHURCH OF CHRIST MEMBERS CAN GO TO HEAVEN

Those persons associated with Stone referred to themselves as "Christians." The references in the following article to the "Reformed Baptists" or to the "Disciples" are in reference to those people who were associated with the Campbell movement. This article was written the year before the Stone movement combined with the Campbell movement to constitute collectively what we now refer to as the restoration movement.

The question is going the round of society, and is often proposed to us, Why are not you and the Reformed Baptists, one people? or, Why are you not united? We have uniformly answered; In spirit we are united, and that no reason existed on our side to prevent the union in form. It is well known to those brethren, and to the world, that we have always, from the beginning, declared our willingness, and desire to be united with the whole family of God on earth, irrespective of the diversity of opinion among them. The Reformed Baptists have received the doctrine, taught by us many years ago. For nearly 30 years we have taught that Sectarianism was antichristian, and that all Christians should be united in the one body of Christ—the same they teach. We then and ever since, have taught that authoritative creeds and confessions were the strong props of sectarianism, and should be given to the moles and the bats—they teach the same. We have from that time preached the gospel to every creature to whom we had access, and urged them to believe and obey it—that its own evidence was sufficient to produce faith in all that heard it, that the unrenewed sinner must, and could believe it unto justification and salvation—and that through faith the Holy Spirit of promise, and every other promise of the New Covenant, were given. They proclaim the same doctrine. Many years ago some of us preached baptism as a means, in connexion with faith and repentance, for the remission of sins, and the gift of the Holy Spirit—they preach the same, and extend it farther than we have done. We rejected all names, but Christian—they acknowledge it most proper, but seem to prefer another. We acknowledge a difference of opinion from them on some points. We do not object to their opinions as terms of fellowship between us. But they seriously and honestly object to some of ours as reasons why they cannot unite. These we shall name, and let all duly consider their weight.

Objection 1st: That we have fellowship, and commune with unimmersed persons. They contend, (so we understand them) that according to the New Institution, none but the immersed have their sins remitted; and therefore they cannot commune with the unimmersed. On this point we cannot agree with them, and the reason of our disagreement, is, that this sentiment, in our view will exclude millions of the fairest characters, for many centuries back, from heaven. For if the immersed only, receive the remission of sins, all those millions that have died, being unimmersed, have died in their sins, or unwashed from their sins. Jesus said, "If ye die in your sins, where God is, you can never come." Of course they are excluded from heaven. Hell therefore, must be their portion; for protestants do not believe in a purgatory: Why are they sent to hell? For disobedience to the one command of being immersed. Hear the poor creature's complaint, while suffering the vengeance of eternal fire. On earth, says he, in obedience to the King, whom I loved, whose laws I loved, whose family I loved, I denied myself, took up my cross and followed him. I was taught that it was my duty to be baptized, and that baptism meant to be sprinkled with water; in the humble spirit of obedience I submitted, not knowing but that this was the very way the King meant this command to be observed. But now, alas! for my ignorance of the right way of performing one command, I must be forever banished from God into everlasting punishment. What should we think of an earthly king, if a province of loving subjects, being ignorant of the meaning of a certain law, and yet endeavoring to obey it according to their understanding of it, should by his order be cut off by an excruciating death? Surely, we should reprobate his conduct, and should see in his character that which is less amiable than otherwise. Is it possible to divest ourselves of the same thoughts and conclusion respecting the lively King of saints? Should we not, by presenting his character in this view, expose it to the contempt of a scoffing world?

I know our brethren say, We do not declare that they are excluded from heaven, but only from the kingdom on earth. We leave them in the hand of God. But does not the sentiment lead to that conclusion? We believe, and acknowledge, that Baptism is ordained by the King a means for the remission of sins to penitent believers; but we cannot say, that immersion is the *sine qua non,* without maintaining the awful consequence above, and without contradicting our own experience. We therefore teach the doctrine, believe, repent, and be immersed for the remission of sins; and we endeavor to convince our hearers of its truth; but we exercise patience and forbearance towards such pious persons, as cannot be convinced.

2ndly. Another cause or reason, why we and they are not united as one people, is, that we have taken different names. They acknowledge the name Christian most appropriate; but because they think this name is disgraced by us who wear it, and that to it may be attached the idea of Unitarian or Trinitarian, they reject it, and have taken the older name, Disciple. This they have done in order to be distinguished from us. Hence it is concluded that they wish to be a party distinguished from us, and have therefore assumed this name as a party name. This at once bars us from union in the same body, and we cannot but believe it was assumed for this purpose, by some. We should rejoice to believe the contrary. Until a satisfactory explanation be given on this subject, we must view ourselves equally excluded from union with the congregation of the Disciples, as from any other sectarian establishment. We object not to the scriptural name, Disciple, but to the reasons why our brethren assumed it.

We are ready any moment, to meet and unite with those brethren, or any others, who believe in, and obey the Saviour according to their best understanding of his will, on the Bible, but not on opinions of its truth. We cannot with our present views unite on the opinion that unimmersed persons cannot receive the remission of sins, and therefore should be excluded from our fellowship and communion on earth. We cannot conscientiously give up the name Christian, acknowledged by our brethren most appropriate, for any other (as Disciple) less appropriate, and received to avoid the disgrace of being suspected to be a Unitarian or Trinitarian. We cannot thus temporize with divine truth. (We now skip four paragraphs of Stone's article)

Our Brethren, the Disciples, ask us, How can you grant the privileges of the kingdom to such as have not been immersed, when it is plain that by immersion only they are born or made members of the kingdom? How can you commune with such at the Lord's table? I answer, that there are many things done under the New Institution or covenant, which were divinely instituted before that covenant was fully confirmed, and declared;

yet these things were designed to be perpetuated to the end of time. Thus prayer, praise, thanksgiving, teaching, preaching, and even the Lord's supper, were divinely instituted, before Jesus died, was buried and rose again; consequently, before the foundation of the New Institution was fully laid, and of course, before any were built upon it. John's baptism brought none into the new kingdom. The Disciples, and the rest of the 120 on Pentecost, were therefore not inducted into this new kingdom by immersion, yet they prayed, praised and communed with those in it, and these divine acts were reciprocated. As well might we forbid unimmersed persons to pray, to praise, to teach, as to forbid them to commune. These privileges were enjoyed before the kingdom was established, and before the New Institution took place; and we dare not say, they are now taken from them? It was not done at Pentecost. It has not been divinely done at any period since. What authority have we for inviting or debarring any pious, holy believer from the Lord's table? Though it is done by many, we see no divine authority for it. The King's will is, that his friends do this in remembrance of him—and all that his law expressed on the subject is, "Let a man examine himself and so let him eat and drink—If he eats and drinks unworthily, he eats and drinks damnation to himself, (not to others) not discerning the Lord's body. He has no where established a court of inquisition to fence his table, nor to prevent any from praying, praising, or worshipping him, unless they have been immersed. We confess we cannot see why so much more importance should be attached to the Lord's supper, than to the other divine commands. We have long feared that the feast of love has been made by designing men an occasion of discord and division among the saints. We have seen many unimmersed possess the spirit of the kingdom; and we have seen many immersed destitute of it. To receive the latter, and to reject the former, we cannot view divine.

If we philosophize on religion, we may amuse the intelligent, but are unprofitable to all. Nothing but truth, truth felt, truth preached in the spirit, and truth copied in our lives, will arrest the attention, and gain and fix the heart of a drowsy, dying world.

I have long thought, and seriously thought, whether a formal union on the Bible, without possessing the spirit of that book, would be a blessing or a curse to society—whether it would be better than faith without works, or than a body without the

Spirit—whether it would not rather be a stumbling block, a delusive snare to the world. O, my brethren, let us repent and do our first works—let us seek for more holiness, rather than trouble ourselves and others with schemes and plans of union. The love of God shed abroad in our hearts by the Holy Ghost given unto us, will more effectually unite, than all the wisdom of the world combined. Endeavor to walk in peace and love with all. Then shall we feel a reviving from the presence of the Lord, and see, flowing to the Lord, weeping penitents, pleading for mercy, and praising aloud for mercy received through our Lord Jesus Christ. Amen.

Comments by Walter Scott

In 1833 Walter Scott published an article in *The Evangelist* entitled "The Holy Spirit, A Discourse." He also published a list of questions and answers immediately following the article. One of the questions and Walter Scott's answer are given below: (No. 2, Vol. 2, Feb. 4, 1833, p. 49)

(Question No. 6 by the queriest) If christians who have not been baptized for the remission of their sins, have no scriptural evidence that they have received 'the gift of the Holy Spirit', except by an appeal to their feelings and experiences, can they have any solid evidences in a mere opinion, such as, 'whereas I was blind, now I think I see'?

(The answer by Walter Scott) Christians who have not been baptized for the remission of their sins! Strange! Whoever read of such christians in God's word? But the times are peculiar, and as faith does purify the life of a man, and as the man of pure life and pure heart is accepted of God and may receive the Spirit, therefore we must allow, that there are now a days christians in heart and life who have not been baptized for the remission of their sins!

'What evidences, then, have they for themselves and others, that they are possessed of the Spirit? None but the moral graces which have already been quoted, viz: love, joy etc.; they don't need to depend upon an opinion; they feel within themselves and show to those without them by their fruits, that they have been made partakers of the Spirit of Christ.'

But it is not necessary to call the last italicised words in the question, viz: 'I think I see,' au opinion; for no man discerns fairly and to all intents and purposes, that the Kingdom of God is righteousness and peace and joy in the Holy Spirit until he is a partaker of the Holy Spirit: therefore, on the reception of the Spirit, one may with all propriety say, 'I see,' or more modestly, 'I think I see'.

Additional Thoughts on the Limits of Religious Fellowship — A. Campbell

In the *Christian Baptist,* Vol. V., No. 12, July 7, 1828, p. 457, there appears an article by Alexander Campbell entitled "Review of the History of Churches.—No. III." In the previous articles he has been discussing various churches in Europe and America. All except the last two paragraphs of the specified article are included below.

While all of the above churches manifest a scrupulous regard to the grand constitutional principles of the kingdom of Jesus Christ, they seem to differ from each other in their view of the ordinance of the Great King on the subject of naturalization. Some of them receive unnaturalized persons into his realm on the ground of forbearance. On this subject I write with great caution, for I know this question of forbearance has in it some perplexities of no easy solution, and is at least of as difficult solution as that concerning the amalgamation of the Jews and Gentiles in the christian church, decided by the apostles and elders in the city of Jerusalem. On the scriptural propriety of receiving unnaturalized or unimmersed persons into the kingdom into which the Saviour said none can enter but by being born of water and of Spirit, little can be said either from precept or example. For it is exceedingly plain, that from the day on which Peter opened the reign of the Messiah, on the ever memorable Pentecost, no man entered the realm but by being born of water. Jew and Gentile, Barbarian, Scythian, bond and free, could find but one gate into the empire of Immanuel, and with joy they enter in at this door. As yet there was no breach in the walls, no scaling ladders, no battering rams, to find an easier way. Jesus was yet recognized as the living way; and as he came by water and by blood, so he ordained that through faith in his blood and through water, the soldiers of the cross must follow him. There were even in those hale and undegenerate days, matters on which patience and endurance must be exercised; but they were all within the constituted realms. There was none without the gates demanding recognition from those within, on the grounds of charity. But now the walls of this city of refuge, the ramparts of Zion have been broken through; and while the inhabitants of the city of God have gone out and trafficked with the world, the world has come in and trafficked with them. And now they sue for a treaty offensive and defensive. Well they urge their plea with an embassy of weeping mothers and screaming infants, and who is proof against such importunities? But the question of the greatest difficulty to decide, is, whether there should be any laws or rules adopted by the churches relating to the practice of receiving unimmersed in the assemblies of the saints. Whether on the ground of forbearance, as it is called, such persons as have been once sprinkled, or not at all, but who are satisfied with their sprinkling, or without any, are, on their solicitation, to be received into any particular congregation, and to be treated in all respects as those who have, by their own voluntary act and deed, been naturalized and constitutionally admitted into the kingdom. To make a law that such should be received, appears to me, after long and close deliberation, a usurpation of the legislative authority vested in the holy apostles, and of dangerous tendency in the administration of the Reign of Heaven. Again, to say that no weak brother, however honest in his profession, excellent in his deportment and amiable in his character, who cannot be convinced but that his infant sprinkling is christian baptism, and who solicits a participation with us in the festivities of Zion: I say, to say by a stern decree that none such shall on any account be received, appears to be illiberal, unkind, censorious, and opposite to that benevolence which is one of the primary virtues of christianity.

Yet some will urge that if such a person is very solicitous for the enjoyment of the benefits of the church, it is no very difficult or hazardous thing for him to be immersed on his own profession, and for the objects contemplated therein. And that if his love of the christian institution will not make him forbear with himself, or in other words, sacrifice his own partialities, we are not warranted, nor warrantable, in receiving him. Now, although I could feel myself at perfect liberty, in full accordance with the requirements of the Great King, to receive into the most cordial fellowship every one which I have reason to recognize as a disciple of Jesus Christ, with all his weaknesses, as I would call them; yet I could not, and dare not, say to all the members of a christian congregation, that they must do so too; and as I have no right to dispense with any of the institutions of Jesus Christ, I could not approve the adoption of a rule to receive such persons, which, in its direct tendency, aims at the abolition of one of the fundamental laws of the empire. Again, if we are to fritter down the christian institution to suit the prejudices and weaknesses of disciples, it would soon be divested of every prominent feature characteristic of its grand original. There are, indeed, many matters on which there is full scope given for the display of moderation, condescension, and forbearance, without infringing upon the constitutional provisions of the kingdom. We may shew all courtesy, kindness, and hospitality to strangers, but to invest them with the rights and immunities of citizens, without their voluntary submission to the constitutional requirements in order to naturalization, would neither be beneficial to them, nor safe to the empire. Christians were called a sect in the times of the apostles. They had their peculiarities then; and although there were no sects tolerated amongst them, they were a sect as regarded all other religious communities. In divesting christianity of its sectarian character, we must not divest it of the peculiarities which made it a sect in its best days, and which will keep it a sect until all the kingdoms and religions in the world shall bow to our King.

I know that there is something called charity in the world, which is very much flattered; but when dissected, is a hideous thing. To please the taste of any body and every body, it will administer to all their requirements. If medicine or poison is sought after, with equal liberality it bestows on all. Like a too indulgent mother, it defeats itself. If it would be cruel to give a scorpion when a fish is asked, it is no better to give a scorpion when a scorpion is desired, especially if he who desires to obtain it sues for it through mistake. On the same principles, it is not charity, in its true import, to gratify the vitiated humor, or caprice, or prejudice, or weakness of every body. While we are willing to go more than half way, where it is optional with us to go at all, to meet the doubting and the weak, there are certain occurrences and circumstances which compel us not to move at all, and the same charity, properly so called, governs us in both cases. But here we do not argue the merits of this question at all; but only state the result of much examination and reflection on the subject.

The Extra No. I in the *Millennial Harbinger* of 1830, written by Alexander Campbell, is devoted to the support of the concept of baptism by immersion for the forgiveness of sins. In the latter part of this Extra Campbell addresses some anticipated objections to his position. One of the objections and Campbell's response are of interest at this time.

Objection 3. —"Then none of the unimmersed can be saved; for none can enter the Kingdom of God, but those born of water."

This is, or is not true, according as you understand the term saved. If you understand the terms as defined in the preceding pages, they are not saved; for the present salvation of the gospel is that salvation into which we enter, when we become citizens of the Kingdom of God. But whether they may enter into the kingdom of future and eternal glory after the resurrection, is a question much like that question long discussed in the schools; viz. Can infants who have been quickened, but who died before they were born, be saved? We may hope the best, but cannot speak with the certainty of knowledge. One thing we know, that it is not a difficult matter for believers to be born of water; and if any of them wilfully neglect, or disdain it, we cannot hope for their future and eternal salvation. But we have no authority to speak comfortably to them who will not submit to the government of the saviour.

Many persons, I doubt not, who never were informed on these matters, but simply mistook the import and design of the Institution, who were nevertheless honestly disposed to obey, and did obey as far as they were instructed, may, as the devout Jews and Patriarchs who lived before the christian era, be admitted into the Kingdom of future glory. But this by the way, to prevent the calumnies of those who are better disposed to censure every thing we write, than to obey the Lord. I am sure of one thing; because the decree is published: viz. that he that believes the gospel,

ENDANGERED HERITAGE

and is immersed shall be saved; and he who submits not to the government of Jesus Christ shall be condemned.

In 1843 Alexander Campbell debated N. L. Rice, a Presbyterian, on the subject of baptism (among other things). The proceedings of this debate are reprinted by Religious Book Service, Indianapolis. They contain the following comments by Campbell, part of which was quoted in a previous section:

> (p. 556) . . . We send none to perdition but those who disbelieve and reject the gospel. . . .
> No good—no religious, moral, or virtuous man, can perish through our views or principles. Our theory thunders terrors to none but the self-condemned. Human responsibility, in my views and doctrines, always depends upon, and is measured by, human ability. It is so, certainly, under the gospel. The man born blind will not be condemned for not seeing, nor the deaf for not hearing. The man who never heard the gospel, cannot disobey it; and he who, through any physical impossibility, is prevented from any ordinance, is no transgressor. It is only he who knows, and has power to do, his Master's will, that shall be punished for disobedience. None suffer, in our views, but those who are wilfully ignorant, or negligent of their duty. Natural ability, time, place, and circumstances, are all to be taken into the account; and none but those who sin against these, are, on our theory, to perish with an everlasting destruction, "from the presence of the Lord, and from the glory of his power." Infants dying, need neither faith, repentance, nor baptism, in order to their salvation, according to the Bible. They died in the first Adam, but the second Adam died for them, and they shall live with him.
> Great men often believe great nonsense. . . . Neither learning, nor genius, nor talent, nor numbers, are tests of truth, or a proof that any tenet, custom, or tradition is canonical or useful.
> (p. 785) . . . We are so exclusive, however, that we say to every one, without the fold, you must repent and be baptized for the remission of your sins, if you would enjoy the fullness of the blessing of the gospel of Christ. Still we do not so make conditions of ultimate salvation out of the conditions of church membership. We are not now descanting upon the conditions of salvation among the antediluvians, the Jews, the pagans, infants,

and those otherwise incapable of hearing, believing, and obeying the gospel.

Robert Richardson gives what seems like an accurate description of Alexander Campbell's views regarding fellowship on page 138 of the *Memoirs*:

> Remembering the earnestness and faith in which the church at Brush Run sought to know and to do the will of God, while yet mistaken in regard to baptism, his feelings led him to wish to have communion with any similar churches, though they might be yet Paedobaptist. Nevertheless, he remained fully satisfied that the New Testament presented baptism as "indispensably preceding" social communion in religious acts. Thus he was placed in a strait between his conviction on the one hand that there were saints of God in all parties, and on the other that obedience to the ordinances of the Gospel was necessary to church membership. His feelings led him to recognize all as Christians who gave evidence of faith and piety, while his views of the Gospel restricted him to formal communion with those only who had publicly professed to put on Christ in baptism.

SUMMARY

We have seen from the writings that have been quoted that many of the early leaders of the restoration movement wrestled with conflicting sentiments on the issue of religious fellowship with those whom they considered to be in error. On the one hand they had a tendency to be tolerant and forbearing toward other conscientious and sincere professors of the name of Jesus Christ. All of the first generation leaders could remember when they too had believed, taught and practiced false doctrines even while they were honestly searching after truth. They had considered themselves saved even in their previous more imperfect state and therefore they were prone to extend this same consideration to others. On the other hand they were very reluctant to compromise on what they now considered to be divinely revealed truth (such as, for instance, to allow the unimmersed to be members of their congregations). It appears that prior to the merger of the two groups in 1832 that those associated with Stone were much more lenient in this regard than were those associated with Campbell. Even so we saw that Stone expressed in his writings the same perplexities that Campbell did on the subject.

The restoration movement, during its early era of very marked success and dynamic growth, seems to have dealt with this dilemma with a two pronged approach. First to allow none but those who had been immersed for the forgiveness of their sins and who believed in the weekly observance of the Lord's Supper to be accepted as members of their congregations. And second, to believe and acknowledge that there were Christians (sincere believers in Christ who would spend eternity in heaven) to be found among all of the denominations. This approach seems to have provided at least four major advantages:

1. They did not have to compromise any of what they believed to be divinely revealed truth. They could continue to teach New Testament Christianity exactly as they perceived it to be.

2. It kept the lines of communication open so that their teaching could be heard by the other denominations. During the height of Alexander Campbell's career he was invited to speak in the meeting houses of many of the various denominations in the areas through which he traveled.

3. It prevented the reformers from placing themselves in the position of acting as the ultimate judges of other servants of Christ (a position strictly forbidden in Scriptures).

4. It helped to keep them from closing their minds to the possibility of their own errors. The quotations which have been presented reflect a growth or evolution towards the doctrine which they eventually adopted. Without an open mind, this growth would never have been possible.

Of course there were those, even from the early days, who had a much more narrow, sectarian point of view. It was these that occasioned the writing of Barton W. Stone's articles in

1831 and Alexander Campbell's letters of 1837. At first the more narrow-minded, sectarian brethren seem perhaps to not have been very organized in their position. Some apparently thought that one must be immersed in order to have any chance of going to heaven. However there was another contingent who maintained that one must be immersed in order to be a Christian, but their somewhat interesting definition of the term Christian allowed some who were not Christians to go to heaven. Moses E. Lard, in his 1863 article, is an example of one such leader. Somewhere between 1863 and our generation the definitions changed such that only Church of Christ members were "Christians" and only "Christians" could go to heaven. The list of requirements for belonging to the select group grew as time progessed. At first immersion for the forgiveness of sins and the weekly communion constituted the core requirements. Later the requirement to prohibit the use of instrumental music in worship was added. The list of things which must be absolutely prohibited in order for one to go to heaven continued to grow with time. Sunday school classes, multi-cup communion, kitchens in the church building, support for orphans homes and colleges, are a few of the things which eventually were added to the forbidden list by some congregations. The religious reformation that started out as a plea across denominational lines for Christian union gradually became more exclusivistic and sectarian in its nature.

Perhaps it would have been difficult, living in the early 1800s, to decide which side of this issue to take. But we have an advantage over those people. We have 150 years of history recorded for our evaluation. Someone once said, "Those who do not remember the past are condemned to relive it."[28] We have experienced the same kind of evolution from an emphasis on the essentials to a spirit of dogmatism that occurred centuries earlier in the Roman Catholic church. We can look around us

---

28. George Santayana, *The Life of Reason*, 1905.

and observe that the Church of Christ of today has a very bad reputation. We have essentially destroyed our influence within the Christian world. We would be well advised to examine ourselves and our history and try to improve our situation in the future.

Remember that earlier in this chapter the pioneer preachers of the restoration movement were allowed to speak for themselves, to present in their own words their views on this issue of religious fellowship. Since we in the Church of Christ claim to be the only branch of the movement which has remained true to the spirit and goals of our heritage this seemed to be a most appropriate way to proceed in our study.

I will not try, as author of this document, to tell the reader exactly where God draws the line, says no more error can be tolerated even under his abundant grace, and closes off the gates to heaven. I am confident that such a point does exist; however, I have learned that it is not my job to specify this limit. It is God alone who is to judge his subjects. He, in fact, warns us sternly against trying to usurp this authority. Each person must, at least in his own mind, evaluate the issue and come to at least some tentative conclusion. However, we must remember that this will be a personal opinion, based on interpretations of and inferences from things which the Scriptures tell us. And we should be very careful to remember just how strongly our ancestors in the restoration movement warn us about the dangers of personal opinions and inferences.

I feel that it is appropriate at this time to present some personal observations on this subject. It is often productive when investigating any concept to first look at the extremes. In this case there are two extremes at either end of a spectrum. The first extreme could be described as: "It doesn't matter what religious doctrine a person has or what he believes as long as he is sincere." I totally reject this position. If this were true, a person could go to heaven even if he were an atheist, as long as he was sincere in his belief. The Lord provides each of us (to each in varying degrees) with certain intellectual capabilities and places each of us in a set of environmental circumstances all of which combine to create a situation which determines how quickly, how easily, and how completely and accurately we can ascertain the truth of God's word as revealed in the Bible. I believe that the Lord is satisfied with nothing less than that we continually, throughout our lives, make the maximum use of our capabilities to learn all of his truth and to live it in our lives. I believe that it is this kind of total commitment to a Christlike life which the Lord looks for most. So I say it matters a lot what we believe. The second extreme in our case would be: "Only members of the 'yellow pages' Church of Christ can possibly go to heaven." One believing this extreme position makes two totally false assumptions. One, the assumption that a person must be perfect in his doctrine in order to go to heaven, and the other the assumption that the Church of Christ has the perfect doctrine (the perfectly restored New Testament Church, perfect in the most minute detail). Based on my study of the Bible and my study of our religious history, it is impossible for me to believe that this extreme is true. And so we are still left with the question. Who is going to heaven? And at the risk of being repetitious I will say once again—it is not our job to answer this question. That job belongs only to our Lord. It is our job to learn his will as completely as we possibly can, to live it in our lives to the maximum possible extent, and to teach it boldly to any and all who will listen.

I, for one, reject the idea that all persons outside of our religious group are going to hell. I will never say that all persons in the other religious denominations have no hope of salvation. Even if this were true (which it isn't) it would probably not be in the interest of good public relations, nor would it contribute in a positive way to the spread of the truth, to say it. I believe that we must approach people who are members of other denominations under the assumption that they are (at least potentially) Christians. They may be Christians in error (we are all Christians in error) and we can try to correct them. Some are certainly greatly in error, regarding such things as baptism. Perhaps they are so greatly in error that they will be lost. If they are in error because of voluntary ignorance, then, perhaps there is no hope for them. But what if they are dedicated to learning the truth and sincere but still in grave error? Can they then be lost? Perhaps, but we should tread lightly here. We in the Church of Christ have been dedicated to learning the truth and we have been sincere, but we have been wrong in some areas, so what about us? But an even more fearful thing to consider is that many of our people have been very harsh and have judged others without mercy. The Bible seems to teach that to the extent that we judge others without mercy to that same extent will the Lord judge us without mercy on the judgment day (James 2:13, Romans 2:1). If we could step back and look objectively at the whole situation we might observe that not only might there possibly be some persons in the other denominations going to heaven, but it might also be that for approximately the last 100 years there might be (because of our harsh, merciless, judgmental attitude) fewer people going to heaven from the Church of Christ than from any other denomination. This should be a very sobering thought.

But I hope, and fervently pray, that the Lord, through his grace and mercy, will forgive such of our brethren as fall in this category. I hope that he will remember that they were sincere and that they honestly thought that they were doing his will in all things. I pray for this and I think that we have reason to hope that it will be true. But if we do have reason to hope for his grace and mercy to cover these, our brethren in the Church of Christ, then we must be willing to acknowledge that there may be those in other denominations of whom it may also be said that "He will remember that they were sincere and that they honestly thought they were doing his will in all things."

PART IV

EPILOGUE

11

THE VALIDITY OF THE RESTORATION PRINCIPLE

Some people have argued that because the Church of Christ (or the Stone-Campbell movement in general) has divided many times, over many issues, that this proves that the restoration principle is invalid. They claim that there is something inherently divisive about the concept of attempting to restore New Testament Christianity in the present age. I want to suggest that this is not the case at all. These divisions do not indicate that restorationism has failed, rather they indicate that we have failed restorationism. We, in our imperfect human condition, have failed in our efforts at the restoration of New Testament Christianity.

The restoration principle, the concept of restoring New Testament Christianity in the present age, is not a panacea, and a pledge of support for restorationism will not guarantee Camelot. It will not immediately end all divisions within Christendom and it will not cause all Christians to agree on every issue. If all men agreed to be restorationists they would still disagree on what it means to be a restorationist. They would still disagree on what needs to be restored and what can be ignored. They would still disagree on the role of Biblical commands and Biblical examples in determining modern Christian doctrine. They would not agree as to which commands apply to Christians today and which were directed only to those of the first century. They would not agree on which Biblical examples, if any, apply to the 20th century church and which were only incidental to the first century cultural situation. These issues, and probably others as well, would continue to present problems. But problems and disagreements and divisions are not by-products unique to restorationist movements. They are, rather, manifestations of the imperfect state of man and of the efforts of Satan to confound the attempts of man to follow Christ. All religious movements of any kind are plagued by imperfections, therefore one must not reject restorationism simply because it has not produced a utopia. Acceptance or rejection of the concept must be based on more sound criteria.

The restoration principle, stated simply, pleads for the restoration of the Bible as the sole source of authority in religion. This is a noble and lofty ideal, and also a very realistic and practical approach to the implementation of modern day Christianity. Consider the alternatives. If one religious group looks to Rome for their source of authority, if another group relies on a modern day prophet who claims to receive new direct revelations from God, if yet another group claims to derive their truth from a book other than the Bible, and if only some claim the Bible as the only source of authority then only confusion can ever result. There is no hope, either at the present time or in the future, of the four groups used in this example ever achieving a meaningful unity. They are like four ships lost in the night, each trying to sail toward a different lighthouse on a different shore. They have no hope of ever arriving at the same destination. Consider now four other groups, each restorationists and each claiming to take the Bible as the only source of authority in religion and each striving to restore New Testament Christianity in the modern world. Consider further that these four groups disagree on many things, so much so even that they will not associate with each other in any way. Again we have four ships tossed about on a stormy sea, each currently headed in a perhaps somewhat different direction; however, this example differs significantly from the previous one. Here each ship has in view, however brightly or dimly, the same lighthouse on the same distant shore. Each sees the Bible as a beacon to guide the wayfaring Christian to a safe harbor, to the truth of God's word. Each has the same declared objective, even if they do currently disagree somewhat on which way to steer the rudder. If each group continues to become more Christ-like in their lives and more Biblical in their doctrine, there is at least a hope and a chance that at some point in the future their paths will cross. This is what restorationism is all about, and it would seem to be the only solid foundation upon which to build modern Christianity.

With these thoughts in mind we can view our own 19th century Stone-Campbell restoration movement in the proper perspective. We must never claim that they perfectly restored the New Testament church. They made a valiant attempt, however, and were successful to a degree rare (perhaps unique) among major religious movements. We should study their successes and their failures and take heed of the lessons that history offers, to aid us today in our Christian walk.

If we could view time as God might view it, rather than from our limited human perspective, we might say that very little time has passed since Jesus Christ died on the cross—a mere twenty centuries (approximately). And in this limited time man drifted significantly from the practice of Christianity as described in the Scriptures. We don't know when our Lord will return, it might be tomorrow. But it also might be another twenty centuries, or one hundred or one thousand or multiplied thousands of centuries. If the human race is to have any hope of remaining true to Christ and his teaching, we must have a constant, unchanging, standard against which each and every generation can measure their religion. And if (in any given generation) some deviations from the standard are observed, then that generation must make an effort at returning to (restoring) the original standard. This process, whatever other people might choose to call it, we have traditionally called the restoration of New Testament Christianity. It has always been and will always be a valid plea, a reliable guide to direct our study and our lives. Some may abuse it, some may abandon it, and all may not agree on how to implement it, but I believe it to be the only valid approach to the study and the practice of Christianity.

Some have claimed that the plea for the restoration of New Testament Christianity and the plea for Christian unity are not compatible, that they are conflicting goals. I do not believe this to be the case. In fact, I believe that exactly the opposite is true. I believe that the two, unity and restorationism, are completely compatible. In fact, in the long run, I believe that a constant attempt to restore New Testament Christianity is the only approach to Christianity that will precipitate the kind of unity which our Lord desires. We should remember that real, fundamental Christian unity is not something which we can make happen by any of our human effort. We can neither create nor destroy Christian unity. All who are in Christ, throughout the world and across the ages, are united in him. This unity exists whether we recognize it or not and whether we acknowledge it or not. Jesus Christ made this unity a reality by his death on the cross. We may not be able to accurately determine who does and who does not fall into this group, but God did not ordain us as judges of his subjects. The only aspects of unity which our feeble human efforts can influence are those visible, tangible, manifestations of unity among the various groups who claim to be followers of Christ.

What, then, is the effective way for us to contribute toward the kind of visible unity which our Lord desires? I believe that the answer is quite simple, that it is completely consistent with our principle of restorationism, and that it involves the same technique which we should be using in our individual efforts to get to heaven. We should learn the Lord's will, from the Bible, as completely and as accurately as we can, we should apply it in our lives as completely as we possibly can, and we should endeavor to teach all who will listen of its truth. To the extent that we sincerely do these things we will, to just that same extent, achieve Christlikeness in our lives and New Testament Christianity in our doctrine. If, at the same time, some other denomination is also studying the Bible objectively, and applying it sincerely in their lives and in their worship, they too will gradually become more Christlike. If both groups, we and they, continue to become more Christlike then, as time goes by, there will come a point where we are so much alike that we can unite without either party having to sacrifice any of its faith. This now will be the unity of which our Lord speaks, and the only unity for which we should hope. One good example of this type of union happened in 1832 when those reformers associated with Alexander Campbell and those associated with Barton W. Stone united and became one movement, even though the two groups had totally separate and unrelated origins. Thus restorationism and a movement toward meaningful Christian unity are really one and the same thing. And so it is not unity but a Christlike life and faith which should be our constant goal. As we achieve this image of Christ in our lives the unity that we desire will come, true meaningful unity in the spirit of Christ.

But these thoughts are not new with me. Barton W. Stone expressed these same sentiments in 1831 in his article "Union" which was presented earlier in this document. In his last paragraph Stone says:

> I have long thought, and seriously thought, whether a formal union of the Bible, without possessing the spirit of that book, would be a blessing or a curse to society—whether it would be be better than faith without works, or than a body without the

Spirit—whether it would not rather be a stumbling block, a delusive snare to the world. O, my brethren, let us repent and do our first works—let us seek for more holiness, rather than trouble ourselves and others with schemes and plans of union. The love of God shed abroad in our hearts by the Holy Ghost given unto us, will more effectually unite, than all the wisdom of the world combined. Endeavor to walk in peace and love with all. Then shall we feel a reviving from the presence of the Lord, and see, flowing to the Lord, weeping penitents, pleading for mercy, and praising aloud for mercy received through our Lord Jesus Christ. Amen.[1]

---

1. Barton W. Stone, the *Christian Messenger,* "Union," August 1831, p. 185.

12

CONCLUSION

SUMMARY OF OUR PROBLEMS

Robert Haldane, a man of Scottish ancestry whose religious thinking exerted an influence on the Campbells prior to their immigration to America, penned a thought in the year 1793 which I believe to be one of the most profound quotes in the English language. He wrote:

> Christianity is everything or nothing. If it be true, it warrants and commands every sacrifice to promote its influence. If it be not, then let us lay aside the hypocrisy of believing it.[1]

Almost two hundred years later, in the year 1987, we in the Churches of Christ seem to be "straddling the fence." We claim to believe that Christianity is true, we certainly dare not

---

1. Robert Haldane, as quoted by Robert Richardson, *Memoirs of Alexander Campbell*, Vol. 1, p. 151.

ENDANGERED HERITAGE

lay it aside, and yet we are obviously not being effective in promoting its influence. None can deny the truth of this most disturbing observation. Our numbers are not increasing, in fact, many reports say that they may be decreasing. We seem to be floundering like a man thrown overboard in a boundless sea. We seem to thrash about, first in one direction then another, perhaps a little evangelism in one area or a little missionary work in another, but never seeming to make any significant, overall, forward progress. If Christianity is really true, and I believe it to be, and if we are really to be counted among our Lord's people, as we claim to be, then we must make whatever sacrifice is necessary to correct this most unfortunate situation.

Approximately two thousand years ago our Lord and Saviour Jesus Christ, beginning with only a small group of twelve good men and true, turned the then known world upside down with the gospel message of salvation. But Satan would not sit quietly by and as the centuries rolled on Christianity became encumbered with the personal opinions and the traditions of men until it scarcely was a shadow of its original form. But then a little less than two hundred years ago another small group of men, not quite so good nor quite so true, but nevertheless fearing God and to the limits of their human abilities proclaiming righteousness in his name, began a concerted effort to restore again that form of Christianity which they found inculcated on the pages of the New Testament. Theirs was not the only effort at reformation, nor the first, but by building upon the Protestant reformations of the preceding two or three hundred years they made what was perhaps up to that time the most comprehensive effort at restoring the Bible as the sole source of Christian authority. Their religious movement wrote, I honestly believe, one of the most significant pages in the annals of human history. Even in a sparsely populated frontier environment, without modern means of travel or communication, both their numbers and their sphere of influence grew at an astounding rate. If their movement could have continued with the momentum of its early

CONCLUSION

years, it might have well shaped the religious future of the entire nation. But once again Satan would not sit idly by. Once again the Devil made use of men who would establish their own opinions and inferences as traditions for the church, and then require agreement by all men as a condition of salvation, to destroy the unity of the Lord's people.

If we really believe in the restoration principle, in the restoration of the ancient order of things, that our rules of faith and duty must be the same as those of the first century Christians, then we must not keep waiting so long to measure our religious traditions against the teachings of the New Testament. We cannot wait another fifteen hundred years for another Martin Luther, or another three hundred more after that for an Alexander Campbell. Christians in each and every generation must measure each and every one of their beliefs and traditions against the teaching of the Bible, not against the teaching of their parents or elders or preachers or college professors or the opinions of the editors of their religious periodicals, but against the teaching of the Holy Scriptures.

And so we must, today, measure all of our doctrine, our teachings and our traditions, against the Word of God. The study described in this document has been an attempt to do just that; to examine 20th century Church of Christ doctrine and to compare it against both the history of our movement and against the teachings of the Bible. Unfortunately our current doctrine does not measure up to the level of either our history or our Bible. We knew ahead of time that we had some problems of some kind because we could observe the symptoms, a lack of growth and a bad reputation. We have many problems, as a religious group, which keep us from being what many of us think the Lord's people should be. Many of these problems are not discussed in this document because they are problems that we share with most of the major contemporary religious groups. These are problems that seem to be related to our society and our culture. A few that quickly come to mind are the low priority that religion seems to get in the lives of most of us, the breakdown of the traditional family unit, a generally low level of respect for law and authority, the wide disparity between what is taught from the pulpit on Sunday morning and what we live throughout the week, etc. These are very real and very serious threats to the kingdom of our Lord, but they are not the subject of our present study. We have looked at problems that are unique to the Church of Christ, those that have caused our somewhat unique problems and have brought to a halt a religious reformation (restoration) movement which could have otherwise continued to be effective and dynamic.

I have identified in this document three serious problems with our contemporary 20th century main line Church of Christ doctrine. This is not a case of points of doctrine which have been slightly misapplied or overemphasized. It is a situation where we have actually taught things which are wrong, which are false, which are very simply not true. The most embarrassing thing of all is that these three false doctrines appear at the very top of the list of items of our unofficial creed. These three false doctrines are listed immediately below:

Number One: "You must be a member of the Church of Christ in order to go to heaven." This is not true. There are Christians, people who will spend eternity in heaven, outside of our group. Some of our preachers nowadays will admit this to be true, but when they describe this "other" Christian who is outside of our group it turns out to be almost a Church of Christ clone who just happens, for some strange reason, to find himself in the wrong organization. That is not what I mean. What I mean is that there are some people in other religious groups who are teaching what we consider to be some doctrinal error and who are practicing some of what we consider to be doctrinal error in their lives, but who are still Christians. These are people who love the Lord, who are completely dedicated to his word, who are to the best of their knowledge and ability doing his will and who will spend eternity with him in heaven, despite

CONCLUSION

their doctrinal errors. I certainly hope that one can still go to heaven if his denomination teaches some false doctrine because we in the Church of Christ have taught some false doctrine, but I, for one, sure do want to go to heaven.

Number two: "You must sing a cappella in the Lord's worship in order to go to heaven," or to use an alternate phrasing, "Instrumental music used in worship is a sin." The position that we have taken on this issue is our most flagrant abuse of methods of Biblical interpretation. We have absolutely no Scriptural basis for our position, and unfortunately everyone realizes this except us. We have taken a personal opinion and tried to make it a condition of salvation, and since this is diametrically opposed to our own oft stated philosophy of Bible interpretation it has undermined our credibility with the rest of the religious community. This has probably turned out to be the one single thing which has been most damaging to our reputation and to our effectiveness in our attempts to spread the gospel.

Number Three: "The Church of Christ is not a denomination." Our careful study of the defined meaning of this word and its commonly accepted usage in the English language has shown beyond any doubt that this claim is absurd. In order to be sure that I had used the proper word in this situation I consulted Webster's Third New International dictionary (unabridged) for the exact definition of the word absurd. It reads as follows: "1: marked by an obvious lack of reason, common sense, proportion, or accord with accepted ideas: ridiculously unreasonable, unsound and incongrous. 2: SELF-CONTRADICTORY: fallacious by reason of contradiction SYN see foolish." It is truly amazing how precisely each part of this definition fits our situation. The wide spread use of terminology which embodies this claim has rendered most of our preaching and our writing unnecessarily offensive to the very people that it was designed to reach and has therefore hindered our efforts to spread the gospel.

Except for these three problems, our doctrine is amazingly reflective of what I believe to be sound New Testament gospel. However, these three problems in combination create a disastrous situation. Less than two hundred years after a major effort at restoring New Testament Christianity, we find ourselves badly divided and again somewhat off course. We must make whatever sacrifice necessary to get back on track. And it may hurt. What we have to sacrifice is our human pride, our arrogant self-righteousness. We, a people who have always claimed to be right on every major issue (perhaps on everything) must admit that we have been wrong. Not that we have a different hermeneutics than someone else, or a different exegesis; we must quit using jargon to mask our mistakes. We must admit that we very simply have been wrong on some things—some things that we have taught as major points of doctrine. We must do this and then we must very humbly ask our Lord and our fellow man to forgive us.

The three problem "issues" which were just discussed are the only major artificial man made walls (made by us) which interfere with the interaction of the main line Church of Christ with the rest of the world. However within the Church of Christ we have some other obstacles to overcome. We mentioned in an earlier chapter three problem "concepts" which have caused most of the problem "issues" within the Churches of Christ. You will recall that these three problem concepts are: First, that the Church of Christ has the perfect doctrine (i.e. that we have perfectly restored the New Testament church). Second, that there is Biblical authority in "silence." And third, that there is Biblical authority in "necessary inference." The second and third of these caused our problem with the use of musical instruments. But some of our more "conservative" brethren in some of the smaller splinter groups within the Church of Christ have extended the sphere of influence of these problem concepts even farther. For the same reason that the overall Church

CONCLUSION

of Christ has prohibited instrumental music (silence and necessary inference) they have prohibited Sunday schools, multiple cups for communion, and many other things. The entire Church of Christ must realize that in applying these problem concepts we have often been inconsistent, have sometimes failed to use good judgment, and have not been forbearing with others. I am surprised that our more conservative brethren have not realized that, in general, as the number of issues to which these problem concepts are misapplied increases, the number of people who go along with it decreases. The splinter groups are all smaller than the main line Church of Christ. This should cause thoughtful and prudent men to become introspective and to reexamine their methods. But to come to the defense of our more conservative brethren for a moment, and to prevent any readers who are members of the main line congregations from assuming any air of superiority, I must make one very interesting observation. The methods of Bible interpretation used by the conservative brethren are certainly more consistent than those used by the main line groups. It is grossly inconsistent to prohibit instrumental music and not to also prohibit all of these other things as well.

CHRISTIAN FORBEARANCE

I believe, as I think most of us believe, that the division and the fighting among those who claim to be Christians has been the single most destructive influence against the cause of Christ. This division is the work of Satan. We loathe this division and we long for the day when perhaps it will end. But we must acknowledge that it exists, that the devil is still and will probably remain active in the hearts of men, that because of his influence this division will probably continue for some time, and that we must therefore function under less than ideal conditions. Denominationalism exists and we are a part of it. We are one of the many existing denominations. If we will quit trying to deny this most obvious fact, our efforts for the cause of Christ will become more effective.

We must be very careful that we aim our weapons at the proper target. We should not condemn denominationalism per se, we should condemn the doctrinal errors which are the cause of it. Denominationalism and the religious freedom which we claim to love in these United States are inseparably connected. If we could pass a law today to end denominationalism it would also put an end to religious freedom, since the law would either end all religion or force everyone to belong to the same denomination (a state controlled church). Thus, to end denominationalism today would at the same time put an end to the Church of Christ. Thus, as long as Satan is active in the world we should thank God for denominationalism (it allows us to preach the truth and thus fight Satan), we should freely admit that we are a denomination, and we should simply strive to be the one that most nearly reflects New Testament Christianity.

But we must proceed carefully here. When we say that we should strive to be the denomination which most nearly reflects New Testament Christianity what we really mean is that we want to be the one that most nearly reflects "our interpretation" of what the New Testament teaches. This is all any man can do. We can never "totally" obey what the BIble teaches; it is impossible. We can only obey some man's interpretation (hopefully our own interpretation) of what the Bible teaches. We are all mortal human beings and all that even the best and most intelligent of us can do with a written page is read it, evaluate it in our mind, and form an opinion (i.e., our interpretation) of the message that the writer intended to convey. Those of us who are Christians will expect to receive aid from the Holy Spirit in our study, but we will still end up with a resultant interpretation from our study. And the Lord will measure us on the judgment day by our interpretation of Scripture, not by someone else's interpretation of Scripture (this is assuming

CONCLUSION

that ours was a serious, dedicated effort to learn the truth). This is a point which has not always been clearly understood, even by some of our best scholars. Some of our ancestors decided that everyone else would be judged by their interpretation of Scripture, and unfortunately we inherited that attitude. It is an obviously false concept, which all of the pioneer preachers that we studied in this document fought against. This concept led to the false conclusion that we are the only people going to heaven. We have shown earlier in this document that this is not sound reasoning. We must admit that we are not the only ones going to heaven, that we are not the only Christians. We must acknowledge that there are Christians in the other denominations. And I don't mean just a few somewhere who are almost like us. What I mean is that we must change our entire approach to this whole thing. We must begin to treat the members of all other denominations as Christians; not as so-called Christians or potential Christians but as real Christians, as people who will go to heaven. They don't have full fellowship with us, because they believe, teach, and practice things with which we don't agree, but they still might go to heaven. They also might not go to heaven, but we are not able to determine that. It is not our job to determine that. We don't have all the data necessary to make that determination. There may also be a lot of people sitting in Church of Christ pews who will not go to heaven. And so we must learn to treat all professing Christians with respect, to assume that they might really be (or might not be) going to heaven, just like the person sitting next to us on Sunday morning might really be (or might not be) going to heaven. We must learn to respect other people's opinions. We must learn to respect and acknowledge the prayers and the worship services of those of other denominations. We should be willing and able, if the appropriate situation arose, to perhaps even worship with friends or associates who are members of another denomination, in their church, even if they do some things with which we disagree. This would not make us guilty of any sin.

They might even reciprocate and visit our church and therefore give us a chance to teach them our interpretation of the Bible.

In order to maintain our own distinctive characteristics (i.e., continue to teach and practice what we believe to be the truth regarding Christian doctrine) and at the same time not fall into the ridiculously arrogant and self-righteous position of claiming that our intelligence and understanding are perfect and that we are the only Christians, we are forced to recognize that there are several spheres of fellowship. I don't think that this is some new abstract theological theory, I think that it is merely an observation of reality, an acknowledge of the existing condition of things. I can identify at least three distinct spheres of fellowship. The first sphere, the innermost sphere, consists of ourselves and those who agree with us to the extent that we can claim full fellowship with them. This includes those in our home congregation and those in all congregations freely and willingly identifying themselves as being a part of the same group, sect, fellowship, brotherhood or denomination. The second sphere includes all of the other Christian denominations. This includes all groups who claim to be Christian, who claim the name of Christ and him crucified, who believe that Jesus Christ is the Son of God and that he died for our sins. We must learn to acknowledge that there may be Christians in all, or at least most of these groups. There might be some fringe groups of whom we could say, with all propriety, that we don't see how there could be any Christians among their numbers. But for the most part we must learn to treat all men who claim the name of Christ with the courtesy and respect due to a brother in Christ. We don't have to accept them as a part of our congregation (while they maintain their different opinions and practices) and we would probably not be comfortable in theirs (even if they would accept us, which in many cases they would not) but we must treat them as Christians. The third sphere encompasses everyone else in the world, all who are clearly non-Christian.

CONCLUSION

By assuming an attitude of toleration and forbearance, admitting that there are Christians in the other denominations, we gain many positive benefits. We keep the lines of communication open with all men. We have a much better chance of correcting errors in the doctrines of other people because they will listen to us when we talk. They will listen to us even if they disagree with us because we have not made them mad at us ahead of time by some arrogant and self-righteous reproach. Also, over a long period of time, we avoid accumulating an overall bad reputation. This helps keep our efforts at spreading the truth much more effective both among the other denominations and among the non-Christians.

If you happen to be a member of the Church of Christ who has a problem with this attitude of toleration, try approaching the issue from the opposite perspective for a moment. What if we in the Church of Christ were, actually, absolutely the only Christians? How would this help us? What benefit would we accrue from this? Let's examine this for a moment. Would it make heaven sweeter for us? Would it place more stars in our crown in heaven? Would it give us a seat closer to the right hand of God? There is nothing in the Scriptures to indicate that heaven will be in danger of becoming overcrowded or run short on supplies, real estate or fringe benefits. Would it make hell any less hot for us in case we ourselves should fall from grace? There is certainly nothing to suggest this either. Would it somehow make it easier for us personally to get to heaven? I see no connection here. Would it make it easier to convert people to the Church of Christ fold? This item we need to look at carefully. Some in the last century seemed to think that this was true. They seemed to think that they could scare people into joining their group. They seemed to think that, if they admitted the bare possibility of any being Christians who were outside of their group, it would detract from their efforts at reformation. There are discussions of this idea in the early literature. History shows us that the opposite, in fact, turned out to be true. By assuming an exclusivistic, arrogant, self-righteous attitude (by saying that everyone else is going to hell) they acquired, over a period of time, such a bad reputation that the reputation in the long run had a crippling effect on Church of Christ evangelistic efforts. The only help that I can see that is provided by the exclusivistic attitude is that it aids and abets those human tendencies within men to be proud, arrogant and haughty, all traits which are contrary to the spirit of Christ. Thus Satan seems to be the only one who benefits from this type of attitude.

WHERE DO WE GO FROM HERE?

What area of ministry deserves the most attention for those of us within the Churches of Christ today? In what area can we expend our efforts so as to derive the maximum benefits for the cause of Christ? Is it in deciding which to expand, overseas missions or local evangelism? Is it in embarking on an ambitious building program or in emphasizing house churches and home Bible studies? Is it in emphasizing programs for the youth, for young marrieds, for single adults or for our senior citizens? Is it in deciding whether to add more paid professionals to our church staff or in utilizing more volunteer efforts from our members? Is it in more preaching of first principles or in expounding on psychology, personal motivation and the power of positive thinking? Is it in deciding whether to put the most effort on one-on-one personal evangelism, on our congregational preaching and Bible classes, or on radio and television evangelism?

In other times and under other circumstances it might be difficult to decide where to place our most emphasis, but for us within the Churches of Christ today there is no decision to be made; the answer is clear. Our efforts in all of the areas mentioned above, and our efforts in other important areas, are being severely hindered by the reputation that has been created by our attitudes over the last one hundred years. Our major

CONCLUSION

emphasis, for a time, must be an effort to correct these problems so that our efforts for the cause of Christ can once again be highly effective. Specifically we must address the three problem issues and the three problem concepts which have been discussed in this document. Regarding the three problem issues we must admit that:

1. There are Christians outside of the Church of Christ.
2. We have been wrong in our stand against instrumental music in worship.
3. The Churches of Christ, as our congregations collectively are called, constitute a religious denomination, based upon the commonly accepted current usage of the word in the English language.

Also, in order to avoid these kinds of problem issues, and others in the future, we must correct our teaching on the three problem concepts. We must understand that:

1. The Church of Christ does not have the "perfect" doctrine. No one is perfect in their understanding of the Bible. We have tried to restore the New Testament church but we have not "perfectly" restored it.
2. We must be consistent in our application of, and use good judgment when dealing with, the silence of the Scriptures.
3. We must exercise forbearance and use good judgment when dealing with inferences which we deduce from Scriptural teaching.

We must address these topics in our personal Bible study. We must recognize once again, as the pioneer preachers of our restoration movement taught, that each individual is responsible for his own interpretation of Scripture. We must address these topics in our congregational Bible classes. We must teach them from the pulpits on Sunday morning and Sunday night. We must lecture on them and study them in lectureships, workshops and seminars. We must teach the truth on these topics to our young students on our Christian college campuses. It will take some time, and it won't necessarily be easy, but with the help of our Lord, and his Holy Spirit given to us as Christians for our comfort and aid, it is possible. It is possible because the Lord is on our side. He is on our side because we, like the pioneer preachers of our own restoration movement over one hundred and fifty years ago, are making an honest, conscientious effort to reject the traditions of men and to return to the Bible as our only source of authority in religion. It has taken us over a hundred years to get into the situation that we are in right now. It may take a decade of concentrated effort to get us out of it, but the rewards in our personal lives, in the lives of our families, and for the glorious cause of our Lord and Saviour Jesus Christ will make it all worthwhile, many times over.

At this point I would like to anticipate an objection which will be offered to this document by some who are currently in positions of leadership within the Church of Christ. Many will admit that the positions defended in the document on the major issues are true (most will sooner or later be forced to make this acknowledgment); however, some will say that the document is divisive. They will say, for instance, that since instrumental music is such an intensely emotional issue we must not break the silence regarding the error of our position on this issue. This represents a very unique and interesting kind of logic and deserves a careful examination.

Those who subscribe to this kind of reasoning will say that change is already in the wind and that we must not proceed too hastily, lest we divide the brotherhood. They will say that we must continue to "speak in thought provoking ways" (not clearly and directly as this document attempts to do) and "let truth slowly take its course." Would these same men, had they lived in the early 1800s, have told Alexander Campbell, Barton W. Stone and Walter Scott not to speak out against infant baptism and sprinkling or not to speak in favor of baptism of

CONCLUSION

believers for the forgiveness of sins and the weekly observance of the Lord's supper; because, all of these positions were intensely emotional issues and involved a risk of dividing the existing brotherhoods? Would they have advised these men to "speak in thought provoking ways" (not clearly and directly) and "let truth slowly take its course"? Would these men also have advised such great reformers as John Huss, Martin Luther and Huldreich Zwingli not to speak out openly and clearly against certain teachings of the Catholic Church; because, the things they taught were certainly divisive and ran the risk of dividing the contemporary Christian brotherhood? If this kind of thinking had prevailed throughout the ages there never would have been a Protestant Reformation, there never would have been a Stone-Campbell restoration movement, and therefore there would not be anything resembling the Church of Christ as we know it today.

As interesting as these parallels might appear I do not want to dwell on them at any great length, for one very basic reason. I do not believe that the positions taken in this document are divisive at all. In fact, in the final analysis they will be conciliatory and healing, rather than divisive. They will appear divisive in the beginning to a small group that is solidly devoted to some of the problem issues. However, in the long run, many who previously have been driven from our numbers will return, many new people will be attracted because of our more Christ-like attitudes, and a phenomenal growth in our numbers will result. What may appear to some, in the beginning, to be painful and divisive will, in fact, be healing and constructive in the long run. What all within the Church of Christ must realize is that what is actually divisive is the attitude of the sectarian spokesman who make schismatic statements such as to claim that the use of instrumental music in worship is sinful, or that none outside of the Church of Christ have any hope of salvation.

I would like to suggest another equally interesting possibility. Could it be that what is also divisive, in relation to the overall body of Christ, is the silence of those leaders among us who realize that error is being taught, but who refuse to lift a voice against it? Could it be that to remain silent, and to rationalize this behavior for whatever reason, is to be an accomplice, an accessory to this transgression?

It is truly amazing that a situation has evolved within our brotherhood wherein it is considered by some to be divisive to speak the truth. We truly should be ashamed at this situation. We are the very ones who have insisted that those of all other denominations accept the truth as we see it at all costs. We have insisted that truth is important above all things. We have insisted that others reject their previous religious associations, even friends and family, if any of these stand in the way of truth. But now the shoe is on the other foot; and some dare to suggest that the whole truth should not be spoken, because it might be a little embarrassing, or slightly painful, or might be considered divisive in some quarters. May the Lord be merciful.

But that is enough space devoted to those who would discourage our efforts to further the cause of Jesus Christ. The message that I wish to convey to the members of the Church of Christ through the pages of this document is one of hope, of optimism and of encouragement for a glorious future in service to our Lord. I believe that if we consider the general membership in the Church of Christ, many are hungering for a more open and objective approach to Bible study. Many will agree immediately with this document on every point, and be thankful that someone has at last expressed, on paper, concerns which they themselves have had for many years. For many others, some of these concepts will be new because our Church of Christ Bible study classes have not been characterized by this kind of objective examination of the issues. After having time to study and evaluate these issues for themselves, a large percentage of this second group will be thankful for the new freedom of thought.

CONCLUSION

The time has come for a turn of events in the life of the Church of Christ. This document is my offering to the cause of truth in Christ Jesus. I believe that the time is ripe for such a work and that it will be greeted with eagerness by a host of our people. It may not so much shape the thinking of our people as it will reflect their own thinking and provide a medium through which they can evaluate and discuss concerns which they have had for many years. It has been my goal to prepare a document suitable for circulation among, and study by, all members of the Church of Christ. If we, as a people, can come to grips with our problems in these few areas, we will experience a growth beyond our wildest imagination. Our basic Christian doctrine is sound and true. We have avoided most of the doctrinal errors that have plagued the religious world. We cherish in our bosom a message for which millions are searching. But we often have hidden the truth behind some artificial walls which have obscured the precious story of our Saviour's sacrifice for mankind. We have made it unnecessarily hard for men to accept the truth. If we can remove these barriers, if we can once again release the power of the gospel to save men's souls, we will have multitudes of penitent sinners beating down our doors in search of that old and beautiful story of eternal salvation through Jesus Christ our Lord.

May God bless our continuing efforts to be His people, to teach only His truth, to reflect His image in our lives and to bring the gospel message of salvation to a lost and dying world.

BIBLIOGRAPHY

Bales, James. D., *Instrumental Music and New Testament Worship*, copyright 1973, Searcy, Arkansas 72143.

Bales, James D., *The Holy Spirit and the Christian*, copyright 1966 by Gussie Lambert; Lambert Book House, Box 4007, Shreveport, Louisiana 71104.

Boles, H. Leo, *The Holy Spirit*, copyright 1942 by Gospel Advocate Company, Nashville, Tennessee.

Bruner, Frederick Dale, *A Theology of the Holy Spirit*, copyright 1970 by William B. Eerdmans/Publisher, Grand Rapids, Michigan.

Campbell, Alexander, editor, *Millennial Harbinger;* published monthly from 1830-1870, reprinted in a forty-one volume set by College Press, Box 1132, Joplin, Missouri 64801, in 1976.

Campbell, Alexander, editor, the *Christian Baptist;* published monthly from Aug. 1823 to July, 1830. An original copy of the D.S. Burnet Revised Edition, published in 1835, was obtained for this study.

The *Christian Baptist* was reprinted in seven volumes by the Gospel Advocate Company, Nashville, Tenn. in 1955-56.

The *Christian Baptist* was most recently reprinted in a single volume, a copy of the 1835 D.S. Burnet Revised Edition, by the College Press Publishing Co., Inc., Box 1132, Joplin, Missouri 64801, in 1983.

Campbell, Alexander, *The Christian System*, written 1835; reprinted by Gospel Advocate Company, Nashville, Tenn. 1980.

Campbell, Alexander, compiler, *The Living Oracles*, 1826; reprinted by Gospel Advocate Company, Nashville, Tennessee, 1974.

Campbell/Owen Debate, 1829; reprinted by McQuiddy Printing Company, 1957.

Campbell/Purcell Debate, published 1837; reprinted by McQuiddy Printing Company, Nashville, Tenn. 1914.

Campbell/Rice Debate, published 1844; reprinted by Religious Book Service, 722 North Payton Road, Indianapolis, Indiana 46219.

Campbell, Thomas and Acheson, Thomas, Declaration and Address, first published in 1809 at Washington, Pennsylvania. My source was the third printing by Mission Messenger, 139 Signal Hill Drive, St. Louis, Missouri, 1978. This document also contains The Last Will and Testament of the Springfield Presbytery by Barton W. Stone and others, written in Cane-Ridge Kentucky on June 28th, 1804.

Cox, John D., *Church History*, copyright 1951 by Dehoff Publications, Murfreesboro, Tenn. Printed 1980.

Ferguson, Everett, *Church History, Early and Medieval*, Second edition, copyright 1966 by Biblical Research Press, 774 East North 15th Street, Abilene, Texas 79601.

Ferguson, Everett, *A Cappella Music,* Abilene: Biblical Research Press, copyright 1972.

Ferguson, Everett, *Church History, Reformation and Modern,* Second edition, copyright 1967 by Biblical Research Press, 774 East North 15th Street, Abilene, Texas 79601.

Garrett, Leroy, *The Stone-Campbell Movement,* copyright 1981 by College Press Publishing Company, Box 1132, Joplin, Missouri 64802.

Grimm, Hans, *Tradition and History of the Early Churches of Christ in Central Europe,* Firm Foundation Publishing House, P.O. Box 610, Austin, Texas 78767.

Hadwin, M.R., *The Role of New Testament Examples as Related to Biblical Authority,* copyright 1974, Firm Foundation Publishing House, Box 610, Austin, Texas 78767.

Hailey, Homer, *Attitudes and Consequences,* my copy dated 1975, Cogdill Foundation Publications, P.O. Box 403, Marion, Indiana 46052. Authors preface dated Oct. 18, 1945.

Hayden, A.S., *A History of the Disciples on the Western Reserve,* written approx. 1871; reprinted by Religious Book Service, 722 North Payton Road, Indianapolis, Indiana 46219.

Humble, B.J., *The Story of the Restoration,* copyright 1969 by Firm Foundation Publishing House, Box 610, Austin, Texas 78767.

Kurfees, M.C., *Instrumental Music in the Worship,* Nashville: Gospel Advocate Co. (Author's preface dated 1911, my copy dated 1975).

Lard, Moses E., *Commentary on Romans,* written 1875; reprinted by Gospel Light Publishing Company, Delight, Arkansas.

Lard, Moses E., editor, *Lard's Quarterly,* Vol. I, original publishing date 1864; reprinted by The Old Paths Book Club, Box V, Rosemead, Calif., second printing 1952.

MacArthur, John F. Jr., *The Charismatics,* copyright 1980; published by Zondervan Publishing House, Grand Rapids, Michigan 49506.

MacClenny, W.E., *The Life of Rev. James O'Kelly,* written 1910; reprinted by Religious Book Service, 722 North Payton Road, Indianapolis, Indiana 46219.

Mathes, Elder James M., *Works of Elder B.W. Stone,* second edition 1859; reprinted by The Old Paths Book Club, Box V, Rosemead, Calif., 1953.

Mattox, F.W., *The Eternal Kingdom,* copyright 1961 by Gospel Light Publishing Company, Delight, Arkansas.

Morrison, Matthew C., *Like a Lion* (Daniel Sommer's Seventy Years of Preaching), Dehoff Publications, Murfreesboro, Tennessee 37130, Copyright 1975.

Richardson, Robert, *Memoirs of Alexander Campbell,* 1897, reprinted by Religious Book Service, 722 N. Payton Road, Indianapolis, Indiana 46219.

BIBLIOGRAPHY

Scott, Walter, *The Evangelist,* in ten volumes dated 1832-1842; reprinted by College Press Publishing Company, Box 1132, Joplin, Missouri 64802.

Shelly, Rubel, *I Just Want to Be a Christian,* copyright 1984 by Rubel Shelly; 20th Century Christian, 2809 Granny White Pike, Nashville, Tennessee 37204.

Stevenson, Dwight E., *Voice of the Golden Oracle* (a biography of Walter Scott), written in 1946; College Press Publishing Company, Box 1132, Joplin, Missouri 64802.

Stone, Barton W., the *Christian Messenger,* in fourteen volumes dated 1826-1844; reprinted 1978, Star Bible & Tract Corp., Fort Worth, Texas 76118.

Stone, Barton W., *A Short History of the Life of Barton W. Stone*; reprinted in the Cane Ridge Reader, Cane Ridge, Kentucky, July 6, 1972.

Warren, Thomas B., *Christians Only-and the Only Christians,* copyright 1984 by National Christian Press, Inc., P.O. Box 1001, Jonesboro, Arkansas 72401.

Warren, Thomas B., *335 Crucial Questions on Christian Unity,* copyright 1984 by National Christian Press, Inc., P.O. Box 1001, Jonesboro, Arkansas 72401.

West, Earl Irvin, *Elder Ben Franklin: Eye of the Storm,* Religious Book Service, 722 N. Payton Rd., Indianapolis, Indiana 46219, 1983.

West, Earl, *The Search for the Ancient Order,* Vol. 1; Gospel Advocate Company, Nashville, Tennessee.

West, Earl, *The Search for the Ancient Order,* Vol. 2; copyright 1950, Religious Book Service, 722 N. Payton Rd., Indianapolis, Indiana.

West, Earl, *The Search for the Ancient Order,* Vol. 3; 1979, Religious Book Service, 722 N. Payton Rd., Indianapolis, Indiana 46219.

ADDITIONAL RELATED LITERATURE

The following books were acquired for my personal library during and as a direct result of my study of restoration history. They are not included in the Bibliography because they were not involved in the development of this document. However I remember only too vividly the difficulty I experienced in the early part of my study in trying to identify the books which were available on Church of Christ history or indeed on the history of Christianity in general. For this reason I am including this additional list. I hope that this information will be of some benefit to other students of our Christian heritage.

Campbell, Alexander, *Family Culture,* first printing 1850; reprinted by College Press Publishing Company, Box 1132, Joplin, Missouri 64802.

ENDANGERED HERITAGE

Campbell, Alexander, at Glasgow University, 1808-1809, transcribed by Lester G. McAllister, copyright 1971 by Christian Theological Seminary. Published by Disciples of Christ Historical Society, Nashville, Tenn., 1971.

Donan, P., *Life of Jacob Creath, Jr.,* published by Religious Book Service, 722 N. Payton Rd., Indianapolis, Indiana 46219.

Dungan, D.R., *Hermeneutics,* Gospel Light Publishing Company, Delight, Arkansas.

Errett, Isaac, *Elements of the Gospel and Letters to a Young Christian,* published in 1869; Reprinted by College Press, Box 1132, Joplin, Missouri 64802.

Foxe, John, *Foxe's Book of Martyrs,* Whitaker Houst, Pittsburgh and Colfax Streets, Springdale, Pennsylvania 15144.

Hawley, Monroe, *The Focus of our Faith,* copyright 1985 by 20th Century Christian, 2809 Granny White Pike, Nashville, Tenn. 37204.

Josephus, *Josephus Complete Works,* translated by William Whiston, A.M., Grand Rapids, Kregel Publications.

McMillon, Lynn A., *Restoration Roots,* copyright 1983; published by Gospel Teachers Publications, Inc., P.O. Box 210888, Dallas, Texas 75211.

Milligan, Robert, *The Great Commission,* published 1873; reprinted by College Press, Box 1132, Joplin, Missouri 64802.

Roberts, Lawrence H., *Trials and Triumphs,* copyright 1975; printed by Gospel Light Publishing Company, Delight, Arkansas.

Schaff, Philip, *History of the Christian Church;* This is an eight volume set tracing the history of Christianity from apostolic times through the German and Swiss reformations; Eerdmans Publishing Company, Grand Rapids, Michigan.

Wallace, Foy E. Jr., *The Instrumental Music Question,* copyright 1980 by Foy E. Wallace Jr. Publications, P.O. Box 7410, Fort Worth, Texas 76111.

West, Earl Irvin, *The Life and Times of David Lipscomb,* copyright 1954; Religous Book Service, 722 North Payton Road, Indianapolis, Indiana 46219.

Williams, John A., *Life of Elder John Smith,* copyright 1870; Reprinted by Religious Book Service, 722 North Payton Road, Indianapolis, Indiana 46219.

The Ante-Nicene Fathers. This is a ten volume set of the writings of the uninspired church fathers who wrote prior to the Nicene council of 325 A.D., Eerdmans Publishing Company, Grand Rapids, Michigan.

Volume I of, *The Nicene and Post-Nicene Fathers,* the writings of Eusebius; Eerdmans Pubishing Company, Grand Rapids, Michigan.

The Apostolic Fathers, Volumes I & II, translated by Kirsopp Lake, the Loeb Classical Library, Harvard University Press, Cambridge, Mass.

BIBLIOGRAPHY

The Christian Preacher's Companion by Alexander Campbell and *Christian Evidences* by James Challen; reprinted by College Press Publishing Company, Box 1132, Joplin, Missouri 64802. The Christian Preacher's Companion is also reprinted by Lambert Book House, Box 4007, Shreveport, Louisina 71104.

A Brief Treatise on Prayer, by R. Milligan 1883 and *Communings in the Sanctuary,* by R. Richardson 1888; reprinted by College Press, Box 1132, Joplin, Missouri 64802.

Autobiography of Elder Samuel Rogers, edited by his son, Elder John I. Rogers, copyright 1909 and *Where the Long Trail Begins,* by S.S. Lappin, copyright 1913; reprinted by College Press, Box 1132, Joplin, Missouri 64802.

Index

A Cappella 32, 33 (Chapter Eight; 125-162), 245
Adopted 86
A History of the Disciples on the Western Reserve, by A. S. Hayden 55
"A Letter Concerning Toleration," by John Locke 139, 140
Alters, Abraham 46, 136
American Christian Bible Society 61
American Christian Missionary Society 61, 62
"An Address and Declaration," from Sand Creek, Illinois 62
"Ancient Gospel," by A. Campbell 55, 56
"AND" Theology 83
"Anecdotes, Incidents and Facts No. 1," by A. Campbell 142
Antioch 41
"Any Christians among Protestant Parties," First Lunenburg Letter, by A. Campbell 195-199
"Any Christians Among the Sects?" Third Lunenburg Letter, by A. Campbell 201-204
Apostasy 215
Approved Example - see Example
"A Restoration of the Ancient Order of Things":
  No. VII, "On the Breaking of Bread - No. II" 101-106, 142-143
  No. VIII, "On the Breaking of Bread - No. III" 107-110
  No. XXVIII, "On the Discipline of the Church - No. V" 132-133
  No. XI 189
A Short History of the Life of Barton W. Stone, Autobiography 39, 40, 41, 42, 43, 44, 45, 184-185
Asbury, Francis 37

Associate Synod of North America 46
Atheist 52, 230
Atonement 125, 165
Attitudes and Consequences, by Homer Hailey 61
Auricular Confession 148
Authority - see Biblical Authority
Authority of(in) Silence - see Silence
Autonomous - see Congregational Autonomy

Babylon 202, 205, 206, 215
"Back to the Bible for it All," hymn 17
Baptism - see Baptize
Baptism for the Forgiveness of Sins (Remission of Sins) 44, 52, 57, 58, 65, (Chapter Four; 73-92), 125, 126, 130, 174, 175, 177, 185, 191, 192, 221, 225, 226, 254-255
Baptism of the Holy Spirit 67, 118
Baptist 38, 40, 50, 51, 52, 54, 56, 101, 190, 191, 192, 193, 194, 196, 206, 215
Baptisteries 60
Baptists, Regular 56
Baptize, Baptized, Baptism 32, 33, 34, 43, 44, 49, 50, 52, 54, 55, 56, 57, 58, 67, 72, (Chapter Four; 73-92), 92), 102, 118, 161, 165, 174, 177, 178, 182, 187, 188, 191, 192, 193, 195, 197, 199, 200, 201, 202, 204, 205, 206, 207, 208, 214, 216, 217, 218, 220, 221, 223, 226, 227, 232
Bentley, Adamson 54, 55
Biblical Authority 134, 139, 140, 141, 145, 147, 150, 163
Big Four 54, 177
Blood of Christ 74, 76, 77, 78, 79, 87, 88, 90, 91, 92, 101
Blood of Goats and Bulls 75, 76
Blueprint 129, 130
Braceville 54

265

Break Bread, Breaking Bread, Breaking of Bread   96, 98, 99, 101, 102, 104, 106, 107, 108, 109, 110, 111, 112, 113, 114
Brewer, G. C.   64
"Bro. Hayden on Expediency and Progress," by J. W. McGarvey   60
Brush Run Church   49, 50, 51, 187, 188, 227
Buried   80
Burnet, D. S.   61
Burning of Incense   148

Caldwell, Dr. David   38
Calvin, John   36
Calvinism   39, 40, 41, 57
Campbell, Alexander   11, 22, 23, 24, 26, 44, 45, 46, 47, 48, 50, 51, 52, 53, 54, 55, 56, 58, 61, 84-92, 100, 101-106, 107-110, 111, 130-132, 133, 136, 139, 142, 143, 144, 148, 177, 178, 182-183, 186, 188-189, 190, 192, 193, 194, 194-204, 206, 208, 210, 217, 222-227, 228, 229, 239, 243, 254
Campbell, A. W.   53
Campbell, Thomas   24, 25, 26, 45, 46, 47, 48, 50, 54, 58, 135, 136, 137, 139, 140-141, 143-144, 146, 150, 157-158, 161-162, 177, 180-181, 185-186, 186-188, 206, 217
Campbellites   26, 184
Cane Ridge Kentucky   39, 40
Cardinal Principles of the Christian Church   37
Catholic Church (Roman)   18, 19, 22, 36, 66, 74, 75, 163, 229
Catholicism   74
Charismatic   67, 118
Choirs   152
Christendom   51, 57, 75, 95, 99, 100, 158, 161, 235

Christian Baptist   22, 23, 52, 53, 54, 55, 56, 101-106, 107-110, 130-132, 132-133, 142-143, 188-189, 190, 209, 222-225
Christian Church (Disciples of Christ)   10, 62, 63, 64, 68
Christian Fellowship - see Fellowship
Christian Messenger   44, 111-115, 178, 192, 213-221, 239-240
"Christians Among the Sects," Second Lunenburg Letter, by A. Campbell   199-201
Christians in Error   207, 231-232
Christians Par Excellence   208
Christians Simply   37
Christlike Character, Life   38, 66, 74, 179, 231, 237, 239
Circumcision, Circumcised   80, 200, 202, 207
Civil War   27, 28, 61, 62
Clergy   19, 49, 66, 118
Co-editors, of *Millennial Harbinger*   53
Comforter   67
Command   101, 110, 112, 128, 132, 133, 138, 139, 140, 141, 142, 143, 145, 149, 150, 152, 179, 180, 185, 236
"Communion With the 'Sects'," by Geo. W. Elley   204
Confession   74, 193
Congregational Autonomy   65, 118, 163, 165, 167
Congregational Singing   151, 152, 153, 154, 158, 160
Constantinople   210
Contribution   98
"Co-operation," by A. Campbell   133
Corporate Worship   94, 129
Covenants, Old and New   75, 76, 77, 217

Creath, Jacob Jr.   62
Creed   37, 41, 66, 186, 210, 217, 244
Custom   89

Dancing   60, 145
David Lipscomb College   63
Debates - Alexander Campbell   51
  1. John Walker   51, 52
  2. Mr. McCalla   52
  3. Robert Owen   52
  4. Bishop Purcell   52
  5. N. L. Rice   52
"Declaration and Address"   24, 25, 48, 49, 58, 137, 140-141, 142, 143-144, 146, 157-158, 161-162, 180-181, 185-186
Definite Article   105
Definition of a Christian   177-179
Denomination   25, 32, 33, 36, 40, 46, 61, 64, 66, 96, 130, 159, (Chapter Nine; 163-171), 183, 185, 186, 190, 191, 194, 208, 210, 228, 229, 231, 232, 239, 245, 248, 249, 250, 251, 253, 256
Denominationalism (Chapter Nine; 163-171), 208, 247, 248
Dictionary(ies)   166-168
Disciples   41, 64, 68, 217, 219
Disciples of Christ   27, 62, 63, 64, 65
Disfellowship   63
Divisions   59
Divisive   151, 254, 255, 256
Doctrine   102, 104, 112
"Do the Unimmersed Commune?" by Moses E. Lard   211-213
Dunlavy, John   41, 43

Ecclesiastical Organizations   66, 118, 147
Edinburgh University, Scotland   54
Editors   59, 60, 62, 63, 243
Election   39

Elley, Geo. W.   204, 209
English Baptists   211
Errett, Isaac   53, 62, 204-209, 211
Eternal Life   55, 56, 58, 66, 77, 82, 117, 140
Euphemisms   169
Evangelist upon the Western Reserve   54
Example   101, 105, 110, 111, 128, 129, 132, 139, 141, 142, 143, 145, 149, 152, 185, 236
Exclusivism, Exclusiveness, Exclusivistic   175, 205, 208, 212, 213, 252
Exegesis   246
Expiation   74, 117, 176
Explicit Command - see Command
Express Command - see Command
Express Terms - see Command
External Conversion   85
Extra No. I, by A. Campbell   84-92, 199, 225-227
Extra No. II, by A. Campbell   110-111

Faith   55, 56, 57, 66, 67, 74, 75, 80, 83, 86, 87, 88, 90, 91, 92, 117, 118, 147, 156, 161, 179, 180-181, 182, 186, 193, 201, 216, 217, 226, 239
Faith Healing   67, 118
Fasting   75
Fellowship   45, 63, 73, 79, 84, 98, 99, 102, 104, 112, 118, 124, 126, 130, 144, 151, 160, 184, 186, 188, 204, 205, 207, 208, 212, 214, 216, 217, 218, 219, 224, 227, 230, 249, 250
Fellowship, Spheres of - see Spheres of Fellowship
Figurative   89, 90
First Day of the Week - see Lord's Day
First Generation   141, 144, 145, 146, 177, 183

Five Steps (of the gospel) - also see Six Steps   55, 56, 57
Forbearance   42, 43, 47, 48, 50, 60, 138, 146, 156, 181, 183, 191, 215, 222, 223, 224, 247, 251, 253
Foreign Christian Missionary Society   62
Forgiveness   57, 87, 88
Forgiveness of Sins (also see Remission of Sins)   50, 56, 57, 67, (Chapter Four; 73-92), 118, 130, 161, 177, 178, 229
Forrester, George   54
Franklin, Benjamin   60, 61, 62, 63, 145, 208

Gano, John Allen   111-115
Georgetown, Kentucky   44, 58
Get Religion   39, 57
Gift of the Holy Spirit   56, 81, 217, 221
Gospel Advocate   63
Grace   67, 74, 82, 83, 87, 88, 91, 92, 117, 176, 210, 232, 251
Greek Lexicons   149, 150

Hafferty, Rev. Mr.   37
Haggard, Rev. Rice   37, 38, 41
Hailey, Homer   61
Haldane, Robert   241
Haldanians   132
Hamilton Seminary   190
Hardeman, N. B.   64
Hayden, A. S.   55
Hebrews, Chapter Nine   76
Hermeneutics   246
Holy Spirit   39, 40, 41, 42, 43, 44, 55, 56, 57, 66, 67, 76, 81, 82, 87, 89, 101, 104, 118, 131, 139, 140, 165, 182, 192, 196, 206, 217, 221, 222, 248, 254
Howland   54

Humble, Bill   61, 62, 63, 64
Huss, John   255

Immersed   43, 50, (Chapter Four; 73-92), 175, 187, 198, 199, 200, 202, 205, 207, 212, 215, 216, 218, 219, 220, 223, 228, 229
Immersion   43, 47, 49, 50, 55, 56, 57, 64, 67, (Chapter Four; 73-92), 118, 130, 177, 178, 191, 192, 196, 197, 198, 199, 203, 207, 212, 214, 216, 219, 220, 229
Independent Christian Church   10, 27, 65
Independent Churches in Scotland   49
Infant Baptism   43, 47, 49, 50, 101, 147, 151, 207, 223, 254
Inference   98, 124, 129, 138, 143, 144, 153, 160, 181, 230, 243, 253
Instrumental Music   60, 61, 62, 63, 65, (Chapter Eight; 125-162), 194, 229, 253, 254, 255
"Instrumental Music in Churches," by J. W. McGarvey   60
"Instrumental Music in Churches and Dancing," by Moses E. Lard   60
Instrumental Music in the Worship, by M. C. Kurfees   149
Instruments   33, (Chapter Eight; 125-162)
Ireland   45
Itinerate Preacher   54

Jerusalem   184, 206
Jewish Sabbath - see Sabbath, Jewish
Johnson, John T.   44
Jones, Abner   38
Jones, W. (of London)   210, 211
Josephus   20
Judge   155-158, 180-181, 230, 232, 249

INDEX

Judging 155-158, 177, 228
Judgment (as in Judging) 155-158, 176, 180-181, 207, 247, 253
Judgment (Day) 77, 232, 248
Justification 87, 88, 179, 217
Justified 78, 86

Kingdom of Christ 75, 158
Kurfees, M. C. 149, 150

Laity 19, 118, 161
Landmark Baptists 205
Lard, Moses E. 60, 63, 145, 151, 159, 211-213, 229
Lard's Quarterly
  "Instrumental Music in Churches and Dancing" 60, 145
  "Do the Unimmersed Commune?" 211-213
Last Supper 96
Law of Moses 75, 76, 77
Lebanon Church, Surry County 37
"Letter to Bishop Semple. - No. I," by A. Campbell 190
Levitical Priests 75
Lexington Kentucky 58
Lighting of Candles 148
Like a Lion, by Matthew C. Morrison 62, 63
Like Kind 149
Lipscomb, David 63
Liturgy 129, 131, 132
Located Preachers 60, 139
Locke, John 139, 140
Logan County Kentucky 40
Loos, C. L. 53
Lord's Day 66, 93, 94, 95, 96, 99, 101, 104, 109, 110, 111, 113, 114, 117, 130, 143
Lord's Supper 32, 33, 34, 49, 64, 66, 72, (Chapter Five; 93-115), 117, 125, 130, 131, 133, 153, 165, 174, 188, 209, 211, 220, 228, 229

Louisville Plan 62
"Lunenburg Letters," by A. Campbell 194-204
  First Letter: "Any Christians among Protestant Parties" 195-199
  Second Letter: "Christians Among the Sects" 199-201
  Third Letter: "Any Christians Among the Sects?" [excerpts only] 201-204
Luse, Matthias 36, 50
Luther, Martin 212, 243, 255

MacClenny, W. E. 37
Magna Carta 24
Mahoning Baptist Association 51, 54
Marshall, Robert 41, 43
Martyrs 24
McCalla 52
McGarvey, J. W. 60, 63, 145
McGready, James 38
McNemar, Richard 41, 43
Memoirs of Alexander Campbell 22, 38, 46, 47, 49, 51, 52, 53, 55, 136, 137, 148, 178-179, 182-183, 186-188, 192, 193, 194, 227, 241
Mercy 156, 157, 215, 216, 232, 240
Methodist 37, 40
Methodists General Conference in Baltimore in 1792 37
Midway, Kentucky 61
Millennial Harbinger 24, 53, 60, 84-92, 133, 139-140, 142, 144, 145, 178, 183, 192, 194-204, 204-211, 213, 225-227
Milligan, R. 53
Missionary Societies 60, 61, 63
Modern Biblical Criticism 64
Moore, W. T. 62
Morrison, Matthew C. 62, 63
Mourners Bench 43
Mutliple Cups (for Communion) 60, 64, 134, 229, 247

Munro, Andrew 47
Musical Instruments 61, (Chapter Eight; 125-162)

Nashville Bible College 63
Naturalization 222
"Nature of the Christian Organization," by A. Campbell 24
Necessary Inference 123, 128, 129, 138, 139, 141, 145, 146, 147, 246, 247
New Lisbon 57
Non-cooperation 64
North American Christian Convention 65

O'Kelly, James 37
Old Landmark Baptists - see Landmark Baptists
One Cup - see Multiple Cups
"On the Breaking of Bread - No. II," by A. Campbell 101-106
"On the Breaking of Bread - No. III," by A. Campbell 107-110
"On the Discipline of the Church No. V," by A Campbell 132-133
Open Communion 60, 211
Open Membership 64
Opinion 179-183
"Opinion," by Barton W. Stone 213-216
Opinionists 214
"OR" Theology 83
Original Sin 74
Osborne, Jacob 54
"Our Position to American Slavery, No. V," by A. Campbell 144
Owen, Robert 52

Pardoned 86
Paris, Kentucky 58
Passover 96, 97, 208
Pattern 129, 130

Pedobaptist(s) 196, 204, 206, 211, 227
Pendleton, W. K. 53, 61, 204, 209-211, 212
Pentecost 86, 102, 104, 112, 153, 220, 222
Pentecostal 67, 118
Pew Renting 60, 145
Philip (pen name for Walter Scott) 54
Philip (and the Eunuch) 81
Pinkerton, L. L. 61
Pouring 81, 214
Prayer 67, 98, 99, 102, 104, 112, 118, 130, 207
Precedent(s) - see Example(s)
Precept - see Command
Predestination 39
Presbyterian 38, 39, 40, 41, 43, 49, 50, 52, 56, 142, 184, 226
Presbyterian Seceder Synod 135
Presbytery of Chartiers 45
Presbytery of Transylvania 39
Priest 74, 76, 77, 109, 188
Proposition (of "Declaration and Address")
  Three 140
  Five 137
  Six 141
  Seven 141
Protestant 36, 61, 64, 74, 75, 195, 199, 202, 203, 204, 206, 209, 210, 218, 242
Protestant Reformation 36, 242, 255
Psallo 149, 150
Purcell, Bishop 52, 209
Purviance, David 41, 42, 43

Quaker 56, 214
Quarterly 110

Reconcile, Reconciled 86
Redemption 76, 77, 78, 210

2

20TH CENTURY CHURCH OF CHRIST DOCTRINE

The method of study which is used in this document is to first identify the major items of doctrine of the contemporary 20th century Church of Christ, and then to carefully examine each item. Each item is measured against both Biblical teaching and against the teachings of the Church of Christ of the early restoration movement some 150 years ago. Since the Church of Christ claims to have no creed there is no official list of doctrinal items to which reference can be made. Of course, most members will admit privately to themselves that the Church of Christ does have a creed, a very strong creed (in fact probably stronger than that of most other religious groups), to which both individuals and congregations must subscribe in order to be accepted as a member of the community. The creed appears in countless books, sermons, periodicals, Sunday school literature and other places where Church of Christ people write about their doctrine. But there is, indeed, no official list.

The list of doctrinal items to be used in this study will be a list such as that which might be assembled by a person who is not a member of the Church of Christ. This would be a person in the community who knows of or about the Church of Christ through association with friends, neighbors, relatives or business associates but who is not himself a member. This is an appropriate perspective because the present study is concerned, in part, with the reputation of the Church of Christ within the community. However, this same list probably reflects the effective order of priority placed on doctrinal items by a composite profile of at least the vocal elements of contemporary Church of Christ leadership. The five most important items on this list, listed in descending order of importance (i.e., most important first) are suggested to the reader as follows:

1. You must be a member of the Church of Christ in order to go to heaven.
2. You must sing a cappella in the Lord's worship in order to go to heaven.
3. The Church of Christ is not a denomination.
4. You must partake of the Lord's supper each Sunday in order to go to heaven.
5. You must be baptized in the proper way by the proper people in order to go to heaven.

This list, of course, does not stop with the fifth item and could be increased until it was quite lengthy. The five items listed, however, are the ones which will be given specific attention in the present study. This is my list, of course, and although I believe it to be very representative of existing conditions some readers might prefer to make some slight adjustments to the contents or the order of arrangement of the items in the list. That is perfectly acceptable and appropriate. The reader is welcome to make any alterations he chooses to such a list based on his personal background and experience. Neither the study presently undertaken nor any of the conclusions drawn from it would suffer in any significant way from some slight rearrangement of the list.

An explanation is in order at this time of why the items in the list are arranged in the particular order given. Each item will be addressed separately and in the order given.

ITEM 1. "You must be a member of the Church of Christ in order to go to heaven." Anyone who knows anything at all about us knows that we think we are the only ones going to heaven. It might be argued that not everyone in the Church of Christ believes this, and not everyone does, but at least for the last 30 to 60 years most have appeared to believe it. At least most teaching from the pulpit during this period has been to this effect. It is the one thing which is most widely known about us. I think that there is no question but that this item belongs at the top of the list.

ITEM 2. "You must sing a cappella in the Lord's worship in order to go to heaven." This item ranks high on the list for two reasons. First, because it is so conspicuous in our assemblies. Anyone visiting one of our congregations for the first time can plainly see that we do not use mechanical instruments of music. A person might visit us several times without hearing our views on baptism. And even though he would, on a first visit, see us partaking of the Lord's supper he might not know that we do that on every Sunday. But he can certainly see, even in a single visit, that we sing a cappella. The second reason that this item ranks so high on the list is because we have emphasized it so much in our teaching and practice. Sometimes it seems that we have almost made it the most important sign of a Christian people or assembly. No matter how close some other group of people might come to mirroring our teaching and practice in every other regard, we would never even consider the possibility of fellowshipping them as Christians if they used an instrument to accompany their singing.

ITEM 3. "The Church of Christ is not a denomination." This item ranks so high on the list because this concept is so ever present in our writing and in our rhetoric. There is scarcely a sermon, a paper, or a chapter in one of our books that does not reference this idea in some way.

ITEM 4. "You must partake of the Lord's supper each Sunday in order to go to heaven." Any visitor who attends our assemblies two or more weeks in a row will realize that we partake of this memorial feast on a weekly basis. This is contrary to the practices of many of the other major religious organizations. Thus this practice sets us apart.

ITEM 5. "You must be baptized in the proper way by the proper people in order to go to heaven." This item might seem to be the most important of the five to us. It is ranked fifth here because it is probably not as apparent to the casual outside observer as the other four items. He might have to know us a little longer or study with us a little more in order to understand this concept. It is ranked below the Lord's supper only because a visitor might not see a baptism or hear a lesson on baptism every Sunday, but he will see that the Lord's supper is observed weekly.

The basic framework for the study which is done throughout the remainder of this document is the careful analysis of the validity of each of these five items.

3

19TH CENTURY CHURCH OF CHRIST DOCTRINE

BRIEF HISTORICAL BACKGROUND

Introduction

Several of the major leaders of the restoration movement are quoted throughout this study. Some familiarity with the history of the Church of Christ will help the reader to get the maximum benefit from this study, but space permits only a cursory presentation at this time. For the reader who wishes to move on to an in-depth study of restoration history, the bibliography lists several references which are still in print.

A starting place for this study is an introduction of the men whose writings are referenced, and a discussion of the general historical framework surrounding these pioneer preachers and the manuscripts which they have bequeathed to us.

The American restoration movement did not occur in a vacuum nor was it the first attempt to reform Christianity and to restore it to something nearer its original form. In the centuries following the death of the apostles of Jesus Christ, the practice of Christianity gradually evolved in form. What appears to have begun as a very personal religion, based on faith in Jesus Christ, gradually evolved into a highly institutionalized religion encumbered with centuries of man-made traditions. For many centuries this highly structured organization, the Catholic Church, was essentially the only expression of Christianity. Eventually the church leaders themselves, rather than the sacred writings of the Bible, constituted the ultimate authority in religion. The common people were not encouraged to read the Bible and in many cases the Scriptures were not even available to the people in their native language.

In the sixteenth century there appeared on the scene men who were determined to reform the Catholic Church and to make the Bible once again available to the common people. Notable among these great reformers were Martin Luther in Germany and Huldreich Zwingli and John Calvin in Switzerland. What we know as the Protestant Reformation was the result of the efforts of these men and others of the period. Several Protestant groups, denominations, eventually resulted from these efforts. In time, over the next two or three hundred years, there emerged other men who felt that even the Protestant denominations were in need of further reformation. It was in the midst of this amelioration that the American, Stone-Campbell, restoration movement was born.

Early Beginnings

It is not particularly important what date we establish as the beginning of the restoration movement, but the year 1792 is often referenced. This date derives its significance from the actions of the Rev. James O'Kelly, a Methodist from North Carolina and Virginia. O'Kelly had become very unhappy with the autocratic rule exercised over the Methodists by Francis Asbury. At the Methodist General Conference in Baltimore, in 1792, James O'Kelly introduced a motion designed to make the Methodist Church government more democratic. The motion was not approved. As a result O'Kelly and several of his associates walked out of the conference and organized the "Republican Methodists." In 1794 a general meeting of the "Republican Methodist Church" was held on August 4, at Lebanon church, Surry County, Virginia. In this meeting the Rev. Rice Haggard is said to have stood up in the meeting with a copy of the New Testament in his hand and said: "Brethren, this is a sufficient rule of faith and practice, and by it we are told that the disciples were called *Christians,* and I move that henceforth and forever the followers of Christ be known as Christians simply."[1] The motion was unanimously adopted. In the same meeting a Rev. Mr. Hafferty, of North Carolina, moved to take the Bible itself as their only creed.[2] This motion was adopted. W. E. MacClenny, writing in 1910, sums up the proceedings of this meeting as follows:

> The reader will see that the motions by Revs. Rice Haggard and Hafferty, and adopted at this conference, had in them the embodiment of the same truths that are found in the *Cardinal Principles of the Christian Church* of to-day. We mention these here, to show that there has been no necessity for a change since they were first adopted:
> 1. The Lord Jesus is the only Head of the Church.
> 2. The name Christian to the exclusion of all party and sectarian names.
> 3. The Holy Bible, or the Scriptures of the Old and New Testament our only creed, and a sufficient rule of faith and practice.

---

1. W. E. MacClenny, *The Life of Rev. James O'Kelly,* written in 1910; Reprinted by Religious Book Service, 722 North Payton Road, Indianapolis, Indiana 46219, p. 116.
2. Ibid., pp. 116, 117.

4. Christian character, or vital piety, the only test of church fellowship and membership.
5. The right of private judgment, and the liberty of conscience, the privilege and duty of all.[3]

Rice Haggard, years later, around 1804, became associated with Barton W. Stone and suggested the name "Christian" to him.

A few years later some similar activity was taking place among the Baptist churches of New England, beginning in New Hampshire and Vermont. Two Baptist preachers, Elias Smith and Abner Jones, separated themselves from the Baptists and established independent churches in the period around 1800-1803. Robert Richardson says that:

> Those concerned in this movement also assumed the title of "Christians" and adopted the Bible as the only standard of faith and practice.[4]

Barton W. Stone

One of the most significant leaders of the restoration movement was Barton W. Stone. He was born near Port-Tobacco, Maryland, on December 24, 1772. His father died soon after he was born and his mother moved their large family to Pittsylvania county, Virginia. In February of 1790 he left his family and entered an academy in Guilford, North Carolina, under the direction of Dr. David Caldwell. Stone was at this time not interested in religion; however a trip with a friend to hear a Presbyterian minister, James McGready, caused him to fear for his lost soul. He resolved soon after to seek religion at the sacrifice of every earthly comfort. Stone describes his situation at this time in his autobiography:

---

3. Ibid., pp. 121, 122.
4. Robert Richardson, *Memoirs of Alexander Campbell*, Vol. 2, p. 186.

19TH CENTURY CHURCH OF CHRIST DOCTRINE

According to the preaching, and the experience of the pious in those days, I anticipated a long and painful struggle before I should be prepared to come to Christ, or, in the language then used, before I should get religion. This anticipation was completely realized by me. For one year I was tossed on the waves of uncertainty—laboring, praying, and striving to obtain saving faith—sometimes desponding, and almost despairing of ever getting it.

The doctrines then publicly taught were, that mankind were so totally depraved, that they could not believe, repent, nor obey the gospel—that regeneration was an immediate work of the Spirit, whereby faith and repentance were wrought in the heart.[5]

In the fall of 1798, a call to the Presbyterian ministry from the united congregations of Cane Ridge and Concord Kentucky was presented to Barton W. Stone through the Presbytery of Transylvania. In accepting his ordination Stone would be required to adopt the Westminster Confession of Faith as the system of doctrines taught in the Bible. Stone could not conscientiously subscribe to this Confession. He had doubts regarding its doctrines of the Trinity, election, reprobation and predestination. When Stone appeared publicly before the Presbytery for his ordination he made a qualified endorsement of the Confession. In response to the question, "Do you receive and adopt the Confession of Faith, as containing the system of doctrine taught in the Bible?" Stone replied aloud so that the whole congregation might hear, "I do, as far as I see it consistent with the word of God,"[6] No objection was made and Barton W. Stone was ordained. Even after his ordination Stone still wrestled with the doctrines of Calvinism. He describes his perplexities as follows:

I at that time believed, and taught, that mankind were so totally depraved that they could do nothing acceptable to God, till his Spirit, by some physical, almighty, and mysterious power

---

5. Barton W. Stone, *A Short History of the Life of Barton W. Stone*; Reprinted in the Cane Ridge Reader, Cane Ridge, Kentucky, July 6, 1972, p. 9.
6. Ibid., p. 30.

had quickened, enlightened, and regenerated the heart, and thus prepared the sinner to believe in Jesus for salvation. . . . Often when I was addressing the listening multitudes on the doctrine of total depravity, their inability to believe—and of the necessity of the physical power of God to produce faith; and then persuading the helpless to repent and believe the gospel, my zeal in a moment would be chilled at the contradiction.[7]

Stone describes how he gradually began to resolve his dilemma:

> From reading and meditating upon it, (the Bible) I became convinced that God did love the whole world, and that the reason why he did not save all, was because of their unbelief; and that the reason why they believed not, was not because God did not exert his physical, almighty power in them to make them believe, but because they neglected and received not his testimony, given in the Word concerning his Son. "These are written, that ye might believe that Jesus is the Christ, the Son of God, and that believing, ye might have life through his name." I saw that the requirement to believe in the Son of God, was reasonable; because the testimony given was sufficient to produce faith in the sinner; and the invitations and encouragement of the gospel were sufficient, if believed, to lead him to the Savior, for the promised Spirit, salvation and eternal life.
>
> This glimpse of faith—of truth, was the first divine ray of light, that ever led my distressed, perplexed mind from the labyrinth of Calvinism and error, in which I had so long been bewildered. It was that which led me into rich pastures of gospel-liberty.[8]

This newfound understanding of the gospel eventually led Stone to separate himself from the Presbyterian Church. Stone began to preach some of his new ideas during the great revivals around Logan County and Cane Ridge Kentucky in 1801. Preachers from many denominations, including the Presbyterians, Methodists and Baptists, preached simultaneously to emotional crowds numbering in the thousands. When Barton Stone continued to preach the doctrine that sinners had the power to

---

7. Ibid., p. 31.
8. Ibid., p. 33.

accept Christ and his salvation based solely on their belief of the testimony found in the Bible, without first waiting for some mysterious operation by the Holy Spirit, he was opposed by a number of the strong Calvinistic preachers. There were at this time five Presbyterian preachers who joined with Stone in preaching this doctrine. Their names were Richard McNemar, John Thompson, John Dunlavy, Robert Marshall, and David Purviance (Purviance was only a candidate for the ministry at this time). McNemar was charged with heresy by the Synod at Lexington, Kentucky. Knowing that they would all be similarly charged, the six preachers withdrew from the Synod before official action was taken. They immediately constituted themselves into a Presbytery, which they called the Springfield Presbytery. They soon published a book called *The Apology of Springfield Presbytery.* Stone says:

> In this book we stated our objections at length to the Presbyterian Confession of Faith, and against all authoritative confessions and creeds formed by fallible men. We expressed our total abandonment of all authoritative creeds, but the Bible alone, as the only rule of our faith and practice.[9]

But the Springfield Presbytery was not destined to be long-lived. Stone himself describes the events:

> Under the name of Springfield Presbytery we went forward preaching, and constituting churches; but we had not worn our name more than one year, before we saw it savored of a party spirit. With the man-made creeds we threw it overboard, and took the name *Christian*—the name given to the disciples by divine appointment first at Antioch. We published a pamphlet on this name, written by Elder Rice Haggard, who had lately united with us. Having divested ourselves of all party creeds, and party names, and trusting alone in God, and the word of his grace, we became a by-word and a laughing stock to the sects around; all prophesying our speedy annihilation. Yet from this period I date the commencement of that reformation, which has

---

9. Ibid., p. 49.

progressed to this day. Through much tribulation and opposition we advanced, and churches and preachers were multiplied.[10]

On June 28, 1804, in the process of dissolving the Springfield Presbytery, Stone and his associates wrote a document called "The Last Will and Testament of Springfield Presbytery." It is one of the most famous documents produced by the restoration movement. Several points made in this document are worthy of note by all who are interested in the restoration of New Testament Christianity. Some of these points, from page 51 of Stone's autobiography, are listed below:

> *Imprimis.* We *will,* that this body die, be dissolved, and sink into union with the Body of Christ at large; for there is but one body, and one Spirit, even as we are called in one hope of our calling.
> *Item.* We *will,* that our name of distinction, with its *Reverend* title, be forgotten, that there be but one Lord over God's heritage, and his name one.
> *Item.* We *will,* that our power of making laws for the government of the church, and executing them by delegated authority, forever cease. . . .
> *Item.* We *will,* that candidates for the Gospel ministry henceforth study the Holy Scriptures with fervent prayer, and obtain license from God to preach the simple Gospel, *with the Holy Ghost sent down from heaven,* without any mixture of philosophy, vain deceit, traditions of men, or the rudiments of the world. . . .
> *Item.* We *will,* that each particular church, as a body, actuated by the same spirit, choose her own preacher, and support him by a free will offering, without a written call or subscription—admit members—remove offences; and never henceforth delegate her right of government to any man or set of men whatever.
> *Item.* We *will,* that the people henceforth take the Bible as the only sure guide to heaven. . . .
> *Item.* We *will,* that preachers and people, cultivate a spirit of mutual forbearance; pray more and dispute less. . . .

Of the six men who had signed "The Last Will and Testament of Springfield Presbytery" only two, Barton W. Stone and David

---

10. Ibid., p. 50.

Purviance eventually remained in the Stone movement. Robert Marshall and John Thompson returned to the Presbyterian Church and Richard McNemar and John Dunlavy defected to the Shakers.

As Barton W. Stone and his associates among the Presbyterians struggled to return to the Bible as their only guide in religion, the subject of baptism gradually received more attention. Around the turn of the century Robert Marshall had become convinced that the proper Scriptural mode of baptism was immersion and he ceased from the practice of infant baptism. Barton Stone tried to convince him of his error, but in the process Stone himself was convinced of the error of infant baptism and ceased the practice entirely. The excitement surrounding the great revivals of 1801 caused the subject of baptism to be almost forgotten for a time. However, after the dissolving of the Springfield Presbytery many in the group became dissatisfied with their infant sprinkling, Barton Stone included. First the preachers immersed one another and then they began immersing the members of their congregations. Soon this practice prevailed very generally among the churches, although it was considered a matter of forbearance (not a doctrinal requirement) and their pulpits were silent on the subject. They had not at this time made the connection between baptism and the forgiveness of sins. This connection appears to at one time have been dimly recognized by Stone. On one occasion, while people were praying unsuccessfully before the mourners bench for a direct operation of the Holy Spirit, Stone preached "Repent and be baptized for the remission of sins, and you shall receive the gift of the Holy Ghost" and urged them to comply. The people were shocked at this strange approach and Stone did not pursue it again. Stone himself says:

> The subject of baptism now engaged the attention of the people very generally, and some, with myself, began to conclude that it was ordained for the remission of sins, and ought to be administered in the name of Jesus to all believing penitents. . . .

Into the spirit of the doctrine I was never fully led, until it was revived by Brother Alexander Campbell, some years later.[11]

In 1826 Stone began the publication of a monthly periodical called the *Christian Messenger*. This paper was published from 1826 through 1844. In 1832 John T. Johnson became associated with Stone (for two years) as co-editor of the Messenger. Johnson was associated with the Alexander Campbell movement and he was very instrumental in the efforts with Stone to unite the two groups. The Stone movement was very evangelical and was very successful in establishing churches and adding converts. The early Stone movement was more emotional and less concerned with an exact conformity to a primitive pattern of New Testament Christianity than was the early Campbell movement. The two movements were completely independent of each other in their origin and development. Barton W. Stone first met Alexander Campbell in 1824 at Georgetown, Kentucky, and the two developed a warm and mutual friendship after this meeting. Stone comments on Campbell in his autobiography:

> When he came into Kentucky, I heard him often in public and in private. I was pleased with his manner and matter. I saw no distinctive feature between the doctrine he preached and that which we had preached for many years, except on baptism for remission of sins. Even this I had once received and taught, as stated before, but had strangely let it go from my mind, till brother Campbell revived it afresh. I thought then that he was not sufficiently explicit on the influences of the Spirit, which led many honest Christians to think he denied them. Had he been as explicit then, as since, many honest souls would have been still with us, and would have greatly aided the good cause. In a few things I dessented from him, but was agreed to disagree.
>
> I will not say, there are no faults in brother Campbell; but that there are fewer, perhaps, in him, than any man I know on earth; and over these few my love would throw a veil, and hide them from view forever. I am constrained, and willingly

---

11. Ibid., p. 61.

constrained, to acknowledge him the greatest promoter of this reformation of any man living. The Lord reward him![12]

The union of the Stone movement and the Campbell movement was effected in 1832 and resulted finally in the merging of nearly all congregations influenced by the two reformers. Stone was criticized by some for uniting with the reformers, as the followers of Campbell were called. He defends his actions on the last page of his autobiography in 1843, the year before his death in November of 1844.

> But what else could we do, the Bible being our directory? Should we command them to leave the foundation on which we stood—the Bible alone—when they had come upon the same? By what authority could we command? Or should we have left this foundation to them, and have built another? Or should we have remained, and fought with them for the sole possession? They held the name *Christian* as sacred as we did—they were equally averse from making opinions the test of fellowship—and equally solicitous for the salvation of souls. This union, irrespective of reproach, I view as the noblest act of my life.[13]

Thomas Campbell

The Stone Movement had been under way for several years before the father-son team of Thomas and Alexander Campbell began their efforts at religious reformation in America. Thomas Campbell immigrated to the United States from Ireland in 1807. He had already become somewhat dissatisfied with the existing religious organizations as a member of the Seceder Presbyterians in his native land. Upon his arrival in America he was immediately assigned by the Seceder Synod then in session in Philadelphia to the Presbytery of Chartiers in Southwestern Pennsylvania. He was soon a very popular preacher around Washington, Pennsylvania. However, he was soon reprimanded by his

---

12. Ibid., pp. 75, 76.
13. Ibid., p. 79.

denomination for not adhering to the strict sectarian attitudes of his peers. Among other things he was accused of serving Communion to those who were not of his sect. He endured a series of trials for these offenses. He was censured by the Chartiers Presbytery and his case came before the Associate Synod of North America. Thomas Campbell defended himself in a document addressed to this group. This document, written in 1808, contains some hint of the concepts which were to characterize his lifelong efforts at religious reformation. He says:

> . . . I dare not venture to trust my own understanding so far as to take upon me to teach anything as a matter of faith or duty but what is already expressly taught and enjoined by Divine authority. . . . It is, therefore, because I have no confidence, either in my own infallibility or in that of others, that I absolutely refuse, as inadmissible and schismatic, the introduction of human opinions and human inventions into the faith and worship of the Church. . . . I refuse to acknowledge as obligatory upon myself, or to impose upon others, anything as of Divine obligation for which I cannot produce a 'thus saith the Lord?' This, I am sure, I can do, while I keep by his own word; but not quite so sure when I substitute my own meaning or opinion, or that of others, instead thereof. . . .[14]

The Synod found sufficient grounds to censure Thomas Campbell, although they allowed him to retain his position as a minister among the Seceder Presbyterians. His situation, however, became so uncomfortable, that he soon officially removed himself from the authority of the Synod. He continued to preach and teach, even though he was now a minister without a denomination or congregation. He preached wherever he could, often outdoors, and because of his popularity he had a considerable following. These were people who, like himself, were interested in Christian freedom and Christian union based on the Bible. A special meeting was called, probably sometime in 1807 or 1808 at the home of Abraham Altars. During

---

14. Robert Richardson, *Memoirs of Alexander Campbell,* Vol. 1, p. 226.

19TH CENTURY CHURCH OF CHRIST DOCTRINE

this meeting Thomas Campbell made the most famous statement of the restoration movement. He proposed the rule that "Where the Scriptures speak, we speak; and where the Scriptures are silent, we are silent."[15] Writing in the latter part of the century, Robert Richardson has this to say about the occasion:

> It was from the moment when these significant words were uttered and accepted that the more intelligent ever afterward dated the formal and actual *commencement of the Reformation* which was subsequently carried on with so much success, and which has already produced such important changes in religious society over a large portion of the world.[16]

Richardson continues his description of this same meeting on the next page of his account:

> At length, a shrewd Scotch Seceder, Andrew Munro, who was a bookseller and postmaster at Canonsburg, arose and said: "Mr. Campbell, if we adopt *that* as a basis, then there is an end of infant baptism." This remark, and the conviction it seemed to carry with it, produced a profound sensation. "Of course," said Mr. Campbell, in reply, "if infant baptism be not found in Scripture, we can have nothing to do with it."

Contrary to what his remark above would indicate, Thomas Campbell was very slow to give up the concept of infant baptism. For years he considered it a matter of forbearance and it seems that it was only through the influence of his son Alexander that he finally relinquished the doctrine of infant baptism in favor of the immersion of believers.

In order to better promote their goals of Christian union and peace, Thomas Campbell and his associates held a meeting on August 17, 1809, to form themselves into an association under the name of "The Christian Association of Washington." Soon after this Thomas Campbell wrote a document designed to set forth to the public at large, in a clear and definite manner,

---

15. Ibid., Vol. 1, p. 236.
16. Ibid., Vol. 1, p. 237.

the objective of the movement in which he and those associated with him were engaged. This document is entitled "Declaration and Address" and it became the landmark document of the restoration movement. It was first published at Washington, Pennsylvania, on September 7, 1809. The "Declaration and Address" probably contains more quotable material, statements which illuminate the purpose and character (even the very essence) of the restoration movement, than does any other single document. Much of this material is presented in subsequent chapters, in relation to specific issues, and therefore, to avoid duplication, no quotations will be presented at this point. The document promotes simple evangelical Christianity, free from all mixture of human opinions and inventions of men. It extols religious freedom, unity and a forbearance with the opinions of others. With equal vigor it condemns religious division, the judgmental attitude and the sectarian spirit. It speaks of the vast difference between the essential elements of Christianity, as explicitly stated in the Bible, and matters of mere individual opinion.

Alexander Campbell

In 1809 (about the time that the "Declaration and Address" went to press) Thomas Campbell's family, including his son Alexander, arrived in America. During the intervening time since his father had left the family to go to America, Alexander Campbell had been exposed to religious influences in his homeland which caused him to agree wholeheartedly with the sentiments expressed by his father in the "Declaration and Address." Thus independently, and an ocean apart, the two men had been moving in the same direction. Not long after Alexander Campbell had studied the "Declaration and Address" he informed his father that he had determined to devote himself to the dissemination and support of the principles and views which it contained.[17] Thus the son was destined to labor to put into practice what the father had begun. "The paramount claims of the Bible were to be asserted and defended; the intolerant bigotry of sectarism was to be exposed; the people of God were to be delivered from the yoke of clerical domination, and primitive Christianity, in all its original purity and perfection, was to be restored to the world."[18] Alexander Campbell began a very intensive period of Bible and religious history study to prepare himself for his life's work. He preached his first sermon on July 15, 1810.

Thomas Campbell had no intention of founding a new church. Even though rejected by his own Seceder Presbyterian denomination, he still had every intention that his efforts at reformation and restoration be carried out within the existing religious bodies. In 1810 he asked the regular Presbyterians, through the "Synod of Pittsburg," to accept himself and the "Christian Association of Washington" into their fellowship. The Synod rejected this overture in a meeting on October 4, 1810. The rejection was based on the religious sentiments expressed in the "Declaration and Address" and the opposition of some of the Association members to infant baptism. Having been rejected by the Pesbyterians the Christian Association felt that it was forced to organize itself as a church. The Brush Run church was organized on May 4, 1811. Thomas Campbell was appointed elder, and Alexander was licensed to preach the gospel. Four deacons were also chosen. There were thirty charter members of this congregation. They celebrated the Lord's supper weekly, according to the custom of the Independent churches in Scotland. Immersion, as the Scriptural mode of baptism, was gaining popularity among their numbers, although it was not universal.

In March of 1812, Alexander Campbell's first child was born. Since his wife and her father and mother were still members of

---

17. Ibid., Vol. 1, p. 274.
18. Ibid., Vol. 1, p. 276.

the Presbyterian Church, the subject of infant baptism now attracted his attention. Up to this time, even though they had realized that infant baptism had no explicit Scriptural sanction, the Campbells had considered it to be a subject of very little importance and considered it a matter of forbearance. They had never worried that their infant baptism might have been invalid. After a renewed consideration, however, Alexander became convinced that immersion was the only Scriptural mode of Baptism. He decided to be immersed and he engaged the services of Matthias Luse, a Baptist preacher, for this purpose. This was because he felt, probably without justification, that he must be immersed by a person who had himself already been immersed. On June 12, 1812, Alexander Campbell was immersed, along with six other persons. This included his wife, his father (Thomas) and his mother. They were baptized upon the simple confession that "Jesus is the Son of God." It is worthy of note that at this time they still did not perceive a connection between baptism and the forgiveness of sins, and there was apparently no verbal reference made to the forgiveness of sins at the time of baptism. Despite this fact, neither Thomas nor Alexander Campbell ever felt it necessary to be reimmersed when their understanding of this subject became more complete several years later.

From this occasion when Thomas Campbell decided to follow the example of his son in regard to the baptism of believers by immersion, the father conceded to the son, in effect, the guidance of the whole religious movement. From this point on Alexander Campbell was recognized as the spiritual and intellectual leader. On the Sunday following this occasion, thirteen other members of the Brush Run congregation were immersed. Soon the great majority of the church consisted of immersed believers.

The rejection of infant baptism, and the acceptance of immersion, moved the little church at Brush Run farther from the Presbyterians, but closer to the Baptists. During this time

INDEX

Redstone Association 51
Reformation 36, 41, 45, 47, 49, 52, 53, 55, 56, 57, 74, 76, 92, 186, 188, 191, 193, 206, 207, 214, 215, 229, 242, 251
Reformed Baptist(s) 217
Reformers 45, 51, 57, 68, 184, 185, 191, 193, 194, 228
Regeneration 39, 57, 81, 82, 86, 88
Regular Baptist - see Baptists, Regular
Reimmersed, Reimmersion 50, 191, 192
Religious Freedom 248
Remission 88
Remission of Sins (also see Forgiveness of sins) 43, 44, 52, 54, 55, 56, (Chapter Four; 73-92), 193, 217, 218, 219
"Remission of Sins," by A. Campbell 84-92, 199, 225-227
Repentance 55, 56, 57, 74, 91, 161, 201, 203, 216, 217, 219, 226
Reprobation 39
Republican Methodists 37
Restoration, Restorationism Chapter Eleven; 235-240
Revelation, Biblical 144, 180, 181
Revelations from God to Man; modern day; direct 67, 118, 138
Reverend 42
"Review of the History of Churches. - No. II," by A. Campbell 131-132
"Review of the History of Churches. - No. III," by A. Campbell 222-225
Revivals 43
Rice, N. L. 52, 209, 210, 211, 226
Richardson, Robert 21, 22, 38, 46, 47, 49, 51, 52, 53, 55, 136, 137, 148, 178-179, 182-183, 186-188, 188-189, 191-192, 193, 194, 204, 211, 227, 241
Ritual (also see Liturgy) 131

Roman Catholic Church - see Catholic Church (Roman)
Rosary in Prayer 148

Sabbatarians 104, 105, 106
Sabbath, Jewish 94
Sacrament 75
Sacrifice(s) 75, 76, 77, 92
Salaries for Preachers 60
Salvation 77, 92, 137, 139, 140, 158, 160, 181, 182, 186, 189, 196, 202, 210, 217, 225, 226, 231, 243, 255, 257
Sanctification (Sanctify, Sanctified) 77, 86, 87, 88, 201
Sand Creek Address 62, 63
Sandemanians 132
Satan 79, 236, 242, 243, 247, 248, 252
Saved 86
Saving Faith 39, 83
Scotch Presbyterian 54
Scotch Seceder 47
Scott, Walter 26, 54, 55, 56, 57, 58, 177, 190-191, 193, 221-222, 254
Seceder Presbyterians 45, 46, 49
Seceder Synod 45, 46
Second Generation 60, 63, 144, 146, 177, 183
Sectarian, Sectarianism 48, 151, 188, 196, 206, 208, 214, 215, 217, 219, 224, 228, 229, 255
Sects 195, 199, 201, 202, 203, 204, 206, 213, 215, 224, 250
Semiannual(ly) 105, 110
Septennial 105
Septuagint 149
Shakers 43
Shepherd, J. W. 63
Silence; Silence of Scriptures; Authority of(in) Silence 123, 124, 134, 135, 138, 246, 247, 253

271

Silence of Scriptures - see Silence
Six Steps (of the gospel) - also see
 Five Steps   55, 56
Slavery   62
Smith, Elias   38
Solo Singing   152, 154
Sommer, Daniel   61, 62, 63
Spheres of Fellowship   250
Springfield Presbytery   41, 42, 43
Sprinkling   74, 81, 89, 92, 101, 143,
 147, 151, 192, 196, 214, 218, 223,
 254
Stevenson, Dwight E.   54
Stone, Barton W.   11, 26, 38, 39, 40,
 42, 43, 44, 45, 54, 58, 111, 177, 178,
 182, 184-185, 192, 213-221, 228,
 239-240, 254
Stoneites   184
Sunday - see Lord's Day
Sunday Schools   60, 64, 134, 176,
 229, 247
Surry County, Lebanon Church   37
Synod at Lexington, Kentucky   41
Synod of Pittsburg   49

The Apology of Springfield Presbytery
 41
Theatre Going   60, 145
"The Breaking of the Loaf," by A.
 Campbell   110-111
The Christian Association of
 Washington   47, 49
The Evangelist   190-191, 221-222
"The Holy Spirit, A Discourse," by
 Walter Scott   221-222
"The Last Will and Testament of
 Springfield Presbytery"   42, 184
The Life of Rev. James O'Kelly,
 by W. E. MacClenny   37, 38
"The Limits of Religious Fellowship,"
 by Isaac Errett   204-209
"The Lord's Supper," by John Allen
 Gano   111-115

"The Lunenburg Letters," by A.
 Campbell - see "Lunenburg Letters"
The Search for the Ancient Order,
 by Earl Ervin West (Vol. 2) (Vol. 3)
 60, (Vol. 1) 61, 62, (Vol. 2) 63
The Story of the Restoration, By Bill
 Humble   61, 62, 63, 64
Third Generation   63
Thomas, John   191-192
Thompson, John   41, 43
Tongue Speaking   67, 118
Totally Depraved   39, 40
Trinity   39, 74
Troas   97, 98, 104, 106, 113

Uncircumcised - see Circumcision
Unimmersed   199, 204, 205, 207,
 208, 212, 213, 215, 216, 218, 219,
 220, 222, 223, 225, 227
"Union," by Barton W. Stone   216-
 221, 239-240
Unity   238, 239
U.S. Census Bureau   63

Vital Piety   38, 66
Voice of the Golden Oracle, by
 Dwight E. Stevenson   54

Walker, John   51, 52, 188
Wallace, Foy E. Jr.   64
Wash Away Sins   74
Washington, Pennsylvania   45, 48,
 136, 142
Water Baptism   67, 118, 214
Wellsburg   51
West, Earl Irvin   60, 61, 62, 63
Westminster Confession of Faith   39
"What has been the Custom Among
 Us?" by W. K. Pendleton   209-211
"Where the Scriptures speak, we
 speak; and where the Scriptures are
 silent, we are silent," quote by
 Thomas Campbell   47, 136, 150
Wine; Wine vs. Grape Juice   64, 101

Zwingli, Huldreich   36, 255

NEBRASKA CHRISTIAN COLLEGE LIBRARY